Michael Müller, Brixious Queloz

Purgatorian Consoler

A Manul of Prayers

Michael Müller, Brixious Queloz

Purgatorian Consoler
A Manul of Prayers

ISBN/EAN: 9783744660204

Printed in Europe, USA, Canada, Australia, Japan

Cover: Foto ©Lupo / pixelio.de

More available books at **www.hansebooks.com**

"What! Could you not watch one hour with me?"

Murphy Faltimore

Purgatorian Consoler:

A Manual of Prayers,

CONTAINING A SELECTION OF

DEVOTIONAL EXERCISES,

ORIGINALLY PREPARED FOR THE USE OF THE

Members of the Purgatorian Arch-Confráternity,

Enlarged and Adapted to General Use.

BY A REDEMPTORIST FATHER.

PUBLISHED WITH THE APPROBATION OF
THE MOST REV. THE ARCHBISHOP OF BALTIMORE.

BALTIMORE:
PUBLISHED BY JOHN MURPHY & CO.
182 BALTIMORE STREET.
1868.

PRINTED BY
JOHN MURPHY & CO.,
BALTIMORE.

CONTENTS.

	PAGE
PREFACE	v
MOVABLE FEASTS	vii
WHAT EVERY CHRISTIAN MUST KNOW	ix
PRIVATE BAPTISM	xii
MORNING PRAYERS	13
NIGHT PRAYERS	17
DEVOTIONS FOR MASS	21
———— FOR VESPERS	40
BENEDICTION OF THE BLESSED SACRAMENT	68
DEVOTIONS BEFORE CONFESSION	71
———— AFTER CONFESSION	79
———— BEFORE COMMUNION	80
———— AFTER COMMUNION	84
———— BEFORE AND AFTER CONFIRMATION	134
BEFORE AND AFTER EXTREME UNCTION	188
GENERAL DEVOTIONS TO OUR LORD	90
———— TO THE BLESSED VIRGIN	99, 138
———— TO THE SAINTS	156
PRAYERS FOR VARIOUS OCCASIONS	181
GENERAL DEVOTIONS FOR THE DEAD	221
RULE OF LIFE	315
EXPLANATION OF THE COMMANDMENTS	321
DUTIES OF PARTICULAR STATES	341
INSTRUCTION ON PURGATORY	345
THE PURGATORIAN ARCH-CONFRATERNITY	419
INSTRUCTION ON INDULGENCES	426
ALPHABETICAL INDEX	461
LIST OF INDULGENCES	452
TRANSLATOR'S PROTEST	468

TRANSLATOR'S PREFACE.

The Arch-Confraternity for the relief of the souls in Purgatory, being favored in a most extraordinary manner both by the Holy See and the Heads of several Religious Orders, a quarter of a century had not elapsed after its establishment, when four hundred confraternities were already incorporated with the mother association at Rome, the number of its members exceeding one million. Thus it became an absolute necessity for the Very Rev. Father Brixious Queloz, C.S.S.R., Chief Director of the Arch-Confraternity, to compile, for the use of its members the manual of devotion: "*La Pietà del Christiano verso i Morti.*" This manual has been translated into several languages, and as the Arch-Confraternity has already been established in six dioceses of this country, and continues to spread rapidly, the many and pressing demands of its members have made the translation of this manual an absolute necessity.

The translation is substantially the same as the original, with the exception of some additional prayers, devotions, and instructions, mostly taken from the writings of St. Alphonsus, and more especially adapted to this country.

In the selection of prayers, the translator was guided both by the advice of St. Alphonsus, viz: that our prayers should be petitions rather than affections, especially for the grace of divine love and final perseverance, and by the later and more stringent rules of the Church concerning prayer-books, and as this manual has already become the favorite manual of thousands of pious Catholics throughout Europe, the translator confidently presents it, not only to the members of the Purgatorian Arch-Confraternity, but also to the public in general. As a prayer-book it combines force and solidity, and is well calculated by the pious instructions on Purgatory which it contains, and the extraordinary spiritual advantages and privileges which it holds out to induce the clergy as well as the laity to promote to the best of their power the spreading of this pious Association.

Finally, this manual will not fail, as general experience has proved, to stir up in the hearts of the faithful both great charity toward the suffering souls in Purgatory and true love of Jesus Christ, inspiring them, by the reflections on the Purgatorial torments with a holy fear of the severe chastisements of Almighty God, with a true hatred of sin, both mortal and venial sin, and an effectual desire to perform works of sincere penance and charity whilst they have time and grace to do so.

St. Alphonsus', Baltimore.
March 19, 1868.

Table of Movable Feasts.

A. D.	Ash Wed'y.	Easter Sunday	Ascen. Day.	Whit- Sunday	Corpus Christi.	1st Sun. Advent.
1860	Feb. 22	April 8	May 17	May 27	June 7	Dec. 2
1861	Feb. 13	Mar. 31	May 9	May 19	May 30	Dec. 1
1862	Mar. 5	April 20	May 29	June 8	June 19	Nov. 30
1863	Feb. 18	April 5	May 14	May 24	June 4	Nov. 29
1864	Feb. 10	Mar. 27	May 5	May 15	May 26	Nov. 27
1865	Mar. 1	April 16	May 25	June 4	June 15	Dec. 3
1866	Feb. 14	April 1	May 10	May 20	May 31	Dec. 2
1867	Mar. 6	April 21	May 30	June 9	June 20	Dec. 1
1868	Feb. 26	April 12	May 21	May 31	June 11	Nov. 29
1869	Feb. 10	Mar. 28	May 6	May 16	May 27	Nov. 28
1870	Mar. 2	April 17	May 26	June 5	June 16	Nov. 27
1871	Feb. 22	April 9	May 18	May 28	June 8	Dec. 3
1872	Feb. 14	Mar. 31	May 9	May 19	May 30	Dec. 1
1873	Feb. 26	April 13	May 22	June 1	June 12	Nov. 30
1874	Feb. 18	April 5	May 14	May 24	June 4	Nov. 29
1875	Feb. 10	Mar. 28	May 6	May 16	May 27	Nov. 28
1876	Mar. 1	April 16	May 25	June 4	June 15	Dec. 3
1877	Feb. 14	April 1	May 10	May 20	May 31	Dec. 2
1878	Mar. 6	April 21	May 30	June 9	June 20	Dec. 1
1879	Feb. 26	April 13	May 22	June 1	June 12	Nov. 30
1880	Feb. 11	Mar. 28	May 6	May 16	May 27	Nov. 28
1881	Mar. 2	April 17	May 26	June 5	June 16	Nov. 27
1882	Feb. 22	April 9	May 18	May 28	June 8	Dec. 3
1883	Feb. 7	Mar. 25	May 3	May 13	May 24	Dec. 2
1884	Feb. 27	April 13	May 22	June 1	June 12	Nov. 30
1885	Feb. 18	April 5	May 14	May 24	June 4	Nov. 29
1886	Mar. 10	April 25	June 3	June 13	June 24	Nov. 28
1887	Feb. 23	April 10	May 19	May 29	June 9	Nov. 27
1888	Feb. 15	April 1	May 10	May 20	May 31	Dec. 2
1889	Mar. 6	April 21	May 30	June 9	June 20	Dec. 1
1890	Feb. 19	April 6	May 15	May 25	June 5	Nov. 30
1891	Feb. 11	Mar. 29	May 7	May 17	May 28	Nov. 29
1892	Mar. 2	April 17	May 26	June 5	June 16	Nov. 27
1893	Feb. 15	April 2	May 11	May 21	June 1	Dec. 3
1894	Feb. 7	Mar. 25	May 3	May 13	May 24	Dec. 2
1895	Feb. 27	April 14	May 23	June 2	June 13	Dec. 1
1896	Feb. 19	April 5	May 14	May 24	June 4	Nov. 29
1897	Mar. 3	April 18	May 27	June 6	June 17	Nov. 28

What every Christian must know.

Every Christian, by the *command of the Church*, must know at least: I. The four great truths of Faith. II. The Sacraments; at least, Baptism, Penance and the Blessed Sacrament. III. The Prayers, Our Father, Hail Mary, and the Creed, or, I believe. IV. The Commandments of God and the Church.— *See St. Alphonsus Liguori.*

I. FAITH.

Be very careful to learn these *four great truths;* because no one can go to heaven without knowing them.

1. How many Gods are there?

One God.

† 2. How many persons are there in God?

Three Persons: the Father, the Son, and the Holy Ghost.

† 3. Which of them was made man, and died to save us from hell?

God the Son, the Second Person: or the Son of God.

4. What will God do to the good?

He will make the good happy for ever in heaven.

And what to the wicked?

He will burn the wicked for ever in hell.

II. THE SEVEN SACRAMENTS.

5. What is Baptism for?

It cleanses from original sin, and makes us Christians.

† 6. What is Penance for?

It forgives the sins after baptism.

† 7. What is the Blessed Eucharist?

It is the body and blood of Jesus Christ, under the appearances of bread and wine.

<small>The above short answers on the principal Sacraments, are for those who cannot learn more, the four side crosses † marking the answers least known; the answers of the catechism are below.</small>

How many Sacraments are there?

Seven Sacraments: Baptism, Confirmation, Holy Eucharist, Penance, Extreme Unction, Holy Orders and Matrimony.

1. What is Baptism?

Baptism is a sacrament which cleanses from original sin, and from actual sin if we are guilty of it, makes us Christians, children of God, and heirs of heaven.

2. What is Confirmation?

Confirmation is a sacrament by which we receive the Holy Ghost, to make us strong and perfect Christians, and soldiers of Jesus Christ.

3. What is the Holy Eucharist?

The Holy Eucharist is the body and blood, soul and divinity of Jesus Christ, under the appearances of bread and wine.

4. What is Penance?

Penance is a sacrament which forgives the sins we commit after Baptism.

5. What is Extreme Unction?

Extreme Unction is a sacrament which gives grace to die well.

6. What is Holy Orders?

Holy Orders is a sacrament by which bishops, priests, and the other ministers are ordained, and receive grace and power for their sacred duties.

7. What is Matrimony?

Matrimony is a sacrament which gives grace to married persons to live well in their state, and bring up their children in the fear of God.

III. THE PRAYERS.

1. Our Father, Who art in heaven; hallowed be Thy name; Thy kingdom come; Thy will be done on earth, as it is in heaven. Give us this day our daily bread; and forgive us our trespasses, as we forgive them that trespass against us; and lead us not into temptation, but deliver us from evil. Amen.

2. Hail Mary, full of grace: the Lord is with thee: blessed art thou amongst women: and blessed is the fruit of thy womb, Jesus. Holy Mary, mother of God, pray for us sinners, now, and at the hour of our death. Amen.

3. I believe in God the Father Almighty, creator of heaven and earth; and in Jesus Christ His only Son, our Lord; who was conceived by the Holy Ghost; born of the Virgin Mary; suffered under Pontius Pilate; was crucified, dead and buried. He descended into hell: the third day He arose from the dead: He ascended into heaven: sitteth at the right hand of God, the Father Almighty: from thence He shall come to judge the living and the dead. I believe in the Holy Ghost; the holy Catholic Church; the communion of saints; the forgiveness of sins; the resurrection of the body; and life everlasting. Amen.

IV. THE COMMANDMENTS OF GOD.

1. I am the Lord thy God; thou shalt have no other God but me. 2. Thou shalt not take the name

of the Lord thy God in vain. 3. Remember thou keep holy the Sabbath day. 4. Honor thy father and thy mother. 5. Thou shalt not kill. 6. Thou shalt not commit adultery. 7. Thou shalt not steal. 8. Thou shalt not bear false witness against thy neighbor. 9. Thou shalt not covet thy neighbor's wife. 10. Thou shalt not covet thy neighbor's goods.

THE COMMANDMENTS OF THE CHURCH.

1. To do no work and hear Mass on Sundays and holidays. 2. To abstain from flesh-meat on days of abstinence. 3. To fast on fasting days when you are twenty-one years old. 4. To confess your sins every year. 5. To receive the Blessed Sacrament about Easter. 6. To help to support your pastors when you are able.

Private Baptism.

Any person, whether man, woman or child, may and should baptize an infant in case of danger of death, thus: Take common water, pour it upon the head of the child, and while you are pouring it, say the following words: "*I baptize thee in the name of the Father, and of the Son, and of the Holy Ghost. Amen.*"

These words must be said and the water poured on by **one and the same person**, and care must be taken to pronounce the *words distinctly and* **at the same time** that the water is poured on.

Morning Prayers.

As soon as you awake, make the sign ✝ of the cross, saying:

Glory be to the Father Who hath created me.
Glory be to the Son Who hath redeemed me.
Glory be to the Holy Ghost Who hath sanctified me.

Blessed be the holy and undivided Trinity, now and forever. Amen.

On rising from your bed, say:

In the name of our Lord Jesus Christ, I arise.
May He bless, preserve and govern me and bring me to everlasting life. Amen.

While you are dressing, occupy yourself with pious thoughts. As soon as you are dressed, kneel down and say:

1. My God, I adore Thee and love Thee with all my heart.

2. I thank Thee for all Thy benefits, and especially for having preserved me this night.

3. I offer Thee whatever I may do or suffer this day, in union with the actions and sufferings of Jesus and Mary, with the intention of gaining all the indulgences I can in favor of the souls in Purgatory.

4. I intend that every thought, word and work, and suffering shall be for Thy greater glory, and in honor of the Blessed Virgin Mary, of my Guardian Angel and of all my holy patrons.

5. I resolve to conform myself to Thy holy will, and particularly in those things which are contrary to my inclinations, saying always: May the most just, most high, most adorable will of God be in all things done, and praised, and for ever magnified.

6. I resolve to fly from all sin this day, and especially such a one (here mention the fault into which you fall the oftenest,) and I beg of Thee to give me perseverance for the love of Jesus Christ.

My Jesus, keep Thy hand over me this day! Most Holy Mary, take me beneath thy mantle! And do Thou, Eternal Father, help me for the love of Jesus and Mary!

Then say the following prayers:

The Lord's Prayer. The Hail Mary. The Creed.

Afterwards say three Hail Mary's in honor of the purity of the B. V. M.

HOW TO PASS THE DAY IN A HOLY MANNER.

When you are tempted to sin, say often:

Jesus and Mary.

Morning Prayers.

When the bell rings for the Angelus, at morning, noon and evening, pray as follows:

The Angel of the Lord declared unto Mary,
And she conceived of the Holy Ghost.

      Hail Mary, etc.

Behold the handmaid of the Lord
May it be done unto me according to thy word.

      Hail Mary, etc.

And the Word was made flesh,
And dwelt among us.

      Hail Mary, etc.

PRAYER.

Pour forth, we beseech Thee, O Lord, Thy grace into our hearts, that we to whom the incarnation of Christ, Thy Son, has been made known by the message of an angel, may, by His passion and cross, be brought to the glory of His resurrection, through the same Christ, our Lord. Amen.

Whoever says the Angelus daily for a whole month and goes to confession and communion, in the course of the same month, gains a plenary indulgence.—Benedict XIII.

Before meals, say:

Bless us, O Lord, and these Thy gifts which we are about to receive from Thy bounty, through Christ our Lord. Amen.

After meals, say:

We give Thee thanks, Almighty God, for all Thy benefits, Who livest and reignest world without end. Amen.

May the souls of the faithful departed rest in peace! Amen.

When the clock strikes, say:

My Jesus, I love Thee; never permit me to offend Thee again, and let me never be separated from Thee.

In adverse circumstances, say:

Lord, since Thou hast so willed it, I will it also.

When you know or doubt of some sin you have committed, say immediately:

My God, I am sorry for having offended Thee; I will sin no more.

And if it was a grievous sin, confess it directly.

Night Prayers.

In the name of the ✝ *Father, and of the Son, and of the Holy Ghost. Amen.*

Come, Holy Ghost, fill the hearts of Thy faithful, and enkindle in them the fire of Thy love.

V. Send forth Thy spirit, and they shall be created,

R. And Thou shalt renew the face of the earth.

PRAYER.

O God, Who hast taught the hearts of the faithful by the light of Thy holy spirit, grant us, by the same spirit, to have a right judgment in all things, and everymore to rejoice in His consolation, through Jesus Christ, our Lord. Amen.

ACT OF THANKSGIVING.

I thank Thee, O Lord, for all the graces and benefits which Thou hast bestowed upon me, especially for having given me Jesus Christ for my redeemer, the Blessed Virgin for my mother and for having called me to be a child of the only one true Catholic Church.

Ask yourself then seriously and carefully the following questions, by way of an

EXAMINATION OF CONSCIENCE.

Have I not sinned this day—

In thought? By willingly entertaining some unchaste, uncharitable, or covetous thoughts?

In word? By using immodest language — uttering oaths—curses—lies—passionate, slanderous, profane, or irreverent words? Have I given scandal so?

In action? By being idle?—slow or impatient about my work? Have I not been in evil or dangerous company? Done any immodest action? Been too free in my manners? Been rude, cross, or disobedient towards my parents or superiors? Been unkind, insolent, malicious, cruel or unjust towards my neighbor? Have I given any bad example to my children, my servants, my neighbors?

By omission? Have I refused or neglected to do any act of charity? Been watchful over my children, and others depending upon me, and careful for their salvation? Have I omitted my prayers, my penance, or some other duty?

Finally, examine whether you have kept the resolution you made in the morning. If not, consider well what was the cause of your fall, and seek out the means to preserve you from falling in future. For be assured, that your whole Christian perfection depends upon this diligent examination of conscience.

Having finished this examination, make the following acts of Faith, Hope, Charity and Contrition:

ACT OF FAITH.*

O my God! Who art the infallible Truth! I believe every thing which the Holy Church commands me to believe, because Thou hast revealed it to her. I believe that Thou art the Creator of heaven and earth, that Thou dost reward the just in paradise, and punish the wicked eternally in hell. I believe that Thou art one divine essence in three persons, namely; the Father, the Son, and the Holy Ghost. I believe the carnation and the death of Jesus Christ. In a word, I believe all that the Holy Church believes. I thank Thee for having made me a Christian, and a Catholic, and I protest that I will live and die in this holy faith.

ACT OF HOPE.

O my God! I confide in Thy promises, because Thou art faithful, powerful, and merciful, and hope, through the merits of Jesus Christ, for the pardon of my sins, final perseverance, and the everlasting glory of paradise.

ACT OF CHARITY.

O my God! I love Thee with all my heart, and above all things, because Thou art infinitely

---

* According to a concession of Pope Benedict XIV., granted in December, 1751, an indulgence of seven years and seven quarantines (280 days) may be gained by devoutly repeating these acts. If recited daily for a month, with confession and communion made in the course of the same month, a plenary indulgence is gained.

good, and worthy of infinite love, and for love of Thee I love my neighbor as myself.

ACT OF CONTRITION.

O my God! I am heartily sorry for all my sins, because by them I have lost heaven and deserved hell, but more than all because I have offended Thee, O my God, Who are infinitely good, and worthy of all my love; but now I am firmly resolved, by the help of Thy grace, never to sin against Thee any more, and to avoid all the occasions of sin.

Then say for the repose of the souls of the faithful departed:

One Our Father and one Hail Mary, with

V. Eternal rest give to them, O Lord.
R. And let everlasting light enlighten them.
V. May they rest in peace.
R. Amen.

Go to bed now, with holy thoughts, or repeating with your lips some short fervent ejaculations of love, and continue thus until you fall asleep. If you awake in the night, lift up your thoughts immediately to God, that no evil imaginations may enter your mind, and if they should, say promptly:

O Jesus! O Mary! No, no, let me die rather than do, or wish, or even think of such a thing! In the name of the Father, and of the Son, and of the Holy Ghost. Amen.

Devotions at Mass.

PRAYERS BEFORE MASS.

In the name of the ✠ Father, and of the Son, and of the Holy Ghost. Amen.

Receive, O holy Trinity, one God, the holy sacrifice of the body and blood of our Lord Jesus Christ, which I, Thy unworthy servant, desire now to offer unto Thy divine Majesty by the hands of this Thy minister, with all the sacrifices which have ever been or are to be offered unto Thee, in union with that most holy sacrifice offered by the same our Lord at the last supper, and on the altar of the cross. I offer it unto Thee with the utmost affection of devotion, out of pure love for thine infinite goodness, and according to the most holy intention of the same our Lord, and of our holy mother Church:

1. To the great and eternal glory and love of Thy divine Majesty.

2. In acknowledgment of Thy sovereign excellence and supreme dominion over us, and our subjection to Thee, and dependence upon Thee.

3. In perpetual commemoration of the passion and death of the same Christ our Lord.

4. For the honor and increase of glory of the blessed Virgin, and of all the saints triumphant.

5. In eternal thanksgiving for all Thy benefits, conferred upon the most sacred humanity of our Lord, upon the blessed Virgin His mother, upon the saints my patrons; and for all the benefits hitherto or yet to be conferred upon all the blessed and predestinated, and upon me, the most unworthy of all.

6. In satisfaction for my sins, and for the sins of all the faithful, living or dead.

7. In particular, I offer it for the attainment of these (N N,) or for this (N) grace or blessing, for these (N N) persons particularly recommended to me, and for all for whom I am accustomed or bound to pray; that Thou wouldst grant to the departed rest, and to the living grace, to know, and love, and glorify Thee perfectly now in this life, and hereafter blissfully in heaven. Accept and perfect this my desire, and vouchsafe Thy abundant grace and blessing for its accomplishment.

AT THE CONFITEOR.

O divine Jesus, Thou art the victim charged with all the iniquities of the world; Thou didst weep for them bitter tears; Thou didst expiate them by the most dreadful torments and by the most cruel of deaths. I come to mingle my tears with Thine; I confess to Thee, in the presence of Mary ever Virgin and of all the Saints, that I have sinned exceedingly; that it is my ingratitude that pierced Thy heart, and put Thee to a cruel death. O God, my Saviour, through Thy tears, through Thy agony in the garden, and through Thy precious blood and the wound in Thy Sacred Heart, I beseech Thee to accept this my confession, and mercifully pardon all my deficiencies, that, according to the greatness of Thy mercy, I may be fully and perfectly absolved in heaven; Who livest and reignest, &c.

AT THE INTROIT.

Let us adore the heart of Jesus, which has loved us so much; let us prostrate ourselves before Him, and bewail the sins of which we have been guilty. Grant us, O Lord, a contrite and humble heart; let the homage of our adorations be as acceptable to Thee as if we offered Thee thousands of victims.

AT THE KYRIE.

O Father of infinite mercy, have pity on Thy children; O Jesus, sacrificed for us, apply to us the merits of Thy precious blood; O Holy Ghost, the sanctifier, descend into our hearts, and inflame them with Thy love.

AT THE GLORIA IN EXCELSIS.

What happiness for us that the Son of the Most High should have been pleased to dwell amongst us, and have vouchsafed to offer us a dwelling in His Divine Heart! Suffer us, O Lord, to mingle our voices with those of the angelic choir, to thank Thee for so great a favor; and let us say with them, "Glory to God in the highest heavens." O almighty Father, we praise Thee, we bless Thee, we adore Thee; we give Thee thanks for all the benefits which Thou hast lavished upon us without ceasing. O Jesus, lamb without spot, Who takest away the sins of the world, have mercy on us; Thou only art holy, Thou only art the Lord, Who reignest with the Father and the Holy Ghost in glory, and meritest all our homage on earth.

AT THE COLLECTS.

O Lord, vouchsafe favorably to hear the prayers which Thy priest offers to Thee for the Church and for me.

I earnestly beseech Thee to grant me those graces and virtues of which I have need, in order to deserve Thy love. Fill my heart with eternal gratitude for all the blessings which Thou hast conferred upon me, with a lively horror of sin, and with perfect charity towards my neighbor. Make my whole life worthy of one who is Thy child. I deserve not to be heard for my own sake, O my God, but I beseech Thy mercy through the infinite merits of Thy divine Son.

O divine Jesus, inexhaustible fountain of all good things, open to us, we beseech Thee, the interior of Thy heart; that having entered, by pious meditation, into this august sanctuary of divine love, we may fix for ever there our hearts, as the place wherein are found the treasure, the repose, and the happiness of holy souls.

AT THE EPISTLE.

Thou hast vouchsafed, O Lord, to teach us Thy sacred truths by the prophets and apostles: oh, grant that we may so improve by their doctrine and examples in the love of Thy holy name and of Thy holy law, that we may shew forth by our lives whose disciples we are; that we may no longer follow the corrupt inclinations of flesh and blood, but master all our passions; that we may be ever directed by Thy light, and strengthened by Thy grace to walk in the way of Thy commandments, and to serve Thee with clean hearts. Through our Lord Jesus Christ.

AT THE GOSPEL.

O Lord Jesus, Who, according to Thy Father's will, hast declared unto the world the message of the Gospel; grant that we may receive it into our minds, embrace it with our wills, preserve it in our memory, and practise it in our lives; and being united here with those elect sheep who hear Thy voice, may be numbered with them also at the last day at Thy right hand, and hear Thee say, "Come, ye blessed of my Father, possess you the kingdom prepared for you from the foundation of the world." O Jesus, give holy pastors to thy Church.

PRAYER AT THE SERMON.

I will hear what the Lord will say unto me.

O Jesus, light of the world, enlighten my understanding, that I may understand Thy word; and cleanse my heart, that it may bring forth the fruits of the same.

AT THE CREED.

I firmly believe — because God Who is Infallible Truth hath so revealed it to the Holy Catholic Church, and through the Church to us — I firmly believe that there is one only God, in three divine persons, equal and distinct, whose names are Father, Son, and Holy Ghost: that the Son became man, and through the operation of the Holy Spirit took flesh and a human soul in the womb of the most pure Virgin Mary, died for us upon the cross, rose again, ascended into heaven, and will come from thence at the end of the world to judge all the living and the dead, to give paradise to the good, and hell to the wicked, for ever; and furthermore, upon the same motive, I believe every thing that the holy Church believes and teaches. In this faith and for this faith I desire to live and die. Grant, O Lord, that my life may be conformable with my faith, that my faith may be animated by good works, that I may never be ashamed to declare myself a Catholic, and may constantly maintain the interests of Thy holy religion. Draw closer to me, Lord, the bonds that bind me to Thy holy Church; put into my heart a spirit of perfect obedience to its lawful pastors. In its bosom I became Thy child, and in its bosom I desire to live and die. Amen.

DURING THE OFFERTORY.

I adore Thee, O my God; and, in union with the priest, offer Thee this sacrifice, for Thy honor and glory, in thanksgiving for all the benefits conferred upon myself and upon the whole world; and in satisfaction for my many sins, and the sins of other men. Accept, O Lord, of this holocaust, which is no other than Thy divine Son, at once made priest and victim, offering and offerer, and apply his saving merits to my needy soul.— Be comforted, O my heart, Jesus sacrifices Himself for thee.

O my Lord Jesus Christ, in remembrance and praise of Thy boundless love, with which Thou didst give Thyself wholly to us upon the altar of the cross, behold I offer unto Thee this day this present sacrifice of the Mass, together with all those which are celebrated throughout the world, by the hands of Thy priests, to be presented to Thy eternal Father, in union with, and in the virtue of, that oblation in which Thou Thyself, dying on the cross, didst offer Thy sacred body and blood for the salvation of the world.

Grant that the oblation of the same Thy body and blood, which here is renewed in mystery, and is made under the form of bread and wine, may effectually obtain its proper fruit; that thereby the living may receive grace, and the faithful departed, everlasting rest.

Accept, also, O Lord, this same sacrifice, which contains in itself the fruit of Thy passion and death, as an act of thanksgiving for the innumerable benefits Thou hast conferred upon us, and a propitiation and satisfaction for the countless sins we have committed, the good we have omitted to do, and the punishments we have deserved. Who livest, &c.

AT THE PREFACE.

Lift up, O Lord, do Thou Thyself lift up my heart to Thee. Take from it all unholy thoughts, all earthly affections. Lift it wholly up to heaven, where Thou art worthily adored, and to the altar, where Thou art about to manifest Thyself to me. My life is but one continual succession of Thy mercies; let it be one continual succession of thanksgivings: and as Thou art now about to renew the greatest of all sacrifices, is it not meet that I should burst forth in expressions of heart-felt gratitude? Suffer me then, to join my feeble voice with the voices of all the heavenly spirits, and in union with them to say, in a transport of joy and admiration:

Holy, holy, holy, Lord God of Sabaoth. Heaven and earth are full of Thy glory. Hosanna in the highest.

Blessed is He that cometh in the name of the Lord. Hosanna in the highest.

AT THE CANON.

O eternal and most merciful Father, behold, we come to offer Thee our homage this day: we desire to adore, praise, and glorify Thee, and to give Thee thanks for Thy great glory, joining our hearts and voices with all Thy blessed in heaven, and with Thy whole Church upon earth. But acknowledging our great unworthiness and innumerable sins, for which we are heartily sorry and humbly beg Thy pardon, we dare not venture to approach Thee otherwise than in company of Thy Son, our advocate and mediator, Jesus Christ, Whom Thou hast given us to be both our High Priest and Sacrifice. With Him, therefore, and through Him, we venture to offer Thee this sacrifice; to His most sacred intentions we desire to unite ours; and with this offering which He makes of Himself, we desire to make an offering of our whole being to Thee. With Him, and through Him, we beseech Thee to exalt Thy holy Catholic Church throughout the whole world; to maintain her in peace, unity, holiness, and truth; to have mercy on Thy servant N., our chief bishop, N., our prelate, and on all that truly fear Thee; on our pastor, (parents, children,) friends, and benefactors, &c.; on all those whom we have in any way scandalised, injured or offended, or for whom we are in any other way bound to pray; on all that are in their agony, or under violent temptations, or other necessities, corporal or spiritual; on all our enemies; and, in a word, on all poor sinners; that we may all be converted to Thee, and find mercy, through Jesus Christ Thy Son; through Whom we hope one day to be admitted into the company of all Thy saints and elect, Whose memory we here celebrate, Whose prayers we desire, and with Whom we communicate in these holy mysteries.

When the Priest spreads his hands over the oblation:

(Here the bell is rung.)

Give ear, we beseech Thee, to the prayers of Thy servant, who is here appointed to make this oblation in our behalf; and grant it may be effectual for the obtaining of all those blessings which he asks for us.

Behold, O Lord, we all here present to Thee, in this bread and wine, the symbols of our perfect union. Grant, O Lord, that they may be made for us the true body and blood of Thy dear Son; that, being consecrated to Thee by this holy victim, we may live in Thy service, and depart this life in Thy grace.

AT THE CONSECRATION.

Bow down your body and soul in solemn adoration; make an act of faith in the real presence of your Saviour's body and blood, soul and divinity, under the sacramental veils. Offer your whole self to Him, and through Him to His Father: beg that your heart and soul may be happily changed into Him.

AT THE ELEVATION OF THE HOST.

(Here the bell is rung thrice.)

Hail, true body, born of the Virgin Mary, which didst truly suffer and wast immolated on the cross for man, whose side was pierced, and flowed with water and with blood; may we have a foretaste of Thee in the last agony of death. O kind, O loving one, Jesus, Son of Mary, have mercy on me! Amen.

AT THE ELEVATION OF THE CHALICE.

(Here also the bell is rung thrice.)

Saviour of the world, save us; for by Thy cross and by Thy blood Thou hast redeemed us; help us, we beseech Thee, O our God. Amen.

Have mercy on me, dear Jesus, and grant that Thy blood may not be shed in vain for me, I most humbly beseech Thee. Amen.

AFTER CONSECRATION.

Look down upon me, good and gentle Jesus, while before Thy face I humbly kneel, and with burning soul pray and beseech Thee to fix deep in my heart lively sentiments of faith, hope and charity, true contrition for my sins, and firm purpose of amendment; the while I contemplate with great love and tender pity Thy five wounds, pondering over them within me, whilst I call to mind the words which David, Thy prophet, said of Thee, my Jesus: "Foderunt manus meas et pedes meos; dinumeraverunt omnia ossa mea." "They pierced my hands and my feet; they numbered all my bones," (Ps. xxi. 17, 18.)

O Jesus, give holy pastors to Thy Church.

Pope Pius VII, by a decree of the S. Congr. of Indulgences, dated April 10, 1821, granted—

The Plenary Indulgence to all who shall devoutly say the prayer, p. 477, before a crucifix, with contrite hearts, praying for the wants of Holy Church, after having confessed and communicated, and, by a recent decision, praying according to the intention of the Sovereign Pontiff.

DEVOTIONS AT MASS.

AT THE MEMENTO FOR THE DEAD.

I offer Thee again, O Lord, this holy sacrifice of the body and blood of Thy only Son, in behalf of the faithful departed, and in particular for the souls of (here name whom you chiefly propose to pray for) my parents, (if dead,) relatives, benefactors, neighbors, &c. Likewise of such as I have any ways injured, or been the occasion of their sins; of such as have injured me, and been my enemies; of such as die in war, or have none to pray for them. To these, O Lord, and to all that rest in Christ, grant, we beseech Thee, a place of refreshment, light, and peace, through the same Christ our Lord. Amen.

AT THE NOBIS QUOQUE PECCATORIBUS.

Vouchsafe to grant the same to us, poor and miserable sinners: judge us not according to our demerits; but through the infinite multitude of Thy mercies, in which we hope, liberally extend to us Thy grace and pardon.

We ask it of Thee in the name of Thy dear Son, Who liveth and reigneth eternally with Thee, and in that form of prayer which He Himself hath taught us.

AT THE PATER NOSTER.

O our Father, Who reignest in heaven, come and reign in my soul, come and sanctify it by Thy presence; come and subject it to Thy holy will, and render it obedient to the inspirations of Thy grace. Extinguish in my heart every feeling of hatred and revenge; forgive me as I forgive. Grant to me such wisdom and such strength that I may triumph over all temptations. Deliver me from all those evils which oppress me, and under which I groan, being burdened. I come to Thee, as a child to his father, to be fed; as a subject to his prince, to be protected; as one afflicted to his only succor, to be consoled and comforted.

AT THE LIBERA NOS.

Deliver us, we beseech Thee, O Lord, from all evils, past, present, and to come; and by the intercession of Blessed Mary, ever Virgin, and of all the saints, mercifully grant peace in our days, that by the assistance of Thy holy grace we may be always free from sin and secure from all disturbance.

AT THE PAX DOMINI.

Thy body was broken, and Thy blood shed for us: grant that the commemoration of this holy mystery may obtain for us peace; and that those who receive it may find everlasting rest.

O Lamb of God, pure and spotless victim, Who only canst satisfy the justice of an offended God, vouchsafe to make me partaker of the merits of Thy sacrifice. What lessons of humility, meekness, charity, and patience dost Thou not give me! Impress these virtues upon my heart, that it may be to Thee a pleasant habitation, wherein Thou mayest repose as in an abode of peace.

AFTER THE AGNUS DEI.

In saying to Thy apostles, peace I leave with you, my peace I give unto you; Thou hast promised, O Lord, to all Thy Church, that peace which the world cannot give—peace with Thee, and peace with ourselves.

Let nothing, O Lord, ever interrupt this holy peace; let nothing separate us from Thee, to Whom we heartily desire to be united, through the blessed sacrament of peace and reconciliation. Let this food of angels strengthen us in every Christian duty, so as never more to yield under temptations, or fall into our common weaknesses.

O my good God, and sweet Saviour Jesus, Who art present here for my sake, and givest Thyself to me for daily food, and for the supply of all my necessities; since without Thee, Who art the true food of my soul, I cannot live, I humbly beseech Thee to refresh me spiritually, and make me partaker of that grace which they experience who devoutly receive Thee. O good Jesus, despise me not, but vouchsafe to visit Thy servant, and by Thy grace to work and perfect all the effects and virtues of Thy holy sacrament in me, to Thy honor, O my God, and the eternal salvation of my soul. Amen.

Soul of Christ, sanctify me; Body of Christ, save me; Blood of Christ, inebriate me; Water out of the side of Christ, wash me; passion of Christ, strenghten me. O good Jesus, hear me, hide me within Thy wounds; suffer me not to be separated from Thee; defend me from the malignant enemy; at the hour of my death call me, and bid me come unto Thee, that with Thy saints I may praise Thee for all eternity. Amen.

AT THE DOMINE, NON SUM DIGNUS.

God only can be worthy of receiving God; how, then, can a soul so sinful as mine merit so great a happiness! But Thou, O Lord, regardest not Thy greatness, but Thy mercy. Thou willest that I come to Thee, as one sick to the physician who can heal him, as one poor to the rich lord who can assist him. O God of love, behold at Thy feet the poorest, the most infirm of Thy creatures. Unite me to Thyself, and I shall become rich and whole in Thy sight.— Work, I beseech Thee, this miracle, worthy of Thy omnipotence and charity.

WHILE THE PRIEST COMMUNICATES.

O sacred banquet, in which Christ is received, the memory of His passion is renewed, the mind is filled with grace, and a pledge of future glory is given to us!

Grant, O Lord Jesus, that we may so reverence the sacred mysteries of Thy body and blood, that we may ever find in ourselves the fruits of Thy redemption. Amen.

ACT OF SPIRITUAL COMMUNION FOR THOSE WHO DO NOT INTEND TO COMMUNICATE.

O my most loving Saviour, since I cannot have the happiness of receiving Thee this day, suffer me to gather up the precious crumbs that fall from Thy table, and to unite myself to Thy divine heart by faith, hope, and charity. I confess I do not deserve the children's bread; but I venture humbly to declare that, away from Thee, my soul is dried up with thirst, and my heart cast down with faintness. Come, then, into me, O my divine Jesus, come into my mind, to illuminate it with Thy light; come into my heart, to enkindle in it the fire of Thy love, and to unite it so intimately with Thy own, that it may be no more I that live, but Thou that livest in me, and reignest in me for ever.

AT THE COMMUNION.

Let it be now, O Lord, the effect of Thy mercy, that we, who have been present at this holy mystery, may find the benefit of it in our souls.

Oh, how sweet, Lord, is Thy spirit; Who, to shew Thy sweetness towards Thy children, givest them the most delicious bread from heaven, and sendest the proud away empty.

AT THE POST-COMMUNIONS.

Pour forth upon us, O Lord, the spirit of Thy love, that, by Thy mercy, Thou mayest make those of one mind whom Thou hast fed with one celestial food. Through our Lord Jesus Christ, Who liveth and reigneth with Thee, in the same unity of the holy spirit, &c.

We give Thee thanks, O God, for Thy mercy, in admitting us to have a part in offering this sacrifice to Thy holy name: accept it now to Thy glory, and be ever mindful of our weakness.

For a Saint's Day.

We have received heavenly mysteries, O Lord, in the commemoration of the blessed Mary ever Virgin, N., and all Thy saints; grant, we beseech Thee, that what we celebrate in time, we may obtain in the joys of eternity. Through our Lord, &c.

AT THE LAST GOSPEL.

O Eternal Word, speak to my soul, which adores Thee in profound silence; Thou Who art the great creator of all things, abandon not, I beseech Thee, Thy own creature: be Thou my life, my light, and my all.

O Light Eternal, enlighten me as to this present life, and in the life to come.

Reign in me as in Thine own inheritance; for Thou, O Lord, hast made me; Thou hast redeemed me. May I be ever Thine!

PRAYER AFTER MASS.

I return Thee humble thanks, O Lord, that Thou hast permitted me, the most unworthy of Thy creatures, to bear a part in this great sacrifice. Pardon, O Lord, all my distractions; and may Thy merits enable me to enter the august temple of that heavenly country, where the great sacrifice of Thy love is fulfilled, and where the soul lives eternally in God, and God in the soul.

Devotions at Vespers.

Although there is no express commandment which makes it a mortal sin to be absent from Vespers, yet every good Catholic will make it his duty to attend when he can, and see that his family are present also. We are commanded to sanctify the Lord's day, and the other Holy-days of obligation; but if a Catholic neglects the public service of the Church on Sunday afternoons, without any reasonable excuse, how can it be expected that he will apply himself to sanctify it in other ways?

Be present, therefore, always in the Church at Vespers, and employ the moments you spend there in praying devoutly.

While the priest and choir are singing the Office, you can follow them by using the following translation; or, if you prefer, you may make use of some other prayers, according to your devotion.

PRAYER BEFORE THE OFFICE.

O Lord, open my lips to praise Thy holy name: cleanse my heart also from all vain, perverse and wandering thoughts; enlighten my mind and inflame my heart, so that I may recite this office worthily, attentively, and devoutly, and merit a gracious hearing in the presence of Thy divine Majesty: through Christ our Lord. Amen.

Vespers for Sundays and Festivals.

First recite an Our Father *and a* Hail Mary; *and then begin with the sign of the Cross, thus:*

V. Deus in adjutorium meum intende.
R. Domine, ad adjuvandum me festina.
Gloria Patri, et Filio, et Spiritui Sancto.
Sicut erat in principio, et nunc, et semper, et in sæcula sæculorum. Amen.

V. ✝ Incline unto my aid, O God.
R. O Lord, make haste to help me.
Glory be to the Father, and to the Son, and to the Holy Ghost, as it was in the beginning, is now, and ever shall be, world without end. Amen.

Before and after each Psalm *is sung an* Antiphon, *which varies according to the Festivals.*

Ant. Dixit Dominus.

Antiphon. The Lord said:

PSALM CIX. *Dixit Dominus.*

Dixit Dominus Domino meo: Sede a dextris meis.
Donec ponam inimicos tuos: scabellum pedum tuorum.
Virgam virtutis tuæ emittet Dominus ex Sion: dominare in medio inimicorum tuorum.
Tecum principium in die virtutis tuæ, in splendoribus sanctorum: ex utero ante luciferum genui te.

The Lord said to my Lord: Sit Thou at my right hand, until I make Thy enemies Thy footstool.

The Lord will send forth the sceptre of Thy power out of Sion: rule Thou in the midst of Thy enemies.

With Thee is the principality in the day of Thy strength, in the brightness of Thy saints: from the womb before the day-star I begot Thee.

4*

Juravit Dominus, et non pœnitebit eum: Tu es sacerdos in æternum secundum ordinem Melchisedech.

Dominus á dextris tuis: confregit in die iræ suæ reges.

Judicabit in nationibus, implebit ruinas: conquassabit capita in terra multorum.

De torrente in via bibet: propterea exaltabit caput.

Gloria Patri, &c.

Ant. Dixit Dominus Domino meo, Sede á dextris meis.

Ant. Fidelia.

The Lord hath sworn, and he will not repent: Thou art a priest forever according to the order of Melchisedech.

The Lord at Thy right hand hath broken kings in the day of His wrath.

He shall judge among nations, He shall fill ruins, He shall crush the heads in the land of many.

He shall drink of the torrent in the way: therefore shall He lift up the head.

Glory be to the Father, &c.

Ant. The Lord said to my Lord, Sit Thou at my right hand.

Ant. All His commandments.—

PSALM CX. *Confitebor tibi.*

Confitebor tibi, Domine, in toto corde meo: in concilio justorum, et congregatione.

Magna opera Domini: exquisita in omnes voluntates ejus.

Confessio et magnificentia opus ejus: et justitia ejus manet in sæculum sæculi.

Memoriam fecit mirabilium suorum, misericors et

I will praise Thee, O Lord, with my whole heart: in the assembly of the just, and in the congregation.

Great are the works of the Lord: exquisite and agreeable to all His designs.

His work is His praise and glory: and His justice remaineth forever.

The merciful and gracious Lord hath appointed

miserator Dominus: escam dedit timentibus se.

Memor erit in sæculum testamenti sui: virtutem operum suorum annuntiabit populo suo.

Ut det illis hæreditatem Gentium: opera manuum ejus, veritas et judicium.

Fidelia omnia mandata ejus, confirmata in sæculum sæculi: facta in veritate et æquitate.

Redemptionem misit populo suo: mandavit in æternum testamentum suum.

Sanctum et terribile nomen ejus: initium sapientiæ timor Domini.

Intellectus bonus omnibus facientibus eum: laudatio ejus manet in sæculum sæculi.

Gloria Patri, &c.

Ant. Fidelia omnia mandata ejus; confirmata in sæculum sæculi.

Ant. In mandatis.

PSALM CXI.

Beatus vir qui timet Dominum: in mandatis ejus volet nimis.

a memorial of His wonderful works: He hath given food to them that fear Him.

He will be forever mindful of His covenant: the greatness of His works will He publish to His people.

To give them the inheritance of the Gentiles: the works of His hands are truth and justice.

True and lasting are all His ordinances, confirmed for ever and ever; made in truth and justice.

He hath sent redemption to His people: He hath appointed His covenant forever.

Holy and awful is His name: the fear of the Lord is the beginning of wisdom.

All understand it right, who practise it: His praise endureth for ever and ever.

Glory be to the Father, &c.

Ant. All His commandments are faithful, confirmed for ever and ever.

Ant. He shall delight—

Beatus vir.

Blessed is the man that feareth the Lord: in His commandments He shall take great delight.

Potens in terra erit semen ejus: generatio rectorum benedicetur.

Gloria et divitiæ in domo ejus: et justitia ejus manet in sæculum sæculi.

Exortum est in tenebris lumen rectis: misericors, et miserator et justus.

Jucundus homo qui miseretur et commodat, disponet sermones suos in judicio: quia in æternum non commovebitur.

In memoria æterna erit justus: ab auditione mala non timebit.

Paratum cor ejus sperare in Domino, confirmatum est cor ejus: non commovebitur donec despiciat inimicos suos.

Dispersit, dedit pauperibus, justitia ejus manet in sæculum sæculi: cornu ejus exaltabitur in gloria.

Peccator videbit et irascetur, dentibus suis fremet et tabescet: desiderium peccatorum peribit.

Gloria Patri, &c.

Mighty on earth shall be His seed: the generation of the righteous shall be blessed.

Glory and wealth shall be in His house: and His justice endureth for ever and ever.

He is risen in darkness, a light to the upright: He is merciful, compassionate, and just.

Acceptable is the man that showeth mercy and lendeth: He shall order His words with judgment, and He shall never give way.

The just man shall be in eternal remembrance: He shall not fear an evil report.

His heart is ready to hope in the Lord: his heart is strengthened: he shall not yield till he despise his enemies.

He hath distributed and given to the poor: his righteousness remaineth forever: his power shall be exalted in glory.

The sinner shall see it, and be enraged: he shall gnash his teeth and pine away: the desire of sinners shall perish.

Glory be to the Father, &c.

Ant. In mandatis ejus cupit nimis.

Ant. Sit nomen Domini.

Ant. He shall delight exceedingly in His commandments.

Ant. Blessed be the name—

PSALM CXII. *Laudate pueri.*

Laudate, pueri, Dominum: laudate nomen Domini.

Sit nomen Domini benedictum: ex hoc nunc, et usque in sæculum.

A solis ortu usque ad occasum: laudabile nomen Domini.

Excelsus super omnes gentes Dominus: et super cœlos gloria ejus.

Quis sicut Dominus Deus noster, qui in altis habitat: et humilia respicit in cœlo et in terra?

Suscitans à terra inopem: et de stercore erigens pauperem.

Ut collocet eum cum principibus: cum principibus populi sui.

Qui habitare facit sterilem in domo: matrem filiorum lætantem.

Gloria Patri, &c.

Praise the Lord, ye servants of the Lord: praise ye the name of the Lord.

Let the name of the Lord be blessed: now and for evermore.

From the rising of the sun to the setting thereof: worthy of praise is the name of the Lord.

High is the Lord above all the nations: and above the heavens in his glory.

Who is like unto the Lord our God, who dwelleth on high: and beholdeth what is below in heaven and on earth?

Who from the earth raiseth up the needy one: and from the dunghill lifteth up the poor one:

To place him with the princes: the princes of His people.

Who maketh the barren woman to dwell in her house: the joyful mother of many children.

Glory be to the Father, &c.

Ant. Sit nomen Domini benedictum in sæcula.

Ant. Nos qui vivimus.

Ant. Blessed be the name of the Lord for evermore.

Ant. We who live—

PSALM CXIII. *In exitu Israel.*

In exitu Israel de Ægypto: domus Jacob de populo barbaro.

When Israel came out of Egypt: the house of Jacob from among a strange people.

Facta est Judæa sanctificatio ejus: Israel potestas ejus.

Judah was made His sanctuary: and Israel His dominion.

Mare vidit, et fugit: Jordanis conversus est retrorsum.

The sea beheld and fled: Jordan was turned back.

Montes exultaverunt ut arietes: et colles sicut agni ovium.

The mountains skipped like rams: and the little hills like the lambs of the flock.

Quid est tibi, mare, quod fugisti: et tu Jordanis, quia conversus es retrorsum?

What aileth thee, O thou sea, that thou fleddest: and thou Jordan, that thou wast turned back?

Montes exultastis sicut arietes: et colles sicut agni ovium?

Ye mountains, that ye skipped like rams: and ye little hills like the lambs of the flock?

A facie Domini mota est terra: a facie Dei Jacob.

At the presence of the Lord the earth was moved: at the presence of the God of Jacob.

Qui convertit petram in stagna aquarum: et rupem in fontes aquarum.

Who turned the rock into a standing water: and the stony hill into a flowing stream.

Non nobis, Domine, non nobis: sed nomini tuo da gloriam.

Super misericordia tua, et veritate tua: nequando dicant gentes, Ubi est Deus eorum?

Deus autem noster in cœlo: omnia quæcumque voluit, fecit.

Simulacra gentium argentum et aurum: opera manuum hominum.

Os habent, et non loquentur: oculos habent, et non videbunt.

Aures habent, et non audient: nares habent, et non odorabunt.

Manus habent, et non palpabunt; pedes habent, et non ambulabunt: non clamabunt in gutture suo.

Similes illis fiant qui faciunt ea: et omnes qui confidunt in eis.

Domus Israel speravit in Domino: adjutor eorum et protector eorum est.

Domus Aaron speravit in Domino: adjutor eorum et protector eorum est.

Not unto us, O Lord, not unto us: but unto Thy name give the glory.

For Thy mercy and for Thy truth's sake: lest the gentiles should say, Where is their God?

But our God is in heaven: He hath done whatsoever He would.

The idols of the gentiles are silver and gold: the work of the hands of men.

They have mouths, and they shall not speak: they have eyes, and they shall not see.

They have ears, and they shall not hear: they have noses, and they shall not smell.

They have hands, and they shall not feel; they have feet, and they shall not walk: neither shall they speak through their throat.

Let those that make them become like unto them: and all such as put their trust in them.

The house of Israel hath hoped in the Lord: He is their helper and protector.

The house of Aaron hath hoped in the Lord: He is their helper and protector.

Qui timent Dominum, speraverunt in Domino: adjutor eorum et protector eorum est.

Dominus memor fuit nostri: et benedixit nobis.

Benedixit domui Israel: benedixit domui Aaron.

Benedixit omnibus, qui timent Dominum: pusillis cum marjoribus.

Adjiciat Dominus super vos: super vos et super filios vestros.

Benedicti vos a Domino: qui fecit cœlum et terram.

Cœlum cœli Domino: terram autem dedit filiis hominum.

Non mortui laudabunt te, Domine: neque omnes qui descendunt in infernum.

Sed nos qui vivimus, benedicimus Domino: ex hoc nunc et usque in sæculum.

Gloria Patri, &c.

Ant. Nos qui vivimus, benedicimus Domino.

They that fear the Lord, have hoped in the Lord: He is their helper and protector.

The Lord hath been mindful of us: and hath blessed us.

He hath blessed the house of Israel: he hath blessed the house of Aaron.

He hath blessed all that fear the Lord: the least together with the greatest.

May the Lord add blessings upon you: upon you, and upon your children.

Blessed be ye of the Lord: Who Hath made heaven and earth.

The heaven of heavens is the Lord's: but the earth hath He given to the children of men.

The dead shall not praise Thee, O Lord: neither all they that go down into hell.

But we who live, bless the Lord: from this time forth for evermore.

Glory be to the Father, &c.

Ant. We who live, bless the Lord.

DEVOTIONS AT VESPERS. 49

Then follow the LITTLE CHAPTER *and the* HYMN; *after which is said, with its proper* ANTIPHON:

The Magnificat, or Canticle of the Blessed Virgin.

Magnificat: anima mea Dominum.

My soul doth magnify: the Lord.

Et exultavit spiritus meus: in Deo salutari meo.

And my spirit hath rejoiced in God my Saviour.

Quia respexit humilitatem ancillæ suæ: ecce enim ex hoc beatam me dicent omnes generationes.

For He hath regarded the lowliness of His handmaid: for behold from henceforth all generations shall call me blessed.

Quia fecit mihi magna qui potens est: et sanctum nomen ejus.

For He that is mighty hath done great things unto me: and holy is His name.

Et misericordia ejus a progenie in progenies: timentibus eum.

And His mercy is from generation to generation: unto them that fear Him.

Fecit potentiam in brachio suo: dispersit superbos mente cordis sui.

He hath showed strength with His arm: He hath scattered the proud in the imagination of their heart.

Deposuit potentes de sede: et exaltavit humiles.

He hath put down the mighty from their seat: and hath exalted the humble.

Esurientes implevit bonis: et divites dimisit inanes.

He hath filled the hungry with good things: and the rich He hath sent away empty.

Suscepit Israel puerum suum: recordatus misericordiæ suæ.

He hath received Israel, His servant, being mindful of His mercy.

Sicut locutus est ad patres nostros: Abraham, et semini ejus in sæcula.

Gloria Patri, &c.

As He spoke to our fathers: to Abraham and his seed forever.

Glory be to the Father, &c.

Here follow the proper COLLECT, *and the* COMMEMORATIONS, *if any; after which one of the* ANTIPHONS OF THE BLESSED VIRGIN *is sung, as at page 63.*

[N. B.—The Psalms hitherto given, are sung on Sundays when the Vespers are those *of the Sunday.* When the Vespers are those of a *Saint, &c.*, some changes are made, which we shall now indicate, observing that when only one Psalm is given, as the *last* Psalm, the others are the same as on Sundays.]

COMMON OF APOSTLES AND EVANGELISTS.

First Vespers.

Psalms as on Sundays, with the exception of the last, for which Psalm CXVI., LAUDATE DOMINUM, *is used, as follows:*

PSALM CXVI. *Laudate Dominum.*

Laudate Dominum, omnes gentes: laudate eum, omnes populi:

Quoniam confirmata est super nos misericordia ejus: et veritas Domini manet in æternum.

Praise the Lord, all ye gentiles: praise Him, all ye people:

For His mercy is confirmed upon us: and the truth of the Lord endureth forever.

Second Vespers.

Psalm cix., DIXIT DOMINUS. Psalm cxii., LAUDATE, PUERI.
Then the three following:

PSALM CXV. *Credidi.*

Credidi, propter quod locutus sum: ego autem humiliatus sum nimis.

Ego dixi in excessu meo: Omnis homo mendax.

Quid retribuam Domino: pro omnibus quæ retribuit mihi?

Calicem salutaris accipiam: et nomen Domini invocabo.

Vota mea Domino reddam coram omni populo ejus: pretiosa in conspectu Domini mors sanctorum ejus.

O Domine, quia ego servus tuus: ego servus tuus, et filius ancillæ tuæ.

Dirupisti vincula mea: tibi sacrificabo hostiam laudis, et nomen Domini invocabo.

Vota mea Domino reddam in conspectu omnis populi ejus: in atriis domus Domini, in medio tui, Jerusalem.

I believed, and therefore did I speak: but I was humbled exceedingly.

I said in my excess: All men are liars.

What shall I render unto the Lord: for all He hath rendered unto me?

I will take the chalice of salvation: and call upon the name of the Lord.

I will pay my vows unto the Lord in the presence of all His people: precious in the sight of the Lord is the death of His saints.

O Lord, I am Thy servant: I am Thy servant, and the son of Thy handmaid.

Thou hast broken my bonds: I will offer unto Thee the sacrifice of praise, and will call upon the name of the Lord.

I will pay my vows unto the Lord in the sight of all His people: in the courts of the house of the Lord, in the midst of Thee, O Jerusalem.

PSALM CXXV. *In convertendo.*

In convertendo Dominus captivitatem Sion: facti sumus sicut consolati:

Tunc repletum est gaudio os nostrum: et lingua nostra exultatione.

Tunc dicent inter gentes: Magnificavit Dominus facere cum eis.

Magnificavit Dominus facere nobiscum: facti sumus lætantes.

Converte, Domine, captivitatem nostram: sicut, torrens in austro.

Qui seminant in lacrymis: in exultatione metent.

Euntes ibant et flebant: mittentes semina sua.

Venientes autem venient cum exultatione: portantes manipulos suos.

When the Lord turned again the captivity of Sion: we became like men that are comforted:

Then was our mouth filled with gladness: and our tongue with joy.

Then shall they say among the gentiles: The Lord hath done great things for them.

The Lord hath done great things for us: we are become very joyful.

Turn again our captivity, O Lord: as a river in the south.

They that sow in tears: shall reap in joy.

Going on their way, they went and wept: scattering their seed.

But returning, they shall come with joyfulness: bringing their sheaves with them.

PSALM CXXXVIII. *Domine, probasti.*

Domine, probasti me, et cognovisti me: tu cognovisti sessionem meam, et resurrectionem meam.

Intellexisti cogitationes meas de longe: semitam

O Lord, Thou hast proved me, and known me: Thou hast known my sitting down and my rising up.

Thou hast understood my thoughts long before: my

DEVOTIONS AT VESPERS. 53

meam, et funiculum meum investigasti.

Et omnes vias meas prævidisti: quia non est sermo in lingua mea.

Ecce, Domine, tu cognovisti, omnia novissima et antiqua: tu formasti me, et posuisti super me manum tuam.

Mirabilis facta est scientia tua ex me: confortata est, et non potero ad eam.

Quo ibo a spiritu tuo: et quo a facie tua fugiam?

Si ascendero in cœlum, tu illic es: si descendero in infernum, ades.

Si sumpsero pennas meas diluculo: et habitavero in extremis maris:

Etenim illuc manus tua deducet me: et tenebit me dextera tua.

Et dixi, Forsitan tenebræ conculcabunt me: et nox illuminatio mea in deliciis meis.

Quia tenebræ non obscurabuntur a te, et nox sicut

path and my line hast Thou searched out.

And Thou hast foreseen all my ways: for there is not a word in my tongue.

Behold, O Lord, Thou hast known all things, new and old: Thou hast formed me, and laid Thine hand upon me.

Thy knowledge is become too wonderful for me: it is strong and high, and I cannot attain unto it.

Whither shall I go from Thy spirit: and whither shall I flee from Thy face?

If I go up into heaven, Thou art there: if I go down into hell, Thou art there also.

If I take to me the wings of the morning: and dwell in the uttermost parts of the sea:

Even there also shall Thy hand lead me: and Thy right hand shall hold me.

And I said, Peradventure the darkness shall cover me: and night shall be my light in my pleasures.

But darkness shall not be dark to Thee, and night

5*

dies illuminabitur: sicut tenebræ ejus, ita et lumen ejus.

Quia tu possedisti renes meos: suscepisti me de utero matris meæ.

Confitebor tibi quia terribiliter magnificatus es: mirabilia opera tua, et anima mea cognoscit nimis.

Non est occultatum os meum a te, quod fecisti in occulto: et substantia mea in inferioribus terræ.

Imperfectum meum viderunt oculi tui, et in libro tuo omnes scribentur: dies formabuntur, et nemo in eis.

Mihi autem nimis honorificati sunt amici tui, Deus: nimis confortatus est principatus eorum.

Dinumerabo eos, et super arenam multiplicabuntur: exsurrexi, et adhuc sum tecum.

Si occideris, Deus, peccatores: viri sanguinum declinate a me:

shall be as light as the day: the darkness thereof and the light thereof are alike to Thee.

For Thou hast possessed my reins: Thou hast holpen me from my mother's womb.

I will praise Thee, for Thou art fearfully magnified: marvellous are Thy works, and my soul knoweth them right well.

My bones are not hid from Thee, which Thou didst fashion in secret: and my substance in the lower parts of the earth.

Thine eyes did see my imperfect being, and in Thy book shall all men be written: day by day shall they be formed, while yet there is no one.

But to me Thy friends, O God, are made exceedingly honorable: most firmly is their dominion established.

I will tell them, and they shall be more in number than the sand: I have risen up, and am still with Thee.

Wilt Thou not slay the wicked, O God: ye men of blood, depart from me:

Quia dicitis in cogitatione: Accipient in vanitate civitates tuas.	For ye say in your thoughts: They shall take Thy cities in vain.
Nonne qui oderunt te, Domine, oderam: et super inimicos tuos tabescebam?	Have I not hated them, O Lord, that hated Thee: and pined away because of Thine enemies?
Perfecto odio oderam illos: et inimici facti sunt mihi.	I have hated them with a perfect hatred: and they became as enemies unto me.
Proba me, Deus, et scito cor meum: interroga me, et cognosce semitas meas.	Prove me, O God, and try my heart: examine me, and search out my paths.
Et vide, si via iniquitatis in me est: et deduc me in via æterna.	And look well, if there be in me the way of iniquity: and lead me in the way everlasting.

COMMON OF MARTYRS.

First Vespers: last Psalm, LAUDATE DOMINUM, p. 50. *Second Vespers:* last Psalm, CREDIDI, p. 51.

COMMON OF A CONFESSOR AND BISHOP.

First Vespers: last Psalm, LAUDATE DOMINUM, p. 50. *Second Vespers:* last Psalm, MEMENTO, DOMINE, *as follows:*

PSALM CXXXI.   *Memento, Domine.*

Memento, Domine, David: et omnis mansuetudinis ejus.	O Lord, remember David: and all his meekness.
Sicut juravit Domino: votum vovit Deo Jacob:	How he sware unto the Lord: and vowed a vow unto the God of Jacob:

Si introiero in tabernaculum domus meæ: si ascendero in lectum strati mei:	If I shall enter into the tabernacle of mine house: If I shall go up into my bed wherein I lie:
Si dedero somnum oculis meis: et palpebris meis dormitationem,	If I shall give sleep to mine eyes: or slumber to mine eyelids,
Et requiem temporibus meis: donec inveniam locum Domino, tabernaculum Deo Jacob.	Or rest unto the temples of my head: until I find a place for the Lord, a tabernacle for the God of Jacob.
Ecce audivimus eam in Ephrata: invenimus eam in campis silvæ.	Lo, we heard of it in Ephrata: we found it in the fields of the wood.
Introibimus in tabernaculum ejus: adorabimus in loco, ubi steterunt pedes ejus.	We will go into His tabernacle: we will worship in the place, where His feet have stood.
Surge, Domine, in requiem tuam: tu et arca sanctificationis tuæ.	Arise, O Lord, into Thy resting-place: Thou, and the ark of Thy holiness.
Sacerdotes tui induantur justitiam: et sancti tui exultent.	Let Thy priests be clothed with justice: and let Thy saints rejoice.
Propter David servum tuum: non avertas faciem Christi tui.	For Thy servant David's sake: turn not away the face of Thine Anointed.
Juravit Dominus David veritatem, et non frustrabitur eam: De fructu ventris tui ponam super sedem tuam.	The Lord hath sworn the truth unto David, and He will not make it void: Of the fruit of Thy body I will set upon Thy throne.
Si custodierint filii tui testamentum meum: et testimonia mea hæc quæ docebo eos:	If Thy children will keep My covenant: and these My testimonies which I shall teach them:

Et filii eorum usque in sæculum: sedebunt super sedem tuam.

Quoniam elegit Dominus Sion: elegit eam in habitationem sibi.

Hæc requies mea in sæculum sæculi: hic habitabo, quoniam elegi eam.

Viduam ejus benedicens benedicam: pauperes ejus saturabo panibus.

Sacerdotes ejus induam salutari: et sancti ejus exultatione exultabunt.

Illuc producam cornu David: paravi lucernam Christo meo.

Inimicos ejus induam confusione: super ipsum autem efflorebit sanctificatio mea.

Their children also for evermore: shall sit upon Thy throne.

For the Lord hath chosen Sion: He hath chosen her for His dwelling.

This is My rest for ever and ever: here will I dwell, for I have chosen her.

With blessing, I will bless her widows: I will satisfy her poor with bread.

I will clothe her priests with salvation: and her saints shall rejoice with exceeding joy.

There will I bring forth a horn unto David: I have prepared a lamp for Mine Anointed.

His enemies will I clothe with confusion: but upon himself shall My sanctification flourish.

COMMON OF A CONFESSOR NOT A BISHOP.

First and Second Vespers, same Psalms as on Sundays; last Psalm, LAUDATE DOMINUM, *p. 50.*

COMMON OF VIRGINS, AND OF HOLY WOMEN.

First and Second Vespers, Psalm cix. DIXIT DOMINUS. *Psalm* cxii. LAUDATE, PUERI.

Then the three following:

PSALM CXXI. *Lætatus sum in his.*

Lætatus sum in his quæ dicta sunt mihi: In domum Domini ibimus.	I was glad at the things that were said unto me: We will go into the house of the Lord.
Stantes erant pedes nostri: in atriis tuis, Jerusalem.	Our feet were wont to stand: in thy courts, O Jerusalem.
Jerusalem quæ ædificatur ut civitas: cujus participatio ejus in idipsum.	Jerusalem, which is built as a city: that is at unity with itself.
Illuc enim ascenderunt tribus, tribus Domini: testimonium Israel, ad confitendum nomini Domini.	For thither did the tribes go up, the tribes of the Lord: the testimony of Israel, to praise the name of the Lord.
Quia illic sederunt sedes in judicio: sedes super domum David.	For there are set the seats of judgment: the seats over the house of David.
Rogate quæ ad pacem sunt Jerusalem: et abundantia diligentibus te.	Pray ye for the things that are for the peace of Jerusalem: and plenteousness be to them that love Thee.
Fiat pax in virtute tua: et abundantia in turribus tuis.	Let peace be in thy strength: and plenteousness in thy towers.
Propter fratres meos et proximos meos: loquebar pacem de te.	For my brethren and companions' sake: I spake peace concerning thee.
Propter domum Domini Dei nostri: quæsivi bona tibi.	Because of the house of the Lord our God: I have sought good things for Thee.

DEVOTIONS AT VESPERS.

PSALM CXXVI. *Nisi Dominus.*

Nisi Dominus ædificaverit domum : in vanum laboraverunt qui ædificant eam.

Nisi Dominus custodierit civitatem; frustra vigilat qui custodit eam.

Vanum est vobis ante lucem surgere: surgite postquam sederitis, qui manducatis panem doloris.

Cum dederit dilectis suis somnum : ecce hæreditas Domini filii, merces fructus ventris.

Sicut sagittæ in manu potentis: ita filii excussorum.

Beatus vir qui implevit desiderium suum ex ipsis: non confundetur, cum loquetur inimicis suis in porta.

Unless the Lord build the house: they labor in vain that build it.

Unless the Lord keep the city: he watcheth in vain that keepeth it.

In vain ye rise before the light: rise not till ye have rested, O ye that eat the bread of sorrow.

When He hath given sleep to His beloved : lo, children are an heritage from the Lord, and the fruit of the womb a reward.

Like as arrows in the hand of the mighty one: so are the children of those who have been cast out.

Blessed is the man whose desire is satisfied with them he shall not be confounded, when he speaketh with his enemies in the gate.

PSALM CXLVII. *Lauda Jerusalem.*

Lauda Jerusalem Dominum: lauda Deum tuum, Sion.

Quoniam confortavit seras portarum tuarum: benedixit filiis tuis in te.

Praise the Lord, O Jerusalem : Praise thy God, O Sion.

For He hath strengthened the bars of thy gates: He hath blessed thy children within thee.

Qui posuit fines tuos pacem: et adipe frumenti satiat te.

Qui emittet eloquium suum terræ: velociter currit sermo ejus.

Qui dat nivem sicut lanam: nebulam sicut cineram spargit.

Mittit crystallum suam sicut buccellas: ante faciem frigoris ejus quis sustinebit?

Emittet verbum suum, et liquefaciet ea: flabit spiritus ejus, et fluent aquæ.

Qui annuntiat verbum suum Jacob: justitias et judicia sua Israel.

Non fecit taliter omni nationi: et judicia sua non manifestavit eis.

He hath made peace within thy borders: and filleth thee with the fatness of corn.

He sendeth forth His commandment on the earth: His word runneth very swiftly.

He giveth snow like wool: He scattereth the hoar-frost like ashes.

He sendeth His ice like morsels: who is able to abide His frost?

He shall send forth His word, and melt them: He shall blow with His wind, and the waters shall flow.

He maketh known His word unto Jacob: His statutes and ordinances unto Israel.

He hath not dealt so with any nation: neither hath He showed them His judgments.

COMMON OF THE B. V. MARY.

The Psalms, in both Vespers, as in the COMMON OF VIRGINS; *and the same Psalms are sung at Vespers on* NEW YEAR'S DAY.

CHRISTMAS DAY.

First Vespers: last *Psalm,* LAUDATE DOMINUM, *p.* 50. *Second Vespers (and through the Octave:)* 4th *Psalm,* DE PROFUNDIS, *below. Last do.,* MEMENTO, DOMINE, *p.* 55.

PSALM CXXIX. *De profundis.*

De profundis clamavi ad te, Domine: Domine, exaui vocem meam.

Fiant aures tuæ intendentes: in vocem deprecationis meæ.

Si iniquitates observaveris, Domine: Domine, quis sustinebit?

Quia apud te propitiatio est: et propter legem tuam sustinui te, Domine.

Sustinuit anima mea in verbo ejus: speravit anima mea in Domino.

A custodia matutina usque ad noctem: speret Israel in Domino.

Quia apud Dominum misericordia: et copiosa apud eum redemptio.

Et ipse redimet Israel: ex omnibus iniquitatibus ejus.

Out of the depths have I cried unto Thee, O Lord: Lord, hear my voice.

Oh, let Thine ears consider well: the voice of my supplication.

If Thou, O Lord, shalt mark iniquities: Lord, who shall abide it?

For with Thee there is propitiation: and because of Thy law I have waited for Thee, O Lord.

My soul hath waited on His word: my soul hath hoped in the Lord.

From the morning watch even until night: let Israel hope in the Lord.

For with the Lord there is mercy: and with Him is plenteous redemption.

And He shall redeem Israel: from all his iniquities.

THE EPIPHANY.

First Vespers: last Psalm, LAUDATE DOMINUM, *p.* 50. *Second Vespers; as on Sundays.*

SS. PETER AND PAUL.

First Vespers: last Psalm, LAUDATE DOMINUM, *p.* 50. *Second Vespers: as in* COMMON OF APOSTLES.

ALL SAINTS.

First Vespers: last Psalm, LAUDATE DOMINUM, p. 50. *Second Vespers:* last Psalm, CREDIDI, p. 51.

ASCENSION DAY.

Second Vespers: last Psalm, LAUDATE DOMINUM, p. 50.

CORPUS CHRISTI, AND FEAST OF SACRED HEART.

Second Vespers: 3d Psalm, CREDIDI, p. 51. 4th do., BEATI OMNES, below. Last do., LAUDA JERUSALEM, p. 59.

PSALM CXXVII. *Beati omnes.*

Beati omnes qui timent Dominum: qui ambulant in viis ejus.

Labores manuum tuarum quia manducabis: beatus es, et bene tibi erit.

Uxor tua sicut vitis abundans: in lateribus domus tuæ.

Filii tui sicut novellæ olivarum: in circuitu mensæ tuæ.

Ecce sic benedicetur homo: qui timet Dominum.

Benedicat tibi Dominus ex Sion: et videas bona Jerusalem omnibus diebus vitæ tuæ.

Et videas filios filiorum tuorum: pacem super Israel.

Blessed are all they that fear the Lord: that walk in His ways.

For thou shalt eat the labors of thy hands: blessed art thou, and it shall be well with thee.

Thy wife shall be as a fruitful vine: on the walls of thy house.

Thy children as olive plants: round about thy table.

Behold, thus shall the man be blessed: that feareth the Lord.

May the Lord bless thee out of Sion: and mayest thou see the good things of Jerusalem all the days of thy life.

And mayest thou see thy children's children: peace upon Israel.

The Four Antiphons of the B. V. Mary.

USUALLY SUNG AFTER VESPERS, ACCORDING TO THE SEASON.

(During Advent, and until the Purification.)

ALMA REDEMPTORIS MATER.

Alma Redemptoris Mater, quæ pervia cœli Porta manes, et stella maris, succurre cadenti Surgere qui curat populo; tu quæ genuisti, Natura mirante, tuum sanctum Genitorem, Virgo priùs ac posteriùs; Gabrielis ab ore, Sumens illud Ave, peccatorum miserere.	Mother of Jesus, heaven's open gate, Star of the sea, uphold our fallen state. O thou, whose sacred womb thy Maker bore, Remaining ever virginal and pure, From sinful lips receive that earnest Hail, Which first from Gabriel, hallowed herald, fell.
V. Angelus Domini nuntiavit Mariæ. *R. Et concepit de Spiritu Sancto.*	*V.* The Angel of the Lord declared unto Mary, *R. And she conceived by the Holy Ghost.*

PRAYER.

Gratiam tuam, quæsumus, Domine, mentibus nostris infunde: ut qui angelo nuntiante Christi Filii tui incarnationem cognovimus,

Pour forth, we beseech Thee, O Lord, Thy grace into our hearts, that we, to whom the incarnation of Christ Thy Son has been

per passionem ejus et crucem ad resurrectionis gloriam perducamur. Per eundum Christum Dominum nostrum. Amen.

made known by the message of an angel, may, by His passion and cross, be brought to the glory of His resurrection, through the same Christ our Lord Amen.

(From the Purification until Easter.)

AVE, REGINA CŒLORUM.

Ave, regina cœlorum,

Hail Mary, Queen of heaven above,

Ave, domina angelorum,

Whom radiant Angels own and love!

Salve radix, salve porta,

Hail fruitful root, hail portal bright,

Ex qua mundo lux est orta.

Whence streamed on earth celestial light.

Gaude virgo gloriosa,

Hail glorious Maid, with beauty blessed,

Super omnes speciosa;

Far lovelier than the loveliest;

Vale, ô valde decora,

Oh! crowned with grace and glory thus,

Et pro nobis Christum exora.

Pray, Mary, pray to Christ for us!

V. Dignare me laudare te, Virgo sacrata.

R. Da mihi virtutem contra hostes tuos.

V. O deign to let me praise Thee, Sacred Virgin!

R. And give me power against thy enemies.

PRAYER.

Concede, misericors Deus, fragilitati nostræ præsidium: ut qui sanctæ Dei Gen-

Grant us, O merciful God, a safeguard against all our weakness, that we, who

itricis memoriam agimus, intercessionis ejus auxilio, à nostris iniquitatibus resurgamus. Per eundem Christum Dominum nostrum. Amen.

celebrate the memory of the holy Mother of God, may, by the help of her intercession, rise again from our iniquities, through the same Christ our Lord. Amen.

(From Easter until Trinity.)

REGINA CŒLI.

Regina cœli lætare, Alleluia.
Quia quem meruisti portare, Alleluia.
Resurrexit sicut dixit, Alleluia.
Ora pro nobis Deum, Alleluia.

V. Gaude et lætare, Virgo Maria, Alleluia.
R. Quia surrexit Dominus vere. Alleluia.

Joy to thee, O Queen of heaven, Alleluia!
He whom thou wast meet to bear, Alleluia!
As He promised, hath arisen, Alleluia!
Pour for us to Him thy prayer, Alleluia!

V. Rejoice and be glad O Virgin Mary, Alleluia!
R. For the Lord is truly risen. Alleluia!

PRAYER.

Deus, qui per resurrectionem Filii tui Domini nostri Jesu Christi mundum lætificare dignatus es; præsta quæsumus, ut per ejus genitricem virginem Mariam perpetuæ capiamus gaudia vitæ. Per eundem Christum Dominum nostrum. Amen.

O God, Who, by the resurrection of Thy Son, our Lord Jesus Christ, hast been pleased to fill the world with joy, grant, we beseech Thee, that by His mother, the Virgin Mary, we may receive the joys of eternal life, through the same Christ our Lord. Amen.

(From Trinity Sunday until Advent.)

SALVE, REGINA.

Salve, Regina, mater misericordiæ!—vita, dulcedo, et spes nostra, salve!

Ad te clamamus exules Filii Hevæ.

Ad te suspiramus gementes et flentes in hac lacrymarum valle.

Eia ergo, advocata nostra, illos tuos misericordes oculos ad nos converte. Et Jesum, benedictum fructum ventris tui, nobis post hoc exilium ostende.

O clemens, O pia, O dulcis virgo Maria.

V. Ora pro nobis, sancta Dei genitrix.
R. Ut digni efficiamur promissionibus Christi.

Mother of mercy, hail! O gentle Queen! Our life, our sweetness, and our hope all hail!

Children of Eve, To thee we cry from our sad banishment.

To thee we send our sighs, Weeping and mourning in this tearful vale.

Come then, our Advocate, O! turn on us those pitying eyes of thine:
And, our long exile past,
Show us at last
Jesus, of thy pure womb the fruit divine;

O Virgin Mary, Mother blest!
O sweetest, gentlest, holiest!

V. Pray for us, O holy Mother of God.
R. That we may be made worthy of the promises of Christ.

PRAYER.

Omnipotens sempiterne Deus qui, gloriosæ Virginis Matris Mariæ corpus et an-

Almighty and eternal God! Who, by the co-operation of the Holy Ghost,

imam, ut dignum Filii tui habitaculum effici mereretur, Spiritu Sancto co-operante, præparisti: da ut cujus commemoratione lætamur ejus pia intercessione ab instantibus malis et a morte perpetua liberemur. Per eundem Christum Dominum nostrum. Amen.

didst prepare the body and soul of the glorious Virgin Mother, Mary, that she might become a worthy habitation for Thy Son, grant, that as with joy we celebrate her memory, so by her pious intercession we may be delivered from present evils, and from eternal death, through the same Christ our Lord. Amen.

V. Divinum auxilium maneat semper nobiscum.

R. Amen.

V. May the divine assistance remain always with us.

R. Amen.

CONCLUDING PRAYER.

To the most Holy and undivided Trinity, to the crucified humanity of our Lord Jesus Christ, to the most blessed and glorious and ever-faithful virginity of the Virgin Mary, and to the assembly of all the Saints in heaven, may everlasting praise, honor, power, and glory be given, by every creature, and to us, also, the remission of all our sins, through never-ending ages. — Amen.

V. Blessed be the womb of the Virgin Mary, which bore the Son of the eternal Father!

R. And blessed be the breasts which nourished Christ our Lord.

"Our Father," *and* "Hail Mary."

BENEDICTION OF THE BLESSED SACRAMENT.

Ordinarily at the close of the Sunday Vespers, and sometimes on other occasions, is given the Benediction with the Blessed Sacrament. This is done in the following manner:

The Priest, or sometimes a Deacon assisting the Priest, goes up to the altar, and opening the tabernacle, takes out the *Most Blessed Sacrament* which is kept there, and leaves it thus on or above the altar, exposed in full view to the adoration of the faithful. The Priest then descends from the altar, and, while he incenses the *Sacred Host*, the Choir sing the following hymn, the people remaining all the while on their knees, in prayer and adoration.

Hymn.—*O Salutaris Hostia.*

O Salutaris Hostia,	O saving victim! opening wide
Quæ cœli pandis ostium:	The gate of heaven to man below:
Bella premunt hostilia:	Our foes press on from every side;
Da robur, fer auxilium.	Thine aid supply, Thy strength bestow.
Uni trinoque Domino.	To Thy great name be endless praise,
Sit sempiterna gloria:	Immortal Godhead, one in three!
Qui vitam sine termino,	Oh, grant us endless length of days
Nobis donet in patria.	In our true native land with Thee!

Sometimes, also, other Anthems are here sung, or the *Litany of the Blessed Virgin*, during which time you can make use of that *Litany*, or of one of the *Visits to the Blessed Sacrament*, &c. (To be found in this book.) Last of all is sung the following

Hymn.—*Tantum ergo Sacramentum.*

Tantum ergo sacramentum,	Down in adoration falling,
Veneremur cernui;	Lo! the sacred Host we hail;
Et antiquum documentum	Lo! o'er ancient forms departing,
Novo cedat ritui;	Newer rites of grace prevail;
Præstet fides supplementum,	Faith for all defects supplying.
Sensuum defectui.	Where the feeble senses fail.
Genitori, Genitoque,	To the everlasting Father,
Laus et jubilatio,	And the Son Who reigns on high,
Salus, honor, virtus quoque,	With the Holy Ghost proceeding
Sit et benedictio:	Forth from each eternally,
Procedenti ab utroque,	Be salvation, honor, blessing,
Compar sit laudatio.	Might, and endless majesty.
Amen.	Amen.

V. Panem de cœlo præstitisti eis.

R. Omne delectamentum in se habentem.

V. Thou hast given them bread from heaven.

R. Replenished with all sweetness and delight.

PRAYER.

Deus qui nobis, sub sacramento mirabili, passionis tuæ memoriam reliquisti: tribue, quæsumus, ita nos corporis et sanguinis tui

O God, Who hast left us in this wonderful Sacrament a perpetual memorial of Thy passion: grant us, we beseech Thee, so to

sacra mysteria venerari, ut redemptionis tuæ fructum in nobis jugiter sentiamus. Qui vivis et regnas in sæcula sæculorum. *Amen.*	reverence the sacred mysteries of Thy Body and Blood, that we may continually find in our souls the fruit of Thy Redemption: Thou Who livest and reignest world without end. *Amen.*

After the Priest has sung this prayer, the white veil is laid over his shoulders, and he then mounts the steps of the altar, and, taking in his hands the monstrance which contains the Blessed Sacrament, gives the Benediction, by making with it over the Congregation the sign of the cross. At this moment kneel more profoundly than before, to receive this divine blessing of your Saviour, and say:

O my God, I am sorry—I am sorry for my sins: forgive me them, and give me my part in this heavenly blessing! I love Thee, I will love Thee always, and seek to please Thee in every thought, in every word, and every action of my life. ✠ In the name of the Father, and of the Son, and of the Holy Ghost. *Amen.*

Devotions for Confession.

How to get Ready and go to Confession.

I. ASK GOD TO HELP YOU.

O my God, help me to make a good Confession, to know my sins, and to be truly sorry for them, because they have offended Thee. Keep me from sin for the time to come. Help me that I may sincerely and humbly confess all my sins, and that I may keep back nothing in my heart. Hail Mary, etc. My dear Angel Guardian, to your care I am given, watch over me and help me. Come, O Holy Spirit, etc.

<small>You may say also a decade of the Rosary.</small>

II. EXAMINE YOUR CONSCIENCE.

Read over the following examination of conscience, and when you come to any sin that you have done, especially if it is a great one, try to find out *how many times* you did it, at least how many times each day, or week, or month. Sometimes in one action there are more sins than one. If a child strikes its parent, there are two sins, one against the fourth Commandment, and another against the fifth. If by one detraction you injure the characters of many persons, then there are many sins.

EXAMINATION OF CONSCIENCE.

First Commandment. — Ignorance of the great truths, prayers, etc., — neglecting to say your morning or night prayers — going to sermons or prayers in Protestant churches — giving scandal by it, or joining with them in worship — reading Protestant books — wilfully doubting, denying, or disbelieving the Catholic Faith, or speaking against it — despairing of God's help, or expecting it without doing what He commands you — murmuring against God or His Providence — not helping the poor — leading others into sin — asking fortune-tellers or those who use charms, signs, toss cups, cut cards — reading books about such things — behaving ill in Church, or to any holy thing or person — neglecting your penance — receiving the blessed sacrament after breaking your fast — receiving any sacrament with bad dispositions. *How often each sin?*

Second Commandment. — Speaking ill of God, or the Saints, or what is sacred — cursing, especially if from your heart, or with God's name — an oath, in a lie, or to do what is sinful — a custom of swearing, breaking a lawful oath?

Third Commandment. — Working on Sundays or holidays without necessity — losing mass on Sundays or holidays by your own neglect, or playing or talking during mass—stopping away from Sunday school, catechism, questions, etc.?

Fourth Commandment.—Not loving or helping your parents—striking them, or disrespect to them, especially in their presence—cursing them or calling them bad names, especially in their hearing—disobedience to them, if in any great thing, for example, by going into dangerous company—stopping from school, or being idle there.

Fifth Commandment.—Evil wishes on yourself or another, especially if from your heart—quarreling, hatred, keeping spite, revenge, fighting, doing harm to the life or health of yourself or another—drunkenness?

Sixth and Ninth Commandments. — Immodest thoughts, (if wilful,) immodest desires, words, looks, actions, alone or with others, with married persons or relations, or with any thing — going into bad company, to bad dancing houses, etc.,—keeping dangerous company with persons of the other sex — reading or keeping bad books?

Seventh and Tenth Commandments.—Stealing, what did you steal, and how often—helping others to steal, receiving stolen things, cheating, injuring others in their goods or any way—not restoring to another what is his, or not paying your debts when able — breaking a promise of marriage, or any agreement without just reason?

Eighth Commandment.— Lies, did they do great harm?—speaking ill of others—rash judgments, unjust suspicions—using bad language to others, reading their letters, etc.,—causing quarrels by tale-bearing?

Commandments of the Church.—Breaking the abstinence or fast—neglecting the Sacraments, or your Easter duties—being in secret or forbidden societies? Pride, covetousness, lust, anger, gluttony, envy, sloth—wilfully concealing a sin in confession through shame?— *How many times each sin.*

For Married Persons.— Invalid marriages with relations, etc.,— marrying in any way against the regulations of the Church—cruelty or bad behaviour to one another—giving their affections to another—leaving one another without just cause—wasteful spending of money— wife not taking care of the household—a wrong or improper use of marriage—wife not obeying her husband in the lawful duties of marriage— any thing which might scandalize children.— *How often?*

For Parents.—Care before and after birth— allowing children to be brought up in a false religion — cruelty to, or cursing them — putting brothers and sisters in the same bed—not sending them to a good school, but to Protestant or other schools forbidden by the Priest—neglect about their baptism, or their prayers—not sending them when seven years old to confession, mass or catechism—letting them say bad words, read bad books, go into bad company, play about the streets with any one or keep dangerous company with persons of the other sex—not letting them follow their vocation to be nuns, etc.,—without just reason hindering their marriage, or forcing them to marry. *How often?*

For Masters and Mistresses.—Ill treatment of servants—over-working them—not giving them food enough—not paying their wages—breaking the agreement—allowing them to commit sin, or go into bad company, or asking them to do what is sinful—letting them neglect their religious duties, mass, or the sacraments. *How often?*

III. CONTRITION.

You must detest your sins and be sorry for them, because you offended God by them. Also you must make up your mind not to sin any more, and to keep away from the places or people who led you into sin before, as the burnt child keeps away from the fire. This is contrition. Say, then, the following Acts of Contrition, and tell God how sorry you are for having offended Him.

Say these Acts of Contrition.—O my God! I am heartily sorry for having offended Thee;

and I detest my sins most sincerely, because they displease Thee, my God, Who art so deserving of all my love, for Thy infinite goodness and most amiable perfections; and I firmly purpose by Thy holy grace never more to offend Thee, and carefully to avoid all the occasions of sin.—*The Irish Catechism.* (See *O'Reilly's Catechism, page 32.*)

O my God! for the sake of Thy sovereign goodness and infinite perfections, which I love above all things, I am exceedingly sorry from the bottom of my heart, and am grieved for having offended by my sins this Thy infinite goodness; and I firmly resolve by the assistance of Thy grace never more to offend Thee for the time to come and carefully to avoid the occasions of sin.—*Douay Catechism.*

O my God, I am very sorry that I have sinned against Thee, because Thou art so good, and I will not sin again.—*Blessed Leonard of Port Maurice.*

O Jesus, my Creator, my Redeemer! I remember how Thou wert nailed to the hard cross — how Thy poor head was torn by the sharp thorns — how the holy blood came from Thy blessed body. And why didst Thou suffer all these cruel pains? O Jesus, Thy blessed heart speaks to me, and tells me that Thou didst die a bitter death on the cross for the love of me, Thy poor child, to wash away my sins with Thy blood, and to save me from hell. Yes, it was my sins which nailed Thee to the cross, and made Thee die. O wicked sins, I hate and detest you. My good Jesus, I love Thee, and I am sorry with all my heart for sinning against Thee, because Thou art so good, and I promise Thee with a sincere heart that I will never sin again; let me die rather than sin again. Jesus, have pity on my poor soul—Thou didst not turn away Thy face from those who struck it and spit upon it; wilt Thou turn away from a soul that wants to love Thee? O Jesus, think how much it cost Thee to save my soul—how Thou didst buy it with Thy own blood, and die for it, and now, when Thou needest not die any more to save me—when Thou hast only to say the word—I forgive you—wilt Thou refuse to forgive Thy poor repenting child? Wilt Thou refuse to save a soul which Thou didst die to save? No, my Jesus, Thy heart is too kind and too good to refuse me pardon. I hope, I am sure, Thou wilt pardon me.

Dear Mary, Mother of Jesus, speak to Jesus, and ask Him to have pity on me, and forgive me.

IV. CONFESSION.

1. When you have said the Acts of Contrition, wait patiently till you can get to Confes-

sion; if you have to wait some time, you can say your beads or any prayer. It is good, just before you go to Confession, to make the Act of Contrition again. 2. When you begin your Confession, say, "Pray, Father, give me your blessing, for I have sinned," and half the "I confess;" then tell the Priest all your sins, especially the great sins, and how many times you did them as well as you can—at least, how many times each day, or week, or month. When you have confessed your sins, say: "For these and all other sins which I cannot remember I am heartily sorry, purpose amendment, and humbly beg pardon of God, and penance and absolution of you, my Father,"—then the other half of the "I confess," then listen while the Priest tells you what is good for your soul; receive the penance which he gives you, and do not forget it.— 3. Then, if the Priest sees that you are fit, he will give you the pardon of your sins, which is called *Absolution*. While the Priest is giving you absolution, it is well to say again the Act of Contrition. "O my God, I am very sorry that I have sinned against Thee, because Thou art so good, and I will not sin again," or any Act of Contrition. Remember that in the moment when the Priest says over you the great words of pardon and absolution, your sins are forgiven, the pains of hell are taken away, your soul is made bright and beautiful like an angel of God, and the kingdom of heaven is yours. 4. If you wilfully conceal a mortal sin in Confession, it cannot be forgiven till you are willing to tell it, and you will have to make the Confession over again, at least say, "Father, there is something I do not like to tell." If you doubt whether something you do is good or bad, say, "Father, I have a doubt." For those who have only venial sins to confess, it is well to confess over again some great sin of their past life. 5. When you have done your Confession, go and kneel down again, and thank God for His great mercy to you, you may say, *an act of thanksgiving*. "O my God, I thank Thee for Thy great mercy to me, a poor sinner, and I beg of Thee to strengthen my weakness, that I may never sin any more." Hail Mary, etc.; or a decade of the Rosary.

OR,

O Jesus, how worthy art Thou of my love, and what thanks do I not owe! I hope that through the merits of Thy blood, Thou hast forgiven me my sins. For this I thank Thee with my whole heart, and I burn with the desire to praise Thy mercy in heaven through all eternity. Until now, O my God, I have offended Thee often, but for the time to come, I will never offend Thee again. I am anxious to change my life. Thou dost merit all my love, and therefore I will love Thee truly and dearly. I will never again be separated from Thee. I have already promised Thee rather to die than offend Thee again. Once more I make this promise, and hope through Thy mercy to keep it.

I promise also to shun the occasions of sin, and to take the following means to keep me from falling again; (*here name the means.*) But Thou knowest my weakness, O my God. Give me Thy grace, that I may remain true unto Thee until my death, and teach me, in the hour of temptation, to have recourse to Thee. Mary, help me! Thou art the Mother of perseverance, I place my hopes in Thee.

Preparation for Holy Communion.

There is no means more efficacious in freeing us from our sins, and in enabling us to advance in the love of God, than the Holy Communion. Why is it, then, that some souls find themselves always in the same tepidity, and committing the same faults, notwithstanding the many communions they make? This happens through the want of a proper disposition and preparation. Two things are requisite for this preparation. The first is to disengage our heart from all affections which are an impediment to the divine love. The second is to have a great desire to love God. And this, says St. Francis de Sales, should be our chief intention when we communicate, namely, to increase in divine love. Out of love alone, says the saint, ought our God to be received, Who out of love alone gives Himself to us.

Before you receive the most holy Sacrament of the body and blood of Jesus Christ, you must cleanse your conscience from any mortal sin by the sacrament of penance. You must fast from the midnight before. When the time for Holy Communion is come, go up to the altar respectfully, kneel down there, take the cloth into your hands and hold it before your breast, do not wipe your mouth with it, let your head be raised up, the eyes shut, the mouth open, the tongue forward and resting on the under lip. Shut your mouth after receiving the blessed sacrament, and when it is a little moistened on your tongue swallow it. If it stops on the roof of your mouth, do not remove it with your hand, but with your tongue.

PRAYERS BEFORE HOLY COMMUNION.
By St. Alphonsus.

My beloved Jesus, true Son of God, Who didst die for me on the cross in a sea of sorrows and ignominy, I firmly believe that Thou art present in the most holy Sacrament; and for this faith I am ready to give my life.

My dear Redeemer, I hope by Thy goodness, and through the merits of Thy blood, that when Thou dost come to me this morning, Thou wilt inflame me with Thy holy love, and wilt give me all those graces which I need to keep me obedient and faithful to Thee till death.

Ah, my God, true and only Lover of my soul, what couldst Thou do more to oblige me to love Thee? Thou wert not satisfied, my Love, with dying for me, but Thou wouldst also institute the most holy Sacrament, making Thyself my food, and giving Thyself all to me; thus uniting Thyself most closely to such a miserable and ungrateful creature. Thou dost Thyself invite me to receive Thee, and dost greatly desire that I should receive Thee. O infinite Love! A God gives Himself all to me! O my God, O infinite Love, worthy of infinite love, I love Thee above all things; I love Thee with all my heart; I love Thee more than myself, more than my life; I love Thee because Thou art worthy of being loved; and I love Thee also to please Thee, since Thou dost desire my love! Depart from my soul, all ye earthly affections; to Thee alone, my Jesus, my Treasure, my All, will I give all my love. This morning Thou dost give Thyself all to me, and I give myself all to Thee. Permit me to love Thee; for I desire none but Thee, and nothing but what is pleasing to Thee. I love Thee, O my Saviour, and I unite my poor love to the love of all the angels and saints, and of Thy Mother Mary, and the love of Thy Eternal Father! Oh, that I could see Thee loved by all! Oh, that I could make Thee loved by all men, and loved as much as Thou dost deserve!

Behold, O my Jesus, I am now about to draw near to feed on Thy most sacred Flesh! Ah, my God, who am I? and Who art Thou? Thou art a Lord of infinite goodness, and I am a loathsome worm, defiled by so many sins, and who have driven Thee out of my soul so often.

Domine, non sum dignus. Lord, I am not worthy to remain in Thy presence; I ought to be in hell for ever, far away, and abandoned by Thee. But out of Thy goodness Thou callest me to receive Thee: behold, I come, I come humbled and in confusion for the great displeasure I have given Thee, but trusting entirely to Thy mercy and to the love Thou hast for me. I am exceedingly sorry, O my loving Redeemer, for having so often offended Thee in time past! Thou didst even give Thy life for me; and I have so often despised Thy grace and Thy love, and have exchanged Thee for nothing. I repent, and am sorry with all my heart for every offence which I have offered Thee, whether grievous or light, because it was an offence against Thee, Who art infinite goodness. I hope Thou hast already pardoned me; but if Thou hast not yet forgiven me, pardon me, my Jesus, before I receive Thee. Ah, receive me quickly into Thy grace, since it is Thy will soon to come and dwell within me.

Come, then, my Jesus, come into my soul, which sighs after Thee. My only and infinite Good, my Life, my Love, my All, I would desire to receive Thee this morning with the same love with which those souls who love Thee most have received Thee, and with the same fervour with which Thy most holy Mother received Thee; to her communions I wish to unite this one of mine. O Blessed Virgin, and my Mother Mary, give me Thy Son; I intend to receive Him from Thy hands! Tell Him that I am Thy servant, and thus will He press me more lovingly to His heart, now that He is coming to me.

Prayers after Communion.

By St. Alphonsus.

The time after communion is a precious time for gaining treasures of grace, because the acts and prayers made whilst the soul is thus united to Jesus Christ have more merit, and are of more value, than when they are made at any other time. St. Teresa says, that our Lord then dwells in the soul enthroned as on a mercy-seat, and speaks to it in these words: My child, ask of Me what you will; for this end am I come to you to do you good. Oh, what great favors do those receive who converse with Jesus Christ after communion! The Ven. F. Avila never omitted to remain two hours in prayer after communion; and St. Aloysius Gonzaga continued his thanksgiving for three days. Let the communicant, then, make the following acts, and try during the rest of the day to go on making acts of love and prayer, in order to keep himself united to Jesus Christ, Whom he has received in the morning.

Behold, my Jesus, Thou art come, Thou art now within me, and hast made Thyself all mine. Be Thou welcome, my Beloved Redeemer. I adore Thee, and cast myself at Thy feet; I embrace Thee, I press Thee to my heart, and thank Thee for that Thou hast deigned to enter into my breast. O Mary, O my patron saints, O my guardian angel, do you all thank Him for me! Since then, O my divine King, Thou art come to visit me with so much love, I give Thee my will, my liberty, and my whole self. Thou hast given Thyself all to me, I will give myself all to Thee; I will no longer belong to myself; from this day forward I will be Thine, and altogether Thine. I desire that my soul, my body, my faculties, my senses, should be all Thine, that they may be employed in serving and pleasing Thee. To Thee I consecrate all my thoughts, my desires, my affections, and all my life. I have offended Thee enough, my Jesus; I desire to spend the remainder of my life in loving Thee, Who hast loved me so much.

Accept, O God of my soul, the sacrifice which I, a miserable sinner, make to Thee, and who desires only to love and please Thee. Work Thou in me, and dispose of me, and of all things belonging to me, as Thou pleasest. May Thy love destroy in me all those affections which are displeasing to Thee, that I may be all Thine, and may live only to please Thee!

PRAYER TO BE SAID EVERY DAY, TO OBTAIN THE GRACES NECESSARY FOR SALVATION.

Eternal Father, Thy Son has promised that Thou wilt grant us all the graces which we ask Thee for in His name. In the name, therefore, and by the merits of Jesus Christ, I ask the following graces for myself and for all mankind.— And first, I pray Thee to give me a lively faith in all that the holy Roman Church teaches me. Enlighten me also, that I may know the vanity of the goods of this world, and the immensity of the infinite good that Thou art; make me also see the deformity of the sins I have committed, that I may humble myself and detest them as I ought; and, on the other hand, show me how worthy Thou art by reason of Thy goodness, that I should love Thee with all my heart.— Make me know also the love Thou hast borne me, that from this day forward I may try to be grateful for so much goodness. Secondly, give me a firm confidence in Thy mercy of receiving the pardon of my sins, holy perseverance, and finally, the glory of paradise, through the merits of Jesus Christ and the intercession of Mary.— Thirdly, give me a great love towards Thee, which shall detach me from the love of this world and of myself, so that I may love none other but Thee, and that I may neither do nor desire any thing else but what is for Thy glory. Fourthly, I beg of Thee a perfect resignation to Thy will, in accepting with tranquillity sorrows, infirmities, contempt, persecutions, aridity of spirit, loss of property, of esteem, of relations, and every other cross which shall come to me from Thy hands. I offer myself entirely to Thee, that Thou mayest do with me and all that belongs to me what Thou pleasest; do Thou only give me light and strength to do Thy will; and especially at the hour of death help me to sacrifice my life to Thee with all the affection I am capable of, in union with the sacrifice which Thy Son Jesus Christ made of His life on the Cross on Calvary. Fifthly, I beg of Thee a great sorrow for my sins, which may make me grieve over them as long as I live, and weep for the insults I have offered Thee, the Sovereign Good, Who art worthy of infinite love, and Who hast loved me so much. Sixthly, I pray Thee to give me the spirit of true humility and meekness that I may accept with peace, and even with joy all the contempt, ingratitude and ill-treatment that I may receive. At the same time I also pray Thee to give me perfect charity, which shall make me wish well to those who have done evil to me, and to do what good I can, at least by praying, for those who have in any way injured me. Seventhly, I beg of Thee to give me a love for the virtue of holy mortification, by which I may chastise my rebellious senses, and cross my self-love; at the same time, I beg Thee to give me holy purity of body, and the grace to resist all bad temptations, by ever having recourse to Thee and Thy most holy Mother.— Give me grace faithfully to obey my spiritual father and all my superiors in all things. Give me an upright intention, that in all I desire and do I may seek only Thy glory, and to please Thee alone. Give me a great confidence in the Passion of Jesus Christ, and in the intercession of Mary immaculate. Give me a great love towards the most Adorable Sacrament of the Altar, and a tender devotion and love to Thy holy Mother. Give me, I pray Thee, above all holy perseverance, and the grace always to pray for it, especially in time of temptation and at the hour of death.

Lastly, I recommend to Thee the holy souls of Purgatory, my relations and benefactors; and in an especial manner I recommend to Thee all those who hate me or who have in any way offended me; I beg of Thee to render them good for the evil they have done, or may wish to do me. Finally, I recommend to Thee, all infidels, heretics, and all poor sinners; give them light and strength to deliver themselves from sin. Oh, most loving God, make Thyself known and loved by all, but especially by those who have been more ungrateful to Thee than others, so that by Thy goodness I may come one day to sing Thy mercies in paradise; for my hope is in the merits of Thy blood, and in the patronage of Mary. O Mary, Mother of God, pray to Jesus for me! So I hope; so may it be!

PRAYER TO CONSECRATE ONESELF TO THE BLESSED VIRGIN.

Most holy Virgin Mary, Mother of God, I, N. N., although most unworthy of being thy servant, nevertheless, moved by thy wonderful compassion, and by a desire to serve thee, choose thee this day, in presence of my angel guardian, and of all the heavenly court, for my special lady, advocate, and mother; and I firmly resolve to serve thee always, and to do every thing in my power to make others serve thee also. I beseech thee, then, most merciful mother, by the blood of thy Son, which was shed for me, to take me into the number of thy clients as thy servant for ever. Protect me in my actions, and obtain for me grace so to measure my thoughts, words, and works, that I may never offend thy most pure eyes, nor those of thy Divine Son Jesus. Remember me, and abandon me not at the hour of my death.

Visit to the Blessed Sacrament.

PRAYER BEFORE EACH VISIT.

My Lord Jesus Christ, Who, for the love which Thou bearest to men, dost dwell day and night in this Sacrament, full of goodness and love, awaiting, inviting, and welcoming all those who come to visit Thee, I believe that Thou art present in the Sacrament of the Altar. From the deep abyss of my own nothingness, I adore Thee, and I thank Thee for all the graces Thou hast granted to me, and especially for having given me Thyself in this Sacrament, for having given me also Thy holy Mother Mary, to be my advocate, and for having called me to visit Thee in this church. I adore Thy most loving heart this day, and I adore it with this threefold intention: first, in thanksgiving for so great a gift; secondly, to make satisfaction for the many injuries Thou hast received from Thy enemies in this Sacrament; and thirdly, by this visit I wish to adore Thee in all those places throughout the world, where Thou art least honored, and most neglected in this divine Sacrament. My Jesus, I love Thee with my whole heart! I am sorry for having offended Thy infinite goodness so often in time past. I am resolved, by the help of Thy grace, to offend Thee no more for the future; and at this present moment, all miserable as I am, I consecrate myself entirely to Thee. I give and abandon to Thee my whole will, all my affections, my desires, and all I have. Hereafter, do with me, and with mine, whatever Thou wilt. I ask of Thee nothing but Thy holy love, final perseverance, and the grace to fulfil in all things Thy holy will. I recommend to Thee the souls in purgatory, especially those who have been most devout to Thee in this Holy Sacrament, and to the blessed Virgin Mary. I recommend to Thee, moreover, all poor sinners. Finally, my dear Redeemer, I unite all my desires to the desires of Thy own most loving heart; and I offer them, thus united, to Thy eternal Father, and beseech Him in Thy name, for the love of Thee, to receive them and to grant them.

(His Holiness Pius IX. grants an Indulgence of three hundred days, as often as the above prayer is recited, with a contrite heart, before the Blessed Sacrament. Those who recite it as above every day for a month, may gain a Plenary Indulgence on any one day, at choice, on the ordinary conditions.)

PETITIONS TO JESUS CHRIST IN THE MOST HOLY SACRAMENT.

By St. Alphonsus.

O my Jesus, now that Thou, Who art the true Life, art come to me, make me die to the world, to live only to Thee, my Redeemer; by the flames of Thy love destroy in me all that is displeasing to Thee, and give me a true desire to gratify and please Thee in all things.

Give me that true humility which shall make me love contempt and self-abjection, and take from me all ambition of putting myself forward. Give me the spirit of mortification, that I may deny myself all those things that do not tend to Thy love, and may lovingly embrace that which is displeasing to the senses and to self-love.

Give me a perfect resignation to Thy will, that I may accept in peace, pains, infirmities, loss of friends or property, desolations, persecutions, and all that comes to me from Thy hand. I offer Thee all myself, that Thou mayest dispose of me according to Thy pleasure. And give me grace always to repeat this entire offering of myself, especially at the time of my death. May I, then, so sacrifice my life to Thee, with all my affection, in union with the sacrifice that Thou didst make of Thy life for me to the Eternal Father. My Jesus, enlighten me, and make me know Thy goodness, and the obligation I am under to love Thee above all, for the love Thou hast borne me in dying for me, and in leaving Thyself in the Most Holy Sacrament.

I pray Thee to give Thy light to all infidels who know Thee not, to all heretics who are out of the Church, and to all sinners who live deprived of Thy grace. My Jesus, make Thyself known, make Thyself loved. I recommend to Thee all the souls in purgatory, and especially N. N.; alleviate the pains they suffer, and shorten the time of their banishment from Thy sight: do this through Thy merits, and those of Thy most holy Mother and all the Saints.

My God, enkindle the flame of Thy love within me, so that I may seek nothing but Thy pleasure, that nothing may please me but pleasing Thee; I drive from my heart every thing which is not agreeable to Thee. May I always be able to say with real affection: O God, my God, I wish for Thee alone and nothing more. My Jesus, give me a great love for Thy Most Sacred Passion, that Thy sufferings and death may be ever before my eyes to excite me to love Thee always, and to make me desire to give Thee some grateful compensation for Thy so great love. Give me also a great love for the Most Holy Sacrament of the Altar, in which

Thou hast made known the exceeding tenderness Thou hast for us. I also beg of Thee to give me a tender devotion to Thy most holy Mother: give me grace always to love and serve her, always to have recourse to her intercession, and to induce others to honor her and confide in her patronage; and grant to me and to all men ever to have a great confidence, first in the merits of Thy Prssion, and then in the intercession of Mary.

I pray Thee grant me a happy death. Grant that I may then receive Thee with great love in the Most Holy Viaticum, that in Thy embrace, burning with a holy fire, and a great desire of seeing Thee, I may quit this life to throw myself at Thy feet the first time it shall be my lot to see Thee.

Above all, I pray Thee, O my Jesus, to give me the grace of prayer, that I may recommend myself always to Thee and Thy most holy Mother, especially in time of temptation: and I pray Thee, by Thy merits, to grant me holy perseverance and Thy holy love.

Bless me, my Jesus, and bless me altogether, my soul, my body, my senses, and my faculties. Bless especially my tongue, that it may only speak for Thy glory. Bless my eyes, that they may not look at any thing that might tempt me to displease Thee. Bless my taste, that it may not offend Thee by intemperance; and bless all the members of my body, that they may all serve Thee and not offend Thee. Bless my memory, that it may always remember Thy love and the favors Thou hast accorded me. Bless my understanding, that it may know Thy goodness, and the obligation I have of loving Thee; and that it may see all that I must avoid, and all that I must do to conform myself to Thy holy will. Above all, bless my will, that it may love no other but Thee, the infinite Good; that it may seek for nothing but to please Thee, and may take delight in nothing but what conduces to Thy glory.

O, my King, come Thou and reign alone in my soul; take entire possession of it, that it may neither serve nor obey any thing but Thy love.

O, my Jesus, that I might spend myself all for Thee, Who hast spend all Thy life for me!

O, Lamb of God, sacrificed on the Cross, remember that I am one of those souls which Thou hast redeemed with so much labor and sorrow. Never let me lose Thee again. Thou hast given Thyself all to me; make me to be all Thine, and let my only wish be to please Thee. I love Thee, O immense Good, in order to give Thee pleasure. I love Thee, because Thou art worthy of my love. I have no greater grief than that of thinking that I have been so long in the world without loving Thee.

My beloved Redeemer, give me a portion of that grief which Thou didst feel for my sins in the garden of Gethsemani. O my Jesus, would that I had died and never offended Thee! O love of my Jesus, Thou art my love and my hope! I will rather lose my life, and a thousand lives, than lose Thy grace.

My God, if I were to die in sin, I could no more love Thee. I thank Thee that Thou givest me time, and dost call me to love Thee. Now, then, that I can love Thee, I will love Thee with all my soul. Thou hast borne with me so long, that I might love Thee. Yes, and I will love Thee. Ah, by the Blood that Thou hast shed for me, suffer me not to betray Thee again. "In Thee, O Lord, have I hoped, let me not be confounded for ever." What is the world? what are riches? what are pleasures? what are honors? God, God, I wish for God alone. My God, Thou art sufficient for me; Thou art an infinite Good.

O my Jesus, bind me wholly to Thy love, and draw all my affections to Thyself, so that I may love none other but Thee. Make me all Thine before I die.

Ah, my God, as long as I live I stand in danger of losing Thee. When shall the day come that I can say: My Jesus, I can no longer lose Thee!

O Eternal Father, for the love of Jesus Christ despise me not; suffer me to love Thee, and give me Thy holy love. I wish to love Thee greatly in this life, that I may love Thee greatly in the next.

O infinite Good, I love Thee; but do Thou make me know the great good that I love, and give me the love Thou dost desire to see in me. Enable me to overcome all things to please Thee.

PRAYER OF ST. BONAVENTURE TO THE MOST HOLY SACRAMENT.

Wound, O my most tender Jesus, the inmost of my soul with the sweet dart of Thy love, that through Thy love and the desire of possessing Thee, my soul may languish and melt within me, and so long to quit this life, to come and unite itself perfectly with Thee in a happy eternity.— Make my soul always to hunger after Thee, the Bread of angels, my Jesus, in the Blessed Sacrament. May it ever thirst after Thee, O fountain of life and light! May it ever desire Thee, seek Thee, speak to Thee alone, find Thee, and do all things to Thy praise and glory to the end! Thou, my Redeemer, art my only hope, my riches, my consolation, my peace, my refuge, my wisdom, my portion, and my treasure. On Thee may my heart and my mind be ever fixed!— Amen.

O Jesus, give holy Pastors to Thy Church.

EJACULATION:

O Sacrament most holy! O Sacrament divine! All praise and all thanksgiving be every moment Thine.

Pope Pius VI., by a Rescript of the *Segretaria* of the Memorials, May 24, 1776, granted:

I. The Indulgence of one hundred days, once a day, to all the faithful who, with contrite hearts, say the Ejaculation in honor of the Blessed Sacrament.

II. The Indulgence of three hundred days, every Thursday in the year, and in the octave of Corpus Christi, to those who say it three times.

III. The Plenary Indulgence, once a month, on any one day, to those who, having said it every day for a month, shall, after Confession and Communion, pray for the Holy Church, &c.

These Indulgences were confirmed afresh by Pope Pius VII., by a decree of the S. Congr. of Indulgences, June 30, 1818; and he extended the *Indulgence of one hundred days* to all who say the above Ejaculation at Exposition, Benediction, and the Elevation in the Mass.

ACT FOR A SPIRITUAL COMMUNION.
BY ST. ALPHONSUS.

I believe that Thou, O Jesus, art in the Most Holy Sacrament! I love Thee and desire Thee! Come into my heart. I embrace Thee; oh, never leave me!

'May the burning and most sweet power of Thy love, O Lord Jesus Christ, I beseech Thee, absorb my mind, that I may die through love of Thy love, Who wast graciously pleased to die through love of my love.'—*St. Francis of Assisi.*

'O Love Who art not loved! O Love Who art not known!'—*St. Mary Magdalene of Pazzi.*

'O my Spouse, when wilt Thou ravish me in Thyself?'—*St. Peter of Alcantara.*

> Jesus, my good, my sweetest love,
> Strike and inflame this heart of mine,
> Make it all fire for love of Thee!

Hail to the love of Jesus, our Life and our All! Hail to Mary, our hope! Amen.

Visit to Mary.

My Lady, St. Bernard calls thee, 'the ravisher of hearts.' He says, that thou goest about stealing hearts by the charms of thy beauty and goodness. Steal also my heart and will: I give them wholly to thee; offer them to God with thine own.

O Mary, thou dost so much desire to see this thy Son Jesus loved; if thou lovest me, this is the grace I ask of thee, and which thou must procure for me; obtain for me a great love for Jesus Christ, and not to love any other than Him. Thou obtainest from Him all that thou dost wish; listen to me, then, pray for me and comfort me; bind me in such a manner to Jesus that I shall no longer be able to leave off loving Him. Obtain for me also a great love towards thee, who art of all creatures the most loving, the most lovely, and the most loved by God.— I rely greatly on thy compassion, and I love thee my Lady; but I love thee only a little: ask thy God to give me a greater love; for to love thee is a grace which God grants only to those whom thou dost wish to be saved. Live Jesus our love, and Mary our hope!

EJACULATION:

Sweet heart of Mary be my salvation.

Pope Pius IX., by decree of the S. Congr. of Indulgences, dated Sept. 30, 1852, granted to the faithful:

I. The Indulgence of three hundred days, every time they say with contrition, and devotion the above ejaculation.

II. The Plenary Indulgence, once a month, to all who say it daily devoutly for a month; provided that, after Confession and Communion, they visit a church or public oratory, and pray there according to the mind of His Holiness.

Most holy Immaculate Virgin and my Mother Mary, to thee who art the Mother of my Lord, the Queen of the world, the advocate, the hope, the refuge of sinners, I have recourse to day, I, who am the most miserable of all. I worship thee, O great Queen, and I thank thee for all the graces which thou hast hitherto granted me; and especially I thank thee for having delivered me from hell, which I have so often deserved. I love thee most amiable Lady; and for the love which I bear thee, I promise always to serve thee, and to do all that I can that thou mayest also be loved by others. I place all my hopes in thee, and I confide my salvation to thy care; accept me for thy servant, and receive me under thy mantle, O Mother of Mercy. And since thou art so powerful with God, do thou deliver me from all temptations, or rather obtain me strength to triumph over them until death. Of thee I ask the true love of Jesus Christ; through thee I hope to die a good death. My Mother, by the love which thou bearest to God, I beseech thee to help me always, but especially at the last moment of my life; leave me not until thou seest me safe in heaven, blessing thee, and singing thy mercies for all eternity. Amen.

(His Holiness Pius IX, grants an indulgence of three hundred days, as often as the above prayer is recited with a contrite heart, before a picture or image of the Blessed Virgin. Those who recite it every day for a month may gain a plenary indulgence on any one day, at choice, on the ordinary conditions.)

The Way of the Cross.

By St. Alphonsus.

It was a very frequent and most touching devotion of Christians, in former times, to make a pilgrimage to the Holy Land of Palestine, where our Blessed Redeemer lived and died, and there to visit every spot of ground which had been made sacred by His presence, and especially those which were known as the stations of His passion and death, and to honor these holy places by prayer and by penance. Afterwards, when the Holy Land had fallen into the hands of the infidel Saracens, and Christians could no longer make this pilgrimage with safety this exercise of the Way of the Cross was invented as a substitute. Pictures representing the most moving and remarkable events of our Lord's passion, from the time of His sentence to His burial, are hung about the walls of the church, and by visiting these in succession, and praying before each one, we are able in some manner to imitate the devotion of Catholics of other days, although by a pilgrimage far less long and painful. The Way of the Cross, in its present form, was instituted in the middle of the fourteenth century, by the Franciscans. The Sovereign Pontiffs have attached to it many indulgences, which are too numerous to mention here. Any one who is in a state of grace may gain these indulgences by making the round of these fourteen stations, meditating before each one upon the mystery it represents. No form of prayer is required, nor is it necessary that these meditations should be long. (S. C. Ind. 22 Sept. 1829; ditto, 7 April, 1831.) As for those to whom it is impossible to fulfil these conditions, either because they cannot meditate, or are unable to visit the stations, they may make the Way of the Cross in another manner, by means of a crucifix indulgenced for this purpose. These gain all the indulgences by holding the crucifix in their hand, and reciting fourteen times, the *Pater*, *Ave* and *Gloria:* then five times *Pater*, *Ave* and *Gloria*, in honor of the five wounds of our Lord; and finally, one *Pater*, *Ave* and *Gloria*, for the intention of the Sovereign Pontiff.

This devotion is commenced with an act of contrition, which may be made as follows, or in any similar manner:

O my God, my Redeemer, behold me here at Thy feet. From the bottom of my heart I am sorry for all my sins, because by them I have offended Thee, Who art infinitely good. I will die rather than offend Thee again.

FIRST STATION.

Jesus is condemned to Death.

V. We adore Thee, O Christ, and we bless Thee.

R. Because by Thy holy Cross Thou hast redeemed the world.

(*This versicle and response are repeated before each Station.*)

Consider how Pilate condemned the innocent Jesus to death, and how thy Redeemer submitted to this sentence, to free thee from the sentence of everlasting death.

O Jesus, I thank Thee for this Thy great love, and I beseech Thee to take back the sentence of everlasting death which I have deserved by my sins, so that I may be made worthy to attain to everlasting life.

Our Father, Hail Mary, Glory be, &c.

SECOND STATION.

Jesus is made to bear His Cross.

V. We adore Thee, &c. *R.* Because, &c.

Consider how Jesus took upon His shoulders the Cross which thy many sins made so heavy.

O Jesus, grant me the grace not to make Thy Cross heavier by new sins, and cheerfully to carry mine in a true spirit of penance.

Our Father, Hail Mary, Glory be, &c.

THIRD STATION.

Jesus falls the first time.

V. We adore Thee, &c.　　*R.* Because, &c.

Consider how Jesus, overcome by weariness and pain, fell to the ground under the weight of the Cross.

O Jesus, my falls into sin caused Thee this fall. Grant that I may never renew Thy pain by a relapse into sin.

Our Father, Hail Mary, Glory be, &c.

FOURTH STATION.

Jesus is met by His blessed Mother.

V. We adore Thee, &c.　　*R.* Because, &c.

Consider the anguish which filled the hearts of Jesus and Mary at this sorrowful meeting. It was thy sins that caused the Son and the Mother this affliction.

O Jesus, excite in me, through the intercession of Thy holy Mother, a lively sorrow for my sins, that I may bewail them my whole life long, and in the hour of my death find favor with Thee.

Our Father, Hail Mary, Glory be, &c.

FIFTH STATION.

The Cross is laid on Simon of Cyrene.

V. We adore Thee, &c. *R.* Because, &c.

Consider how the Jews, seeing that Jesus was no longer able to drag His Cross along, compelled Simon of Cyrene to carry it after Him.

O Jesus, I ought to carry the Cross, because I have sinned. Give me the grace at least to accompany Thee on the way to Calvary, and for the love of Thee cheerfully to bear the Cross of adversities.

Our Father, Hail Mary, Glory be, &c.

SIXTH STATION.

Veronica wipes the face of Jesus.

V. We adore Thee, &c. *R.* Because, &c.

Consider how this holy woman tried to alleviate the sufferings of Jesus, and how He rewarded her by leaving the print of His sacred face on the towel she had in her hands.

O Jesus, grant me the grace to cleanse my soul from all its defilements, and imprint deep in my heart and mind the image of Thy holy sufferings.

Our Father, Hail Mary, Glory be, &c.

SEVENTH STATION.

Jesus falls the second time.

V. We adore Thee, &c. *R.* Because, &c.

Consider the sufferings Jesus endures in this second fall. Thou hast been the cause of them, by thy frequent relapse into sin.

O Jesus, I stand before Thee full of shame. Give me the grace so to arise from my sins, as never again to fall back into them,

Our Father, Hail Mary, Glory be, &c.

EIGHTH STATION.

Jesus speaks to the women of Jerusalem.

V. We adore Thee, &c. *R.* Because, &c.

Consider how Jesus exhorts these women to weep, not for Him, but for themselves; to teach thee to weep more for thy sins than for His sufferings,

O Jesus, give me tears of true contrition, that the sorrow I feel for Thy sufferings may be profitable to me.

Our Father, Hail Mary, Glory be, &c.

NINTH STATION.

Jesus falls the third time.

V. We adore Thee, &c.   *R.* Because, &c.

Consider how Jesus falls the third time, enduring excruciating pain, to atone for thy obstinacy in continually committing new sins.

O Jesus, now I am firmly resolved to give up sin forever, so as not to cause Thee new suffering. Strengthen me in this my resolution, and by Thy grace make it efficacious.

Our Father, Hail Mary, Glory be, &c.

TENTH STATION.

Jesus is stripped, and receives gall to drink.

V. We adore Thee, &c.   *R.* Because, &c.

Consider the shame Jesus endured in being stripped of His garments, and the bitterness of the wine mixed with myrrh and gall, which they caused him to drink. Thus He atoned for thy immodesty, and thy intemperance in eating and drinking.

O Jesus, I am sorry for all the sins I have committed by sensuality. I promise, with Thy assistance, not to renew Thy shame and suffering, and to live henceforward in modesty and temperance.

Our Father, Hail Mary, Glory be, &c.

ELEVENTH STATION.

Jesus is nailed to the Cross.

V. We adore Thee, &c. *R.* Because, &c.

Consider the dreadful sufferings Jesus endured, when the Jews stretched His bleeding body on the Cross, and fastened it thereon with nails through His sacred hands and feet.

O Jesus, Thou sufferest all this for me; and should I suffer nothing for Thee? Fasten my obstinate will to Thy cross. I firmly resolve never more to offend Thee, and for the love of Thee to suffer everything.

Our Father, Hail Mary, Glory be, &c.

TWELFTH STATION.

Jesus dies on the Cross.

V. We adore Thee, &c.   *R.* Because, &c.

Consider how Jesus, after three hours' agony, dies on the cross for thy salvation.

O Jesus, since Thou hast sacrificed Thy life for me, it is but just that I should spend the rest of my life for Thee And this I firmly purpose to do. Only grant me, by the merits of Thy death, the grace to put my resolution in practice.

Our Father, Hail Mary, Glory be, &c.

THIRTEENTH STATION.

The Body of Jesus is taken down from the Cross.

V. We adore Thee, &c.   *R.* Because, &c.

Consider the grief of the Mother of God, when she received in her arms the body of her divine Son, all pale, covered with blood, and void of life.

O most holy Virgin, obtain for me the grace never more to crucify Jesus afresh by new sins, but by the practice of virtue to keep Him ever alive in me.

Our Father, Hail Mary, Glory be, &c.

FOURTEENTH STATION.

Jesus is laid in the Sepulchre.

V. We adore Thee, &c.   *R.* Because, &c.

Consider how the most sacred body of Jesus was laid, with the greatest reverence, in the new grave prepared for it.

O Jesus, I thank Thee for all Thou hast suffered in order to redeem me; and I beseech Thee, grant that I may prepare myself to receive worthily, in holy Communion, the Body which Thou hast given for me. Take up Thy abode forever in my soul.

Our Father, Hail Mary, Glory be, &c.

Conclude by saying five times *Our Father, Hail Mary, and Glory be, &c.*, to gain the Indulgences.

The Steps of our Saviour's Passion.

(An excellent Devotion for Fridays, and for Lent, composed by St. Augustine.)

I. O dearest Jesus, so sorrowfully praying to Thy Father in the Garden, whilst trembling with agony, and covered with a sweat of blood; have mercy on us.

R. Have mercy on us, Lord, have mercy on us.

II. O dearest Jesus, betrayed by a traitor's kiss into wicked hands, seized upon, and bound like a robber, and abandoned by Thy disciples; have mercy on us.

R. Have mercy on us, Lord, have mercy on us.

III. O dearest Jesus, by the unjust council of the Jews found guilty of death, led to Pilate as a malefactor, spurned and mocked by unjust Herod; have mercy on us.

R. Have mercy on us, Lord, have mercy on us.

IV. O dearest Jesus, stripped of all Thy garments, and most cruelly scourged at the pillar; have mercy on us.

R. Have mercy on us, Lord, have mercy on us.

V. O dearest Jesus, crowned with thorns, buffeted, smitten with a reed, blindfolded, covered with a purple garment, derided in every way, and saturated with contempt; have mercy on us.

R. Have mercy on us, Lord, have mercy on us.

VI. O dearest Jesus, less valued than the robber Barabbas, rejected by the Jews, and unjustly condemned to the death of the cross; have mercy on us.

R. Have mercy on us, Lord, have mercy on us.

VII. O dearest Jesus, laden with the cross, and led to Thy place of punishment like a lamb to slaughter; have mercy on us.

R. Have mercy on us, Lord, have mercy on us.

VIII. O dearest Jesus, ranked among thieves, blasphemed and derided with gall and vinegar, insulted in Thy thirst, and from the sixth to the ninth hour left hanging on the cross in dreadful torment; have mercy on us.

R. Have mercy on us, Lord, have mercy on us.

IX. O dearest Jesus, extended lifeless on the gibbet of the cross, in presence of Thy holy Mother pierced with a lance, and shedding blood and water in one mingled stream; have mercy on us.

R. Have mercy on us, Lord, have mercy on us.

X. O dearest Jesus, taken down from the cross, and by Thy virgin Mother bathed with tears of most bitter sorrow; have mercy on us.

R. Have mercy on us, Lord, have mercy on us.

XI. O dearest Jesus, shrouded with stripes, marked with five wounds, embalmed with spices, and laid in the sepulchre; have mercy on us.

R Have mercy on us, Lord, have mercy on us.

V. Surely He hath borne our infirmities.

R. And carried our sorrows.

PRAYER.

O God, Who for the world's redemption wast pleased to be born, circumcised, rejected by the Jews, betrayed by the kiss of the traitor Judas, bound with chains, led like an innocent lamb to sacrifice, and shamefully presented before Annas, Caiphas, Pilate, and Herod, accused by false witnesses, beaten with whips and buffets, insulted, spit upon, crowned with thorns, smitten with a reed, blindfolded, stripped of Thy garments, fastened with nails to the cross, and lifted up on high, reputed among thieves, made to drink of gall and vinegar, and wounded by a lance:—O! by these most sacred sufferings, which, unworthy as I am, I thus commemorate, and by Thy holy cross and death, deliver me, Lord, from the pains of hell, and deign to lead me where Thou didst lead that thief who was crucified by Thy side: Thou, Who with the Father and the Holy Ghost, livest and reignest world without end. Amen.

Pope Pius VII., by a decree of the S. Congr. of Indulgences, dated Aug. 25, 1820, granted to all faithful Christians who should say with contrition the above-named prayer, composed by St. Augustine, with five *Pater noster*, five *Ave Maria* and five *Gloria Patri*, in memory of the Passion and Death of Jesus Christ:

I. The Indulgence of three hundred days, once a day.

II. The Plenary Indulgence to all who shall have said it every day for a month; to be gained on any one of the three last days of the month when, after Confession and Communion, they shall pray for the intention of the Sovereign Pontiff.

The Steps of our Saviour's Childhood.

(An excellent Devotion for Advent and until Epiphany.)

I. O dearest Infant Jesus, from the bosom of the Father descending for our salvation, conceived of the Holy Ghost, abhorring not the Virgin's womb, Word made flesh, receiving the form of a slave; have mercy on us.

R. *Have mercy on us, Infant Jesus.*

II. O dearest Infant Jesus, with Thy Virgin Mother visiting Elizabeth, filling John the Baptist, Thy forerunner, with the Holy Ghost, and sanctifying Him while yet in His Mother's womb; have mercy on us.

R. *Have mercy on us, Infant Jesus.*

III. O dearest Infant Jesus, nine months imprisoned in the womb, anxiously expected by the Virgin Mary and St. Joseph, and by God the Father offered for the world's salvation; have mercy on us.

R. *Have mercy on us, Infant Jesus.*

IV. O dearest Infant Jesus, born in Bethlehem of the Virgin Mary, wrapped in swaddling clothes, and laid in the manger, heralded by Angels, and visited by Shepherds; have mercy on us.

R. *Have mercy on us, Infant Jesus.*

V. O dearest Infant Jesus, after eight days wounded in Thy circumcision, called by the glorious name of Jesus, and thus foreshadowing both by name and blood a Saviour's office; have mercy on us.

R. *Have mercy on us, Infant Jesus.*

VI. O dearest Infant Jesus, revealed to the three wise men by a star, adored by them on Thy Mother's bosom, and presented with mystical gifts of gold, frankincense, and myrrh; have mercy on us.

R. *Have mercy on us, Infant Jesus.*

VII. O dearest Infant Jesus, presented in the temple by the Virgin Mother, caressed in the arms of Simeon, and by Anna the prophetess made known to Israel; have mercy on us.

R. *Have mercy on us, Infant Jesus.*

VIII. O dearest Infant Jesus, sought for by wicked Herod to be put to death, carried by Saint Joseph with Thy Mother into Egypt, rescued from the cruel slaughter, and glorified by the fame of the martyred innocents; have mercy on us.

R. *Have mercy on us, Infant Jesus.*

IX. O dearest Infant Jesus, in Egypt remaining with most Holy Mary and the Holy Patriarch Joseph, until the death of Herod; have mercy on us.

R. *Have mercy on us, Infant Jesus.*

X. O dearest Infant Jesus, returning back from Egypt to the land of Israel, wearied by many labors in the way, and retiring into the city of Nazareth to dwell there; have mercy on us.

R. *Have mercy on us, Infant Jesus.*

XI. O dearest Infant Jesus, obediently remaining in the holy house of Nazareth, there dwelling piously with Thy parents, and rapidly advancing in wisdom, age, and grace; have mercy on us.

R. *Have mercy on us, Infant Jesus.*

XII. O dearest Infant Jesus, led to Jerusalem at the age of twelve, there sought by Thy Parents with great sorrow, but after three days found with joy among the Doctors; have mercy on us.

R. *Have mercy on us, Infant Jesus.*
V. *The Word was made flesh. Alleluia.*
A. *And dwelt among us. Alleluia.*

PRAYER.

Almighty and everlasting God, Lord of heaven and earth, Who revealest Thyself to the humble; grant, we beseech Thee, that commemorating with due honor, and following with worthy imitation, these most sacred mysteries of Thy Son, the Infant Jesus, we may happily arrive at that heavenly kingdom which Thou hast promised to Thy little ones; through the same Jesus Christ our Lord. *Amen.*

Chaplet of our Lord.*

This Chaplet instituted by divine inspiration about the year 1516, by the blessed Michael of Florence, a Camaldolese monk, who used to say it every day until his death, Jan. 11, 1522, is called the Chaplet of our Lord, because it is said in honor of Jesus Christ, and is composed of thirty-three *Pater noster*, in remembrance and veneration of the thirty-three years which He lived on the earth; to these are added five *Ave Maria*, in honor of His five most holy wounds, three of which are said, one at a time, at the beginning of each of the three sets of ten *Pater noster*, and of the two remaining the first is said previous to saying the three concluding *Pater noster*, and the last after them. The Chaplet finishes with the *Credo* in honor of the holy Apostles who composed it, and which itself contains an epitome of the Birth, Life, Passion and Death of our Divine Lord Jesus Christ. Pope Leo X., at the prayer of the above-named blessed Michael, granted by a Bull, dated Feb. 18, 1516, several Indulgences to any one who should keep about him the said Chaplet, or say it. Gregory XIII. did as much by means of a Brief, dated Feb. 14, 1573; and Sixtus V. by another Brief, dated Feb. 3, 1589. These Indulgences were all confirmed anew by Clement X., in a special brief, *De salute Dominici gregis*, dated July 20, 1674, who also added several more Indulgences as follows:

I. Indulgence of two hundred years every time, to any one who shall say it, being penitent and having Confessed, or who at least shall firmly resolve to confess.

II. Indulgence of one hundred and fifty years to any one who, having Confessed and Communicated, shall carry about him one of these Chaplets, and say it every Monday, Wednesday and Friday, and also on all festivals of obligation.

III. Plenary Indulgence once a year on any one day, to any one who, having Confessed and Communicated, shall have made a practice of saying it at least four times a week.

IV. Plenary Indulgence once a month to any one who shall have said it every day for a month, and shall then, being peni-

---

* The Directors of the Arch-Confraternity have power to bless this Chaplet.

tent, having Confessed and Communicated, pray to God for the Holy Church, &c.

V. Plenary Indulgence to any one who shall die in battle against the Infidels, having been previously accustomed to say the said Chaplet three times a week, and having said it on the day of his death, and the day previous to it; provided he be penitent for his sins, and ask pardon of God for them.

VI. Plenary Indulgence, and remission of all sins in the article of death, to any one who, being penitent and having Confessed, shall then invoke, at least with his heart if he cannot do so with his lips, the most holy Name of Jesus: provided he has said the above-named Chaplet once during his illness with the intention of gaining this Indulgence: in the event of his recovery, he may gain the two hundred years' Indulgence.

VII. Indulgence of twenty days to any one who shall carry about him one of these Chaplets, and invoke the adorable Name of Jesus, after he has made an examination of conscience with contrition for his sins, and said three *Pater noster* and three *Ave Maria* for the good estate of the Church.

VIII. The Indulgence of twenty years to any one who, having examined his conscience and confessed, shall, after his confession, pray to God for the advancement of the Catholic Faith, the extirpation of heresy, and the exaltation of the holy Church, &c.; and

IX. The Indulgence of ten years to any one who, having about him the said Chaplet, shall say three *Pater noster* and three *Ave Maria*, as often as he does any spiritual or temporal good work in honor of our Lord Jesus Christ, the Blessed Virgin Mary, or some saint.

X. Any one who keeps one of the said Chaplets about him, if he be accustomed to do any good work which is done in any religious order, shall participate in all the good works which are done in the order in whose good works he has made the intention of sharing; if he assist at holy Mass by saying five *Pater noster* and five *Ave Maria*, he shall supply for every defect and distraction which has happened to him through inadvertence in the course of the Mass; moreover, if on days of obligation he has been legitimately hindered from hearing Mass, he shall have the same merit as if he had assisted at it, provided he say the five *Pater noster* and five *Ave Maria* as above.

XI. Any one out of Rome keeping one of these Chaplets about him, shall on the days of the Stations, gain the two hundred years' Indulgence on visiting any church he chooses; if hindered from doing so, he shall gain the same Indulgence by saying this Chaplet, the seven Penitential Psalms, with the Litanies and Prayers. The same Indulgence in Rome may be gained by any one who, being legitimately hindered from visiting the Church of the Station, shall say the Chaplet and the Psalms as above.

Pope Benedict XIII. afterwards, by a decree of the S. Congr. of Indulgences, dated April 6, 1727, confirmed all the above Indulgences, and added another:

XII. Plenary Indulgence to any one who, after having Confessed and Communicated, should say this Chaplet on Friday. This Plenary Indulgence can only be gained on the Fridays in March, and that after the works enjoined above have been fulfilled; as was declared by Pope Leo XII., in a decree of the S. Congr. of Indulgences, dated Aug. 11, 1824.

In order to gain the above-named Indulgences, it is necessary that:

1. The Chaplet be blessed by the Reverend Fathers of the Camaldolese order, either hermits or monks, or else by those who have apostolic authority to bless them; once blessed, they cannot be sold, or lent to others for the purpose of communicating to them the Indulgences; in which case they would afterwards be deprived of the Indulgences annexed to them according to the said brief of Pope Clement X.

2. Every one saying the Chaplet must, according to his capacity, meditate on the mysteries of the life of our Lord Jesus Christ. It is not, however, necessary either to read or recite the following short reflections, as they are only added for the greater devotion of any one who might wish to make use of them.

CHAPLET OF OUR LORD.

Begin with an act of Contrition.

First Decade.

The Archangel Gabriel makes known to the Blessed Virgin Mary the Incarnation of the Divine Word in her pure womb.

Ave Maria.

1. The Son of God made man is born of Mary the Virgin and laid in a manger.

Pater noster.

2. The angels make merry and sing, *Gloria in excelsis Deo.*

Pater noster.

3. The shepherds hear the angels' tidings, and come and adore Him.

Pater noster.

4. He is circumcised the eighth day, and called by the most holy Name of Jesus.

Pater noster.

5. Is adored by the Magi, and receives offerings of gold, frankincense, and myrrh.

Pater noster.

6. Is presented in the Temple, and foretold the Saviour of the world.

Pater noster.

7. Flies from the wrath of Herod, and is carried into Egypt.

Pater noster.

8. Herod finds Him not, and murders the Innocents.

Pater noster.

9. He is carried back by Joseph and his Mother into Nazareth His country.

Pater noster.

10. Disputes in the Temple with the doctors, being twelve years old.

Pater noster.

Add the Requiem æternam (if said for the departed.)

Second Decade.

Jesus is most obedient to the Blessed Virgin His Mother, and to St. Joseph.

Ave Maria.

1. Thirty years old, He is baptized by John in Jordan.

Pater noster.

2. Fasts forty days in the desert, and overcomes the tempter.

Pater noster.

3. Practices and preaches His holy law, whereby is life eternal.

Pater noster.

4. Calls His disciples, who forthwith leave all and follow Him.

Pater noster.

5. Works His first miracle of changing water into wine.

Pater noster.

6. Heals the sick, makes the lame to walk, gives hearing to the deaf, sight to the blind, life to the dead.

Pater noster.

7. Converts sinful men and sinful women, and pardons their sins.

Pater noster.

8. When the Jews persecute Him even unto death, He chastises them not, but sweetly chides them.

Pater noster.

9. Is transfigured on Mount Thabor, in the presence of Peter, James and John.

Pater noster.

10. Enters triumphant into Jerusalem sitting on an ass's colt, and drives the profaners from the Temple.

Pater noster.

Requiem æternam, as above.

Third Decade.

Jesus takes leave of His Mother before He goes to die for our salvation.

Ave Maria.

1. Celebrates the Last Supper, washes the Apostles' feet.

Pater noster.

2. Institutes the most holy Sacrament of the Altar.

Pater noster.

3. Prays in the garden, sweats blood, and is comforted by an angel.

Pater noster.

4. Is betrayed by Judas with a kiss, is taken and bound by the officers of justice as a great malefactor.

Pater noster.

5. Is falsely accused, is buffeted and spit upon, and shamefully used before four tribunals.

Pater noster.

6. Looks tenderly on Peter after he had thrice denied Him; whilst Judas despairs, hangs himself, and is lost.

Pater noster.

7. Is cruelly scourged at the pillar, and receives innumerable blows.

Pater noster.

8. Is crowned with thorns, shown to the people, who cry, Crucify Him, crucify Him.

Pater noster.

9. Is condemned to die, carries the heavy cross with grievous pain upon His shoulders to Mount Calvary.

Pater noster.

10. Is crucified between two thieves, dies after three hours' agony, is wounded in the side with a lance, and is buried.

Pater noster.

The Requiem æternam, as above.

Jesus rises the third day, and visits first of all His most holy Mother.

Ave Maria.

1. Appears to the three Marys, and bids them tell the disciples they have seen Him risen from the dead.

Pater noster.

2. Appears to the disciples, shows them His most holy Wounds, bids Thomas touch them.

Pater noster.

3. The fortieth day after His resurrection, blesses most holy Mary His Mother and all His disciples, then ascends into heaven.

Pater noster.

Let us pray to the most holy Virgin to obtain for us also the blessing of her Son Jesus Christ, now and at the hour of our death.

Ave Maria.

The Requiem æternam, as above.

Let us say the Creed in honor of the holy Apostles.

End with the Prayer said to be St. Augustine's.

LET US PRAY.

O my Lord Jesus Christ, Who to redeem the world and to free us from the pains of hell, didst vouchsafe to be born amongst men, subject to pain and to death, to be circumcised, rejected, and persecuted by the Jews, betrayed by Thy disciple Judas with a sacrilegious kiss, and as a lamb, gentle and innocent, bound with cords, and dragged in scorn before the tribunals of Annas, Caiphas, Pilate and Herod; Who didst suffer Thyself to be accused by false witnesses, torn by scourges, crowned with thorns, smitten with blows, insulted with spittings, to have Thy divine countenance covered out of contempt, to be many ways set at naught and outraged, to be filled with reproaches and ignominies, and, last of all, to be stript of Thy clothes, nailed, and raised high upon a cross between two vile thieves, to be drenched with gall and vinegar, and then pierced with a lance, and so to fulfil the mighty work of our redemption: Saviour most tender, by Thy many cruel sufferings borne by Thee out of Thy love for me, which I, unworthy as I am, yet dare to contemplate, by Thy holy cross and by Thy bitter death, free me (and this Thy servant*) from the pains of hell; and vouchsafe to gather me into the garner of Paradise, whither Thou didst lead the penitent thief who was crucified with Thee, my Jesus, Who now, with the Father and with the Holy Ghost, livest and reignest God for ever and ever. Amen.

---

* If said for a soul in its agony.

Prayer to the Sacred Heart of Jesus.

One hundred days' indulgence each time. Applicable to the souls in purgatory.

Behold, O most loving Jesus, to what an excess Thy love has gone! Of Thy own flesh and most precious blood, Thou hast prepared for me a divine banquet, in which Thou givest me Thy whole self. What could have moved Thee to this transport of love? Nothing else, surely, than Thy most loving Heart. O adorable Heart of my Jesus, furnace of divine love, receive my soul into Thy sacred wound, that I may learn in that school of charity how to love my God, Who has given me so wonderful proofs of His love. Amen.

OFFERING TO THE SACRED HEART OF JESUS.

I, N., to show my gratitude to Thee, and to make up for my frequent unfaithfulness, give Thee my heart, and consecrate myself entirely to Thee, my loving Jesus; and, with Thy help, I resolve never more to sin.

Indulgences: one hundred days each day that this offering is recited once before a picture of the Sacred Heart. A plenary indulgence, on the usual conditions, once a month for those who recite it every day in the month, before a picture of the Sacred Heart.

THE PRAYER OF ST. GERTRUDE TO THE HEART OF JESUS.

Hail, O Sacred Heart of Jesus! living and quickening source of eternal life, infinite treasury of the divinity, burning furnace of divine love! Thou art my refuge and my sanctuary. O my amiable Saviour! consume my heart with that burning fire, with which Thine is ever inflamed, pour down on my soul those graces which flow from Thy love, and let my heart be so united with Thine, that our wills may be one, and mine in all things conformed to Thine. May Thine be the standard and rule of my desires, and of my actions. Amen.

ACT OF CONSECRATION TO THE SACRED HEART OF JESUS.

To Thee, O sacred Heart of Jesus, do I devote and offer up my life, my thoughts, words, actions, and sufferings. May my whole being be no longer employed but in loving, serving, and glorifying Thee. O Sacred Heart, be Thou henceforth the sole object of my love, the protector of my life, the pledge of my salvation, and my refuge at the hour of my death. Justify me, O blessed and adorable Heart, at the bar of divine justice, and screen me from the anger which my sins deserve. Imprint Thyself like a divine seal on my heart, that I may never be separated from Thee. May my name also be ever engraven upon Thee, and may I be ever consecrated to Thy glory, ever burning with the flames of Thy love, and entirely penetrated with it for all eternity. This is all my desire, to live in Thee. One thing have I sought of the Lord, and this will I seek, that I may dwell in the Heart of my Lord all the days of my life. Amen.

Litany of the Holy Name of Jesus.*

Lord, have mercy on us.
Christ, have mercy on us.
Lord, have mercy on us.
Jesus, hear us.
Jesus, graciously hear us.
God, the Father of heaven,
God, the Son, Redeemer of the world,
God, the Holy Ghost,
Holy Trinity, one God,
Jesus, Son of the living God,
Jesus, splendor of the Father,
Jesus, brightness of eternal light,
Jesus, King of glory,
Jesus, sun of justice,
Jesus, Son of the Virgin Mary,
Jesus, most amiable,
Jesus, most admirable,

} *Have mercy on us.*

---

* Approved by a decree of the Sacred Congregation of Rites, August 21, 1862.

LITANY OF THE HOLY NAME OF JESUS.

Jesus, mighty God,
Jesus, Father of the world to come,
Jesus, Angel of great counsel,
Jesus, most powerful,
Jesus, most patient,
Jesus, most obedient,
Jesus, meek and humble of heart,
Jesus, lover of chastity,
Jesus, lover of mankind,
Jesus, God of peace,
Jesus, author of life,
Jesus, model of virtues,
Jesus, zealous for souls,
Jesus, our God,
Jesus, our refuge,
Jesus, father of the poor,
Jesus, treasure of the faithful,
Jesus, good shepherd,
Jesus, true light,
Jesus, eternal wisdom,
Jesus, infinite goodness,
Jesus, our way and our life,
Jesus, joy of Angels,
Jesus, king of the patriarchs,
Jesus, master of the apostles,
Jesus, teacher of the evangelists,
Jesus, strength of martyrs,
Jesus, light of confessors,
Jesus, purity of virgins,
Jesus, crown of all saints,
Be merciful unto us. *Spare us, O Jesus!*
Be merciful unto us. *Hear us, O Jesus!*
From all evil,
From all sin,
From Thy wrath,
From the snares of the devil,
From the spirit of uncleanness,
From eternal death,
From the neglect of Thy inspirations,
Through the mystery of Thy holy incarnation,

LITANY OF THE HOLY NAME OF JESUS.

Through Thy nativity,
Through Thy childhood,
Through Thy most sacred life,
Through Thy labors,
Through Thy agony and passion,
Through Thy cross and abandonment,
Through Thy faintness,
Through Thy death and burial,
Through Thy resurrection,
Through Thy ascension,
Through Thy joys,
Through Thy glory,
} *Lord Jesus, deliver us.*

Lamb of God! Who takest away the sins of the world!
Spare us, O Jesus!
Lamb of God! Who takest away the sins of the world!
Hear us, O Jesus!
Lamb of God! Who takest away the sins of the world!
Have mercy on us, O Jesus!

Jesus, hear us. *Jesus, graciously hear us.*

LET US PRAY.

O Lord Jesus Christ, Who hast said: Ask, and you shall receive; seek, and you shall find; knock, and it shall be opened unto you: we beseech Thee, grant to us, who beg of Thee the divine gift of Thy charity, that we may love Thee with our whole heart, in word, and in deed, and never desist from Thy praise.

Make us, O Lord, to have a continual fear and love of Thy holy name; because Thou dost never abandon the care of those whom Thou instructest in Thy solid love. Through our Lord Jesus Christ, Thy Son; who liveth and reigneth with Thee, in the unity of the Holy Ghost, world without end. Amen.

Preparation for Confirmation.

What is Confirmation?

Confirmation is a sacrament by which we receive the Holy Ghost, to make us strong and perfect Christians, and soldiers of Jesus Christ. —*Douay Catechism.*

Confirmation is a sacrament which makes us strong and perfect Christians.—*Butler's Catechism.*

I. *Preparation.* Get ready for Confirmation by prayer and Confession. You must also get a card, with your Confirmation name (a saint's name) on it.

II. *Who are Confirmed?* Confirmation is given only to those who are *baptized*, and commonly not before they have come to the use of reason.

III. *Who gives Confirmation?* It is given by the *Bishop*, but sometimes the Pope gives a Priest power to confirm.

IV. *What the Bishop does?* When all who are to be confirmed are ready in the chapel, the Bishop turns round to them. (N. B.—All who have to be confirmed must be present in the chapel at this moment, and not leave it till after the Bishop's blessing at the end.) Then the

Bishop extends his hands towards them and prays. Then those who have to be confirmed, go up; they give up their card to the Priest, and kneel down before the Bishop. Then the Bishop *makes a cross on the forehead with the holy chrism,* and says these words: *I sign Thee with the sign of the cross, I confirm Thee with the chrism of salvation, in the name of the Father, and of the Son, and of the Holy Ghost. Amen.* Then the Bishop gives you a gentle blow on the cheek, saying: "Peace be with you:" this means that when pains and sufferings come, you must be patient, and the peace of God will be in your heart.

V. *Effects of Confirmation.* 1. In Confirmation the Holy Ghost comes into your soul, and by His grace He makes your *holy faith strong and perfect,* so that you would rather die than deny the holy faith. Also, you are made strong against your own bad dispositions, the temptations of the world, and the devil. 2. The Holy Ghost also makes in your soul a beautiful bright mark called a *character*, which can never be lost. 3. In Confirmation there is a godfather for boys, and a godmother for girls, who *cannot afterwards marry* either the child for whom they stand, or its parents.

When you have been confirmed, you get up, and the holy chrism is wiped from your forehead.

Then you go back to your place and pray. The holy chrism is made of oil of the olive tree, mixed with balm, and is solemnly consecrated by the Bishop on Maundy Thursday. You can receive Confirmation only once.

Prayer before and after Confirmation. O Holy Ghost, Spirit of God! I believe that Thou art the third Person of the most blessed Trinity. I believe that in the Sacrament of Confirmation, I receive Thee, to make me a strong and perfect Christian. Come then, O Holy Spirit, come into my poor soul, and be my light in darkness, my strength in weakness, my joy in sorrow. Come, O Holy Spirit, and fill my heart with the fire of Thy love. Amen.

<small>This prayer may be said before and after Confirmation for several days. Say also the Rosary.</small>

PRAYER FOR THE SEVEN GIFTS OF THE HOLY GHOST.

O Almighty and Eternal God, Thou hast vouchsafed to adopt me for Thy child in the holy Sacrament of Baptism; Thou hast granted me the remission of my sins at the tribunal of penance; Thou hast made me to sit at Thy holy table, and hast fed me with the bread of angels: perfect in me, I beseech Thee, all these benefits. Grant unto me the spirit of Wisdom, that I may despise the perishable things of this world, and love the things that are eternal; the spirit of Understanding, to enlighten me and to give me the knowledge of religion; the spirit of Counsel, that I may diligently seek the surest ways of pleasing God and obtaining heaven; the spirit of Fortitude, that I may overcome with courage all the obstacles that oppose my salvation; the spirit of Knowledge, that I may be enlightened in the ways of God; the spirit of Piety, that I may find the service of God both sweet and amiable; the spirit of Fear, that I may be filled with a loving reverence towards God, and may dread in any way to displease Him. Seal me, in Thy mercy, with the seal of a disciple of Jesus Christ, unto everlasting life; and grant that, carrying the cross upon my forehead, I may carry it also in my heart, and, confessing Thee boldly before men, may merit to be one day reckoned in the number of Thy elect. Amen.

The Litany of the Blessed Virgin.

(Called also the Litany of Loretto.)

Kyrie eleison. — Lord, have mercy upon us.
Christe eleison. — *Christ, have mercy upon us.*
Kyrie eleison. — Lord, have mercy upon us.
Christe audi nos. — Christ, hear us.
Christe exaudi nos. — *Christ, graciously hear us.*
Pater de cœlis Deus, *miserere nobis.* — God, the Father of heaven, *Have mercy upon us.*
Fili Redemptor mundi Deus, *miserere nobis.* — God, the Son, Redeemer of the world, *Have mercy upon us.*
Spiritus Sancte Deus, *miserere nobis.* — God, the Holy Ghost, *Have mercy upon us.*
Sancta Trinitas, unus Deus, *miserere nobis.* — Holy Trinity, one God, *Have mercy upon us.*
Sancta Maria, *ora pro nobis.* — Holy Mary, *pray for us.*

Latin (*Ora pro nobis.*)	English (*Pray for us.*)
Sancta Dei Genitrix,	Holy Mother of God,
Sancta Virgo Virginum,	Holy Virgin of Virgins,
Mater Christi,	Mother of Christ,
Mater divinæ gratiæ,	Mother of divine grace,
Mater purissima,	Mother most pure,
Mater castissima,	Mother most chaste,
Mater inviolata,	Mother undefiled,
Mater intemerata,	Mother inviolate,
Mater amabilis,	Mother most amiable,
Mater admirabilis,	Mother most admirable,
Mater Creatoris,	Mother of our Creator,
Mater Salvatoris,	Mother of our Redeemer
Virgo prudentissima,	Virgin most prudent,
Virgo veneranda,	Virgin most venerable,
Virgo prædicanda,	Virgin most renowned,
Virgo potens,	Virgin most powerful,
Virgo clemens,	Virgin most merciful,
Virgo fidelis,	Virgin most faithful,
Speculum justitiæ,	Mirror of justice,
Sedes sapientiæ,	Seat of wisdom,

LITANY OF THE BLESSED VIRGIN. 139

Causa nostræ lætitiæ,	Cause of our joy,
Vas spirituale,	Spiritual vessel,
Vas honorabile,	Vessel of honor,
Vas insigne devotionis,	Vessel of singular devotion,
Rosa mystica,	Mystical rose,
Turris Davidica,	Tower of David,
Turris eburnea,	Tower of ivory,
Domus aurea,	House of gold,
Fœderis arca,	Ark of the covenant,
Janua cœli,	Gate of heaven,
Stella matutina,	Morning star,
Salus infirmorum,	Health of the weak,
Refugium peccatorum,	Refuge of sinners,
Consolatrix afflictorum,	Comfortress of the afflicted.
Auxilium Christianorum	Help of Christians,
Regina Angelorum,	Queen of Angels,
Regina Patriarcharum,	Queen of Patriarchs,
Regina Prophetarum,	Queen of Prophets,
Regina Apostolorum,	Queen of Apostles,
Regina Martyrum,	Queen of Martyrs,
Regina Confessorum,	Queen of Confessors,
Regina Virginum,	Queen of Virgins,
Regina Sanctorum omnium.	Queen of all Saints,
Regina sine labe originali concepta,	Queen conceived without the stain of original sin,

Ora pro nobis. / *Pray for us.*

Agnus Dei, qui tollis peccata mundi, *parce nobis Domine.*

Lamb of God, Who takest away the sins of the world. *Spare us, O Lord.*

Agnus Dei, qui tollis peccata mundi, *exaudi nos Domine.*

Lamb of God, Who takest away the sins of the world, *Hear us, O Lord.*

Agnus Dei, qui tollis peccata mundi, *miserere nobis.*

Lamb of God, Who takest away the sins of the world, *Have mercy upon us.*

V. Ora pro nobis, sancta Dei Genitrix.
R. *Ut digni efficiamur promissionibus Christi.*

V. Pray for us, O holy Mother of God.
R. *That we may be made worthy of the promises of Christ.*

Oremus.

Gratiam tuam, quæsumus Domine, mentibus nostris infunde; ut qui, angelo nuntiante, Christe Filli tui incarnationem cognovimus, per passionem ejus et crucem ad resurrectionis gloriam perducamur: Per eundem Christum Dominum nostrum.—*Amen.*

Let us pray.

Pour forth, we beseech Thee, O Lord, Thy grace into our hearts, that we to whom the incarnation of Christ Thy Son has been made known by the message of an angel, may by His passion and cross be brought to the glory of His resurrection; through the same Christ our Lord. *Amen.*

A SHORT AND EASY METHOD OF SAYING THE BEADS WITH THE MYSTERIES.

A very good method of reciting the Rosary with the Mysteries, is to express the mystery appropriate to each decade in the middle of each *Ave*, immediately after the name of JESUS.

The following is an example of this method: Begin as usual with the *sign of the Cross*, and recite the *Creed*, the *Pater*, the three *Aves*, and the *Gloria*, and then go on with the recitation of the decades, as follows:

When you make use of the FIVE JOYFUL MYSTERIES, say the Aves of the first decade in this manner: "Hail Mary, full of grace, the Lord is with thee; blessed art thou amongst women, and blessed is the fruit of thy womb, Jesus, *Whom thou didst conceive at the message of an angel*: Holy Mary, Mother of God, pray for us sinners, now, and at the hour of our death. Amen." In the second decade, instead of the words, "*Whom thou didst conceive*," &c., say, "*Whom thou didst carry in thy womb on thy visit to Elizabeth.*" In the third decade, "*Who was born of thee at Bethlehem.*" In the fourth, "*Whom thou didst present in the temple.*" In the fifth, "*Whom thou didst find in the temple.*" Having thus recited the five decades, end with the following:

PRAYER.

O God! Whose only begotten Son, by His life, death, and resurrection, has purchased for us the rewards of eternal life: grant, we beseech

Thee, that while we meditate upon these mysteries in the most holy Rosary of the Blessed Virgin Mary, we may imitate what they contain, and obtain what they promise: through the same Christ our Lord. Amen.

When you select for your devotion the SORROWFUL MYSTERIES, say in the middle of each Ave of the first decade, "*Who sweat blood for us in the garden.*" In the second decade, "*Who was scourged for us.*" In the third, "*Who was crowned with thorns for us.*" In the fourth, "*Who has carried His cross for us.*" In the fifth, "*Who was crucified for us.*"

For the GLORIOUS MYSTERIES, in the first decade, say, "*Who arose from the dead.*" In the second, "*Who ascended into heaven.*" In the third, "*Who sent the Holy Ghost.*" In the fourth, "*Who took thee up into heaven.*" In the fifth, "*Who crowned thee Queen of heaven.*"

This method is perhaps the best of all, especially for those who recite their Rosary often, and alone, because it requires no book, and helps to keep the mind constantly fixed on the mystery to be meditated.

LITTLE ROSARY OF THE IMMACULATE CONCEPTION.

In the name of the Father, &c.

I.

I thank Thee, Eternal Father, because Thou hast by Thy omnipotence preserved the most holy Virgin Mary, Thy daughter, from original sin.

Our Father, and four *Hail Marys*, adding, after each *Hail Mary:* "Blessed be the holy, most pure, and immaculate conception of the Blessed Virgin Mary."

II.

I thank Thee, Eternal Son, because Thou hast by Thy wisdom preserved the most holy Virgin Mary, Thy Mother, from original sin.

Our Father, &c., as above.

III.

I thank Thee, Eternal Holy Ghost, because Thou hast by Thy love preserved the most holy Virgin Mary, Thy spouse, from original sin.

Our Father, &c., as above. Finish by reciting once, *Glory be to the Father*, &c., in honor of the purity of St. Joseph, spouse of the Blessed Virgin Mary.

INDULGENCES.

1. An Indulgence of one hundred days for reciting the above Little Rosary with a contrite heart.—(*Pius IX., Jan. 9th,* 1852.)
2. A Plenary Indulgence once a month, on the ordinary conditions, for reciting it every day for a month.—(*Idem.*)
3. An Indulgence of one hundred days, as often as the versicle, "Blessed be the holy," &c., as above, is recited with a contrite heart.—*Pius VI., Nov. 21st,* 1793.)
4. An Indulgence of one hundred days, for devoutly kissing the medal of the Immaculate Conception, and saying: "Mary, conceived without sin, pray for us who have recourse to thee."

Prayers to the Blessed Virgin.

FOR EVERY DAY OF THE WEEK.

By St. Alphonsus.

Pope Pius VII, of holy memory, at the prayer of the Chapter of the Basilica of St. Mary in Cosmedin here in Rome, by a Rescript of the S. Congr. of Indulgences, dated June 21, 1808, kept in the Archivium of the said Basilica granted:

I. The indulgence of three hundred days, once a day, to all the faithful who, with contrite hearts, say the following prayers to our Blessed Lady, extracted from the spiritual works of the sainted Bishop Alphonsus Maria de' Liguori, each on that day of the week to which it has been assigned, together with three *Ave Maria*, with the intention of making her some reparation for the many blasphemies which have been, and are daily uttered against her, not only by unbelievers, but even by bad Christians.

II. The Plenary Indulgence once a month, to all who say these prayers, with three *Ave Maria*, daily for a whole month, with the intention above named, on any one day when, after having Confessed and Communicated, they shall pray to God for the Holy Church, &c.

PRAYER FOR SUNDAY.

See, Mother of my God, at thy feet a wretched sinner, who has recourse to thee, and puts his trust in thee. I am not worthy that thou shouldst even cast thine eyes upon me; yet well I know that thou, beholding Jesus thy Son dying for sinners, dost thyself yearn exceedingly to save them. O Mother of Mercy, look on my miseries and have pity. Men say thou art the refuge of the sinner, the hope of the desperate, the aid of the lost: be thou then my refuge, hope, and aid. It is thy prayers which must save me. For Jesus' tender love be thou my help, reach forth thy hand to the poor fallen wretch who cries to thee for succor. I know that thy heart delights to aid the sinner when thou canst; help me, then, thou who canst. My sins have forfeited the grace of God and my own soul. Behold me in thy hands; O tell me what to do that I may regain my Saviour's grace, and lo! I do it. My Saviour bids me go to thee for help; He wills that I should seek thy tender pity's refuge, that so, not thy dear Son's merits only, but thine own prayers too, may unite to save me. To thee, then, I have recourse: pray thou to Jesus for me; and make me know and feel what thou canst do for one who trusts in thee. Be it done unto me according to my hope. Amen.

Then say three *Ave Maria* to the Blessed Virgin Mary, in reparation for the blasphemies uttered against her.

PRAYER FOR MONDAY.

Most holy Mary, Queen of Heaven, I who was once the slave of Satan, now dedicate myself to thy service for ever; wherefore, to honor and to serve thee while I live, I give thee all myself. Accept me for thy willing servant, nor cast me from thee as I merit. Mother, in thee I set all my hope. All blessing and thanksgiving be to God, Who in His mercy giveth me this trust in thee. True it is that once I was miserably fallen in sin. But for Jesus' merits, and by thy prayers, I hope God pardoned me my sins. Yet it is not enough, my Mother, to be forgiven, whilst the thought appals me that I may still lose the grace of God. Danger is ever nigh; the devil sleeps not; temptations fresh assail me. Protect me, then, my Sovereign Mistress; help me in the assaults of hell. O never, never let me sin again, or offend Jesus thy Son. No never, never more suffer me to lose my soul, heaven, and my God, by sin. For this one grace I ask thee, Mary; this I desire; this may thy prayers obtain for me. Such is my hope. Amen.

The three Ave Maria as before.

PRAYER FOR TUESDAY.

Holiest Mary, Mother of Goodness, Mother of Mercy, when I reflect upon my sins and upon the moment of my death, trembling and confusion then possess me wholly. My sweetest Mother, in the Blood of Jesus, in thy intercession are my hopes. Comforter of the sad, abandon me not at my death agony; fail not to console me in that great affliction. If even now I am so appalled by remorse for sin committed, the danger of a relapse, and strictness of thy judgments, how will it be with me then? Mother, before death o'ertake me, gain for me great sorrow for my sins, a true amendment and constant fidelity to God in all my life that yet remains to me. And when indeed mine hour is come, then do thou, Mary, be my hope, be thou mine aid in the anguish wherein my soul will be o'erwhelmed; when the enemy sets before my face my sins, O comfort me then, that I may not despair. Obtain for me at that moment to invoke thee often, that with thine own sweet name and thy most holy Son's upon my lips, I may breathe forth my spirit. This grace thou hast granted to many of thy servants: let me not fail of this my hope and my desire.

The three Ave Maria as before.

PRAYER FOR WEDNESDAY.

Mother of God most holy Mary, how oft by sin have I merited hell! Ere now the judgment had gone forth against my first mortal sin, hadst not thou in thy tender pity stayed awhile God's justice, and then drawn me on by thy sweetness to take confidence in thee. And O, how very oft in dangers which beset my steps my feet had well nigh gone, when thou, loving Mother that thou art, didst preserve me by the graces thou by thy prayers didst win me. My Queen, what will thy pity and thy favors still avail me, if in my wilfulness I perish in the flames of hell? Hear thou yet once again. True though it be that once I loved thee not, now, next to God, I love thee before all. Wherefore henceforth for ever suffer me not to turn away contemptuous from thee and from that God Who through thee hath granted me so many mercies. Lady most worthy of all love, let it not be that I thy child hate thee and curse thee for ever racked in endless torments. What! thy servant, thy child, damned to hell-fire, who loves thee? Canst thou bear to see it? O Mary, say not so!— say not I ever can be lost! Yet lost am I assuredly if I abandon thee. But where is he who will have heart to leave thee? Who ever can forget the love which thou hast ever borne me? No: impossible it is for him to perish who hath recourse to thee; and who with loyal heart commits himself to thee. Only save me from myself, my Mother, or I am lost! Let me but cling to thee! Save me, my hope! save me from hell; and before hell itself, save me from sin, which alone gives hell its terrors.

The three Ave Maria as before.

PRAYER FOR THURSDAY.

Queen of Heaven, sitting enthroned above the nine choirs of angels nighest to God, from this vale of tears I, poor sinner, hail thee, praying thee in thy love, to turn on me those gracious eyes of thine. See, Mary, see the dangers wherein I dwell, and shall ever dwell whilst I live upon this earth. I may yet lose my soul, paradise, and God. In thee, Lady, is my hope. I love thee; and I sigh after the time when I shall see thee and praise thee in heaven's courts. O Mary, when will come that blessed day that I shall see myself safe at thy feet? When kiss that hand so oft outstretched to minister to me graces? Alas, too true it is, my Mother, that in my life I have ever been an ingrate; but when I reach heaven's haven, there will I love thee every moment of a whole eternity, and make thee reparation in some sort for my ingratitude by ever blessing and praising thee. Thanks be to God for that He hath vouchsafed to me such trust in Jesus' Precious Blood and in thy powerful intercession. For this heaven thy true lovers have ever hoped, nor has any one of them been defrauded of his hope. No: neither shall I be deceived of mine. O Mary, pray to thine own Son Jesus, and I will pray

Him too, by all the merits of His Passion, to strengthen and increase this hope.

The three Ave Maria as before.

PRAYER FOR FRIDAY.

Mary, of all creation noblest, highest, purest, fairest, holiest work of God! O that all men knew thee, loved thee, my Queen, as thou deservest to be loved! Yet great is my consolation, Mary, that there are blessed souls in heaven's courts, and just souls still on earth, whose hearts thou leadest captive with thy beauty and thy goodness. But above all I joy in this, that our God Himself loves thee alone more than all men and angels. I too, loveliest Queen, I miserable sinner, dare to love thee, mean though my love be; I would I had a greater love, a more tender love: this thou must gain for me, since to love thee is the surest mark of predestination, and a grace which God vouchsafes the children of salvation. Then too, my Mother, when I reflect upon the debt I owe thy Son, I see His love for me demands for Him of me naught less than immeasurable love. Do thou, then, whose desire it ever is to see Him solely loved, pray that I may have this grace: great love of Jesus Christ. Obtain it, thou who obtainest what thou wilt. Nor goods of earth, nor honors, nor riches do I covet, but that which thine own heart desires most, to love my God alone. O, can it ever be thou wilt not aid me in a desire so acceptable to thee? Impossible! even now I feel thy help, even now thou prayest for me.— Pray, Mary, pray; nor ever cease to pray, till thou dost see me safe in paradise, sure of possessing and of loving my God and thee, my dearest Mother, for ever and for ever. Amen.

The three *Ave Maria* as before.

PRAYER FOR SATURDAY.

Mary most holy, on the one hand I see the graces thou hast obtained for me; and on the other, the ingratitude I have shown thee. The ingrate is unworthy of all favors; yet not for this will I distrust thy mercy. Great Advocate, have pity on me. Thou, Mary, art the stewardess of every grace which God vouchsafes us sinners, and therefore did He make the mighty, rich, and kind, that so thou mightest succor us. Behold me now, then, *willing* my salvation: in thy hands I place it; to thee I here consign my soul. I *will* to be of those who are thy special servants; cast me not, then, away. Thou goest up and down seeking the wretched, to console them. Cast not away, then, this poor wretched sinner who has recourse to thee. Speak for me,

Mary; thy Son grants what thou askest. Take me beneath thy shelter, and it is enough; because with thee to guard me I fear no ill. No, not my sins; because thou wilt obtain God's pardon for them: no, nor yet devils; because thou art far mightier than hell: no, nor my Judge Jesus Christ; for at thy prayer He will lay by His wrath. Protect me, then, **my Mother**; obtain for me pardon of my sins, love of Jesus, holy perseverance, good death, and paradise. Too true, I merit not these graces; yet do thou only ask them of our God, and lo! they shall be mine. Pray, then, to Jesus for me. Mary, my Queen, in thee I trust; in this trust I rest, I live; in this trust I hope to die. Amen.

<small>The three *Ave Maria* as before; then the Litanies, it being Saturday, for which there is the Indulgence, as at p. 138.</small>

THE "MEMORARE" OF ST. BERNARD TO THE BLESSED VIRGIN.

Remember, Mary, tenderest-hearted Virgin, how from of old the ear hath never heard that he who ran to thee for refuge, implored thy help, and sought thy prayers, was forsaken of God. Virgin of virgins, Mother, emboldened by this confidence I fly to thee, to thee I come, and in thy presence I a weeping sinner stand. Mother of the Word Incarnate, O cast not away my prayer; but in thy pity hear and answer.—Amen.

An Indulgence of three hundred days may be gained *once a day* by reciting the above prayer, as by Rescript of his Holiness, Pius IX.

EXERCISE IN HONOR OF HER SORROWFUL HEART.

Pope Pius VII., at the prayer of the priests of the Pious Union of the Sacred Heart of Jesus, sometimes called " Pious Union of St. Paul," granted, by a Rescript of Jan. 14, 1815, issued through the Archbishop of Philippi, at that time vicegerent here in Rome, and kept in the *Segretaria* of his Eminence the Cardinal Vicar:

The Indulgence of three hundred days, to all Christians every time they say with devotion, the following pious exercise in honor of the sorrowing heart of most holy Mary.

THE EXERCISE.

V. Incline unto my aid, O God.
R. O Lord, make haste to help me.
Glory be to the Father, &c.

I. I compassionate thee, sorowing Mother, in the grief thy tender heart underwent when the holy old man Simeon prophesied to thee. Dear Mother, by the griefs of thy heart then so wounded, obtain for me the virtue of humility and the gift of holy fear of God.

Ave Maria.

II. I compassionate thee, sorrowing Mother, for the anxiety which thy heart so sensitive underwent in the flight and sojourn in Egypt. Dear Mother, by thy heart then so sorrowful, obtain for me the virtue of liberality, specially towards the poor, and the gift of pity.

Ave Maria.

III. I compassionate thee, sorrowing Mary, for the terrors felt by thy anxious heart when thou didst lose thy dear Son Jesus. Dear Mother, by thy heart then so agitated, obtain for me the virtue of holy chastity, and with it the gift of knowledge.

Ave Maria.

IV. I compassionate thee, sorrowing Mary, for the shock thy Mother's heart experienced when Jesus met thee as He carried His cross. Dear Mother, by that loving heart of thine, then so afflicted, obtain for me the virtue of patience and the gift of fortitude.

Ave Maria.

V. I compassionate thee, sorrowing Mary, for the martyrdom thy generous heart bore so nobly whilst thou didst stand by Jesus agonising. — Dear Mother, by thy heart then so martyred, obtain for me the virtue of temperance and the gift of counsel.

Ave Maria.

VI. I compassionate thee, sorrowing Mary, for the wound with which thy tender heart was riven when Jesus' sacred Side was cleft with the lance. Dear Mother, by thy heart then pierced through, obtain for me the virtue of fraternal charity and the gift of understanding.

Ave Maria.

VII. I compassionate thee, sorrowing Mary, for the anguish felt by thy loving heart when Jesus' Body was buried in the grave. Dear Mother, by all the bitterness of desolation thou didst then know, obtain for me the virtue of diligence and the gift of wisdom.

Ave Maria.

V. Pray for us, Virgin most sorrowful.

R. That we may be made worthy of the promises of Christ.

LET US PRAY.

Grant, we beseech Thee, O Lord Jesus Christ, that the most blessed Virgin Mary, Thy Mother, may intercede for us before the throne of Thy mercy, now and at the hour of our death, through whose most holy soul in the hour of Thine own Passion the sword of sorrow passed. Through Thee, Jesus Christ, Saviour of the world, Who livest and reignest with the Father and the Holy Ghost for ever and ever. Amen.

SHORT PRAYER TO THE MOST HOLY VIRGIN IN HER DESOLATION.

His Holiness our Sovereign Lord, Pope Pius IX., by a decree of the S. Congr. of Indulgences, of Dec. 23, 1847, vouchsafed to grant:

The Indulgence of one hundred days to all the faithful, every time they say with contrite heart the following prayer in honor of the most holy Virgin in her desolation.

Ave Maria doloribus plena: Crucifixus tecum: lacrymabilis tu in mulieribus, et lacrymabilis fructus ventris tui Jesus. Sancta Maria, Mater Crucifixi: lacrymas impertire nobis crucifixoribus Filii tui, nunc et in hora mortis, nostræ. Amen.

TRANSLATION.

Hail Mary, full of sorrows, the Crucified is with thee: tearful art thou amongst women, and tearful is the fruit of thy womb, Jesus. Holy Mary, Mother of the Crucified, give tears to us, crucifiers of thy Son, now and at the hour of our death. Amen.

Devotions to the Saints.

The Holy Church teaches us that it is both lawful and useful to invoke the Saints reigning with God in heaven. We ask the prayers of good men on earth, without any fear of dishonoring the mediatorship of our divine Saviour; and should that fear deter us from asking the Saints in heaven to pray for us, because they are in heaven? Surely not, as long as we acknowledge (as we are always bound to do) that their prayers can avail us nothing except through the merits of Christ.

Neither can we doubt that the Saints receive our invocations. "There is joy in heaven upon one sinner that doth penance." (S. Luke, xv. 7-10.) *How* the blessed in heaven know what is passing on earth, does not concern us: of the *fact* we are certain. Therefore they know when we are asking their prayers. Moreover, being perfect in charity, they are willing, and, as the friends of God, they are abundantly able, to help us.

Let us, then, frequently beg the prayers of these friends of God, not doubting but that this devotion will be pleasing to God Himself, Who is wonderful in His Saints, and Who is honored by the honor we pay to them for His sake.

THE LITANY OF THE SAINTS.

Lord, have mercy on us.
Christ, have mercy on us.
Lord, have mercy on us.
Christ, hear us.
Christ, graciously hear us.
God, the Father of heaven, *Have mercy on us.*
God, the Son, Redeemer of the world, *Have mercy on us.*
God, the Holy Ghost, *Have mercy on us.*
Holy Trinity, one God, *Have mercy on us.*
Holy Mary, *Pray for us.*

LITANY OF THE SAINTS.

Holy Mother of God, \
Holy Virgin of Virgins, \
St. Michael, \
St. Gabriel, \
St. Raphael, \
All ye holy Angels and Archangels, \
All ye holy orders of blessed Spirits, \
St. John Baptist, \
St. Joseph, \
All ye holy Patriarchs and Prophets, \
St. Peter, \
St. Paul, \
St. Andrew, \
St. James, \
St. John, \
St. Thomas, \
St. James, \
St. Philip, \
St. Bartholomew, \
St. Matthew, \
St. Simon, \
St. Thaddeus, \
St. Matthias, \
St. Barnaby, \
St. Luke, \
St. Mark, \
All ye holy Apostles and Evangelists, \
All ye holy Disciples of our Lord, \
All ye holy Innocents, \
St. Stephen, \
St. Laurence, \
St. Vincent, \
SS. Fabian and Sebastian, \
SS. John and Paul, \
SS. Cosmas and Damian, \
SS. Gervasius and Protasius, \
All ye holy Martyrs, \
St. Sylvester, \
St. Gregory, \
St. Ambrose, \
St. Augustine, \
St. Jerome, \
St. Martin, \
St. Nicholas, \
All ye holy Bishops and Confessors, \
All ye holy Doctors, \
St. Anthony, \
St. Benedict, \
St. Bernard, \
St. Dominic, \
St. Francis, \
All ye holy Priests and Levites, \
All ye holy Monks and Hermits, \
St. Mary Magdalen, \
St. Lucy, \
St. Agnes, \
St. Cecily, \
St. Agatha, \
St. Catharine, \
St. Anastasia, \
All ye holy Virgins and Widows,

Pray for us.

All ye men and women, saints of God, *make intercession for us.* \
Be merciful unto us. *Spare us, O Lord.* \
Be merciful unto us. *Graciously hear us, O Lord.* \
From all evil, *O Lord, deliver us.* \
From all sin, *O Lord, deliver us.* \
From Thy wrath, *O Lord, deliver us.*

From sudden and unprovided death,
From the deceits of the devil,
From anger, hatred, and all ill-will,
From the spirit of fornication,
From lightning and tempest,
From the scourge of earthquakes,
From plague, famine and war,
From everlasting death,
Through the mystery of Thy holy incarnation,
Through Thy coming,
Through Thy nativity,
Through Thy baptism and holy fasting,
Through Thy cross and passion,
Through Thy death and burial,
Through Thy holy resurrection,
Through Thy admirable ascension,
Through the coming of the Holy Ghost the Comforter,
In the day of judgment,

> *O Lord, deliver us.*

We sinners, *do beseech Thee to hear us.*
That Thou spare us,
That Thou pardon us,
That Thou vouchsafe to bring us to true penance,
That Thou vouchsafe to govern and preserve Thy holy Church,
That Thou vouchsafe to preserve our Apostolic Prelate, and all ecclesiastical orders in holy religion,
That Thou vouchsafe to humble the enemies of the holy Church,
That Thou vouchsafe to give peace and true concord to Christian kings and rulers,
That Thou vouchsafe to grant peace and unity to all Christian people,
That Thou vouchsafe to confirm and preserve us in Thy holy service,
That Thou lift up our minds to heavenly desires,
That Thou render eternal good things to all our benefactors,
That Thou deliver our souls, and those of our brethren, kinsfolks, and benefactors, from eternal damnation,

> *We beseech Thee to hear us.*

That Thou vouchsafe to give and preserve the fruits of the earth,
That Thou vouchsafe to give eternal rest to all the faithful departed,
That Thou vouchsafe graciously to hear us, Son of God,

We beseech, &c.

Lamb of God, who takest away the sins of the world,
Spare us, O Lord.
Lamb of God, who takest away the sins of the world,
Graciously hear us, O Lord.
Lamb of God, who takest away the sins of the world,
Have mercy on us.

Christ, hear us. *Christ, graciously hear us.*
Lord, have mercy on us. *Christ, have mercy on us.*
Lord, have mercy on us.
Our Father, &c. *(in secret.)*
V. And lead us not into temptation.
R. *But deliver us from evil. Amen.*

PSALM LXIX.

Incline unto my aid, O God: O Lord, make haste to help me.

Let them be confounded and ashamed that seek my soul.

Let them forthwith be turned backward, and blush for shame, that desire evils to me.

Let them be turned backward, and blush and be put to shame, who say to me, It is well! it is well!

Let all that seek thee be glad and rejoice in thee: and let those who love thy salvation say, always, "The Lord be magnified."

But I am needy and poor: O God, assist me.

Thou art my helper and my deliverer! O Lord, make no delay.

V. Glory, &c. *R. As it was, &c.*

V. Save Thy servants.

R. Who put their trust in Thee, my God.

V. Be to us, O Lord, a tower of strength.

R. Against the face of the enemy.

V. Let not the enemy prevail against us.

R. Nor the son of iniquity have power to hurt us.

V. O Lord, deal not with us according to our sins.

R. Nor reward us according to our iniquities.

V. Let us pray for our chief Bishop (N.)

R. May the Lord preserve him, and prolong his life, and make him happy on earth, and deliver him not up to the will of his enemies.

V. Let us pray for our benefactors.

R. Vouchsafe, O Lord, for Thy name's sake, to render eternal life to all those who do us good.

V. Let us pray for the faithful departed.

R. Give them, O Lord, eternal rest; and let perpetual light shine unto them.

V. May they rest in peace. *R.* Amen.

V. For our absent brethren.

Litany of the Saints.

R. Save Thy servants, O my God, who put their trust in Thee.

V. Send them help, O Lord, from Thy sanctuary.

R. And protect them out of Sion.

V. O Lord, hear my prayer.

R. And let my supplication come unto Thee.

V. May the Lord be with you.

R. And with thy spirit.

LET US PRAY.

O God, whose property is always to have mercy and to spare, receive our petition: that we, and all Thy servants, who are bound by the chain of sins, may, by the compassion of Thy goodness, mercifully be absolved.

Hear, we beseech Thee, O Lord, the prayers of the suppliant, and pardon the sins of them that confess to Thee; that in Thy bounty Thou mayest give us pardon and peace.

Out of Thy clemency, O Lord, show Thy unspeakable mercy to us, that so Thou mayest both acquit us of our sins, and deliver us from the punishments we deserve for them.

O God, Who by sin art offended, and by penance pacified, mercifully regard the prayers of Thy people making supplication to Thee, and turn away the scourges of Thy anger, which we deserve for our sins.

O Almighty and Eternal God, have mercy on Thy servant N., our chief Bishop, and direct him, according to Thy clemency, into the way of everlasting salvation; that by Thy grace he may desire those things that are agreeable to Thee, and perform them with all his strength.

O God, from whom are all holy desires, right counsels, and just works, give to Thy servants that peace which the world cannot give, that both our hearts may be disposed to keep Thy commandments, and, the fear of enemies being removed, the times, by Thy protection, may be peaceable.

Inflame, O Lord, our reins and hearts with the fire of Thy holy Spirit, that we may serve Thee with a chaste body, and please Thee with a clean heart.

O God, the Creator and Redeemer of all the faithful, give to the souls of Thy servants departed the remission of all their sins; that through pious supplications they may obtain the pardon which they have always desired.

Forerun, we beseech Thee, O Lord, our actions by Thy holy inspirations, and carry them on by Thy gracious assistance, that every prayer and work of ours may begin always from Thee, and by Thee be happily ended.

O Almighty and Eternal God, Who hast dominion over the living and the dead, and art merciful to all whom Thou foreknowest shall be Thine by faith and good works; we humbly beseech Thee that they for whom we have determined to offer up our prayers, whether this world still detains them in the flesh, or the world to come has already received them out of their bodies, may by the clemency of Thy goodness, and by the intercession of all Thy Saints, obtain pardon and full remission of all their sins, through our Lord Jesus Christ Thy Son, Who liveth and reigneth, etc. Amen.

V. O Lord, hear my prayer.

R. And let my cry come unto Thee.

V. May the Almighty and most merciful Lord graciously hear us.

R. Amen.

V. And may the souls of the faithful departed, through the mercy of God, rest in peace.

R. Amen.

Prayers.

A DEVOUT RECOMMENDATION.

Which may be used every Morning, or at any other time.

I adore and glorify Thee, O blessed Trinity, God Almighty, Father, Son, and Holy Ghost; I offer myself to Thy divine Majesty, humbly beseeching Thee to take from me, and from all Thy faithful, whatever displeases Thee, and to give us that which is grateful in Thy sight. — Grant that we may here do what Thou commandest, and hereafter receive what Thou promisest.

To Thee, O Lord, I commend my soul and body, (my wife and children, my father and mother, my brothers and sisters;) all my relations, benefactors, friends, and acquaintances; all who have injured or offended me, and all whom I have in any way scandalised, injured, or offended; all who have asked my prayers, or for whom I am accustomed or bound to pray; supply all their necessities, comfort and support them in all their trials and afflictions, deliver them from all temptations, make them in this world truly to know, love, and serve Thee, and to enjoy Thee hereafter in heaven.

I pray also for Thy holy Catholic Church; for its chief pastor, N., our Pope, that the spirit of wisdom, fortitude and piety may rest upon him; for the bishops (especially N. our bishop,) and for all the pastors and clergy of Thy Church, that they may direct the faithful in the way of salvation; for all religious orders of men and women (to whose prayers and good works I desire to be associated;) and for all the faithful. I pray for all heretics, that they may be enlightened; for all poor sinners, that they may be converted; and for the universal spread of truth and righteousness. I pray for this our country, that Thou wouldst deliver us from all those evils which we most justly have deserved by our sins, and bring us back into the ways of truth, peace and godliness. I pray for the President, and all who are in authority; for the poor, and all who are tempted, or afflicted; and for all who are in their last agony. Lastly, I commend all universally to Thy divine protection, beseeching Thee to grant to the living forgiveness of their sins, and to the souls departed, rest and peace. Amen.

A DAILY OBLATION.

My God and my all, I most earnestly desire, by my every breath, every thought, every word, every desire, and my every movement of body and soul, to tell Thee a thousand times that I love Thee more than life, or any thing in this world; and I offer and dedicate myself to Thee, renewing my baptismal vows, together with the promises and resolutions of my life past. I offer Thee also (and by every movement of my body and soul I desire to renew the oblation) all the praise, thanks and adoration of the Church militant, triumphant and suffering; all that it has offered Thee, or will offer to the end of time; all the love, complacency and delights Thou possessest in Thy divine essence; all the homage rendered to Thee by my Saviour Jesus Christ in the most adorable Sacrament of the Altar; all the masses that are now celebrating, have been, or will be celebrated to the end of time, to Thy honor and glory, without any other wish or desire but that of pleasing Thee, loving Thee, living for Thee, and dying for Thee. I am Thine, my God and my all; oh, make me so entirely and eternally. Above all, take my heart; extirpate from it all other affections, and make it for the future a furnace of the purest flames of Thy most ardent love.— Amen.

A UNIVERSAL PRAYER FOR ALL THINGS NECESSARY TO SALVATION.

O my God, I believe in Thee; do Thou strengthen my faith. All my hopes are in Thee; do Thou secure them. I love Thee; teach me to love Thee daily more and more. I am sorry that I have offended Thee; do Thou increase my sorrow.

I adore Thee as my first beginning; I aspire after Thee as my last end. I give Thee thanks as my constant benefactor; I call upon Thee as my sovereign protector.

Vouchsafe, O my God, to conduct me by Thy wisdom, to restrain me by Thy justice, to comfort me by Thy mercy, to defend me by Thy power.

To Thee I desire to consecrate all my thoughts, words, actions and sufferings; that henceforward I may think of Thee, speak of Thee, refer all my actions to Thy greater glory, and suffer willingly whatever Thou shalt appoint.

Lord, I desire that in all things Thy will may be done, because it is Thy will, and in the manner that Thou willest.

I beg of Thee to enlighten my understanding, to inflame my will, to purify my body, and to sanctify my soul.

Give me strength, O my God, to expiate my offences, to overcome my temptations, to subdue my passions, and to acquire the virtues proper for my state.

Fill my heart with tender affection for Thy goodness, hatred of my faults, love of my neighbor, and contempt of the world.

Let me always remember to be submissive to my superiors, condescending to my inferiors, faithful to my friends, and charitable to my enemies.

Assist me to overcome sensuality by mortification, avarice by alms-deeds, anger by meekness, and tepidity by devotion.

O my God, make me prudent in my undertakings, courageous in dangers, patient in affliction, and humble in prosperity.

Grant that I may be ever attentive at my prayers, temperate at my meals, diligent in my employments, and constant in my resolutions.

Let my conscience be ever upright and pure, my exterior modest, my conversation edifying, and my comportment regular.

Assist me, that I may continually labor to overcome nature, to correspond with Thy grace, to keep Thy commandments, and to work out my salvation.

Discover to me, O my God, the nothingness of this world, the greatness of heaven, the shortness of time, and the length of eternity.

Grant that I may prepare for death; that I may fear Thy judgments, that I may escape hell, and in the end obtain heaven; through Jesus Christ my Lord. Amen.

Devotion to St. Joseph.

"I do not remember," says St. Teresa, "ever to have asked any thing of St. Joseph, until this moment, which he did not obtain for me. One would be astonished, were I to tell of all the numberless graces which God has granted me by the intercession of this Saint, and of the perils, both of body and soul, from which he has delivered me. It seems to be the privilege of other Saints to assist us in some particular necessities, but experience proves that this Saint assists us in all, as if by this the Lord would have us understand that as He was pleased to be subject to St. Joseph while on earth, so He is resolved to grant all his requests in heaven. This is what other persons have proved, to whom I had given counsel to recommend themselves to him. Such is the long experience I have of the great favors which he obtains from God, that I would gladly persuade the whole world to be devout to this Saint. I have never known any one that rendered some special homage to him, who has not made manifest progress in virtue. For several years I have been accustomed to ask some favor of him on the day of his festival, and always I perceive that I have been heard. If any one does not believe it, I beg of him for the love of God, to make the experiment. For my part, I do not know how any one can think of the Queen of Angels, and of the care which she took of Jesus in His childhood, without thanking St. Joseph for the succor he gave, during this time, to both mother and Son."—*Life of St. Teresa*, ch. vi.

DEVOUT PRAYERS IN HONOR OF ST. JOSEPH.

Choice of St. Joseph as patron.

O blessed Joseph, faithful guardian of my Redeemer Jesus Christ, protector of thy chaste spouse the virgin Mother of God, I choose thee this day to be my especial patron and advocate, and I firmly resolve to honor thee as such from this time forth and always. Therefore I humbly beseech thee to receive me for thy client, to instruct me in every doubt, to comfort me in every affliction, and finally to defend and protect me in the hour of death. Amen.

FOR HIS SAFE-CONDUCT THROUGH LIFE.

O blessed Joseph, father and guide of Jesus Christ in His childhood and youth, who didst lead Him safely in His flight through the desert, and in all the ways of His earthly pilgrimage, be also my companion and guide in this pilgrimage of life, and never permit me to turn aside from the way of God's commandments; be my refuge in adversity, my support in temptation, my solace in affliction, until at length I arrive at the land of the living, where with thee, and Mary thy most holy spouse, and all the Saints, I may rejoice forever in Jesus my Lord. Amen.

FOR GRACE TO COMMUNICATE DEVOUTLY.

O blessed Joseph, how sweet and wonderful a privilege was thine, not only to see, but to carry in thy arms, to kiss and to embrace with fatherly affection that only begotten Son of God, whom so many Kings and Prophets desired to see, but were not able! O that, inspired by thy example and aided by thy patronage, I may often, with like feelings of love and reverence, embrace my Lord and Redeemer in the Blessed Sacrament of the altar, so that when my life on earth is ended, I may merit to embrace Him eternally in heaven. Amen.

FOR OTHER PARTICULAR GRACES.

O blessed Joseph, since Jesus while on earth was subject to thee, rendered prompt obedience to thy commands, and cherished thee with most especial love and honor, how shall He now refuse thee any thing in heaven, where all thy merits receive their full reward? Pray for me, therefore, O holy Patriarch, and obtain for me these necessary graces: first of all, that I may have a sincere contrition for my sins, that I may ever hate and fear all that is evil, and fly from it with firmness and constancy, especially from my most besetting sins; secondly, that I may amend my life daily more and more, and constantly apply myself to the acquirement of virtue, especially those virtues which I need most; and lastly, that I may be kept safe amidst the various temptations and occasions by which my soul may be exposed to the peril of damnation. For these and all other needful graces, O holy Joseph, I commend myself to the goodness and mercy of my God, and to thy fatherly care and intercession. Amen.

FOR A HAPPY DEATH.

O blessed Joseph, who didst yield thy last breath in the fond embrace of Jesus and of Mary,—when the seal of death shall close my career of life, come, holy Father, with Jesus and Mary, to aid me, and obtain for me this only solace which I ask for in that hour, to die encircled by their holy arms. Into your sacred hands, living and dying, Jesus, Mary, Joseph, I commend my soul. Amen.

V. Pray for us, O most blessed Joseph.

R. That we may be made worthy of the promises of Christ.

PRAYER.

We beseech Thee, O Lord, that we may be assisted by the merits of the Spouse of Thy most Holy Mother; so that what we are unable to obtain of ourselves, may be granted us through his intercession; Who livest and reignest world without end. Amen.

THE MEMORARE TO SAINT JOSEPH.

Most glorious Saint Joseph, Virgin Spouse of the Immaculate Mother of God, my loving Patron, remember that it has never been known that any one invoked thy help or solicited thy patronage without obtaining relief. Encouraged by this assurance, I commend my soul and body, my temporal and eternal interests, to thy powerful protection. Oh! Thou, the adopted Father of the Eternal Son, despise not this appeal, but listen to my prayer and plead for my necessities. Amen.

An Indulgence of three hundred days may be gained once a day by reciting the above prayer, as by Rescript of his Holiness, Pius IX.

Devotion to the Holy Angels.

"Are they not all ministering spirits, sent to minister for them who shall receive the inheritance of salvation?" Heb. i, 14.

"The Angels," says St. Augustine, "love us as their fellow-citizens, and hope to see us fill up what has been lost to their own number by the fall of the rebel angels. For this reason they are always present with us, and watch over us with the greatest care. At all times, and in every place, they are ready to help us, and to provide for our wants. They walk with us in all our ways; going out and coming in, they follow us still, anxiously considering whether we live piously and purely in the midst of a wicked world. They assist those who labor; they guard those who rest; they encourage those who fight; they crown those who conquer; they rejoice with the joyful, and sympathize with the suffering. When we do well, the angels are glad, but the devils are sad. When we sin, the devils rejoice, but the angels are cheated of their joy." (Solil. cap. 27.)

We ought, therefore, to honor these blessed spirits with very great reverence and affection, and to pray to them, especially our guardian angels, to whom God has given charge over us, to keep us in all our ways (Ps. xc.,) and we may be sure that this devotion will be most pleasing to them, and most useful to ourselves.

15*

A PRAYER TO ST. MICHAEL.

St. Michael, glorious Prince, chief and champion of the heavenly host, guardian of the souls of men, conqueror of the rebel angels, steward of the palace of God, under Jesus Christ our worthy captain, endowed with superhuman excellence and virtue; vouchsafe to free us all from every ill, who with full confidence have recourse to thee; and by thy incomparable protection enable us to make progress each day in the faithful service of our God.

V. Pray for us, most blessed Michael, prince of the Church of Jesus Christ.

R. That we may be made worthy of His promises.

PRAYER.

Almighty and eternal God, Who in Thine own marvellous goodness and pity didst, for the common salvation of man, choose the glorious Archangel Michael to be the prince of Thy Church; make us worthy, we pray Thee, to be delivered by his beneficent protection from all our enemies, that at the hour of our death no one of them may approach to harm us: rather do Thou vouchsafe unto us that by the same Archangel Michael we may be introduced into the presence of Thy high and heavenly Majesty. Through the merits of the same Jesus Christ our Lord. Amen.

THE ANGEL PSALTER.

(Extracted from various Psalms.)

O ye angels of the Lord, bless the Lord: praise Him and exalt Him above all forever.

Praise the Lord from the heavens: praise ye Him in the high places. Praise him, all ye His angels; praise ye Him, all His hosts.

Bless the Lord, all ye His angels, you that are mighty in strength, and execute His word, hearkening to the voice of His orders.

Bless the Lord, all ye His hosts; ye ministers of His that do His will.

Bless the Lord, O my soul, and never forget all He hath done for Thee.

Who redeemeth thy life from destruction, Who cowneth thee with mercy and compassion.

For He hath given His angels charge over thee, to keep thee in all Thy ways.

In their hands they shall bear Thee up, lest Thou dash Thy foot against a stone.

Thou shalt walk upon the asp and the basilisk, and Thou shalt trample under foot the lion and the dragon.

The Angel of the Lord shall encamp round about them that fear Him, and shall deliver them.

Glory be to the Father, &c.

V. I will sing praise to Thee, O my God, in the sight of the Angels.

R. I will worship towards Thy holy temple and I will give glory to Thy name.

PRAYER.

O God, Who, in most admirable order, dost assign the various offices, both of angels and of men: grant, we beseech Thee, that they who always minister before Thy face in heaven may also defend us in this our life on earth. Through Jesus Christ Thy Son our Lord. Amen.

PRAYER TO ONE'S GUARDIAN ANGEL.

O blessed Angel, my Guardian and defender, since by the kind providence of God I have been committed to thy care, I beseech thee to direct me always in the way of peace, safety and salvation. Remain especially this day (or night) by my side, to defend me from all danger, and every evil temptation. Remember, O dearest guardian, how once the watchful love of God preserved thee with the good angels in grace and glory, while so many others were cast down from heaven for their pride. I beseech thee, therefore, to watch over me in this my lifetime of trial, and bring me such efficacious aid from heaven, that in no danger I may ever fall and lose the grace of my God and Creator, until I come to appear before His face in my heavenly home; there, with thee and all the saints and angels, to praise and adore Him, through the endless ages of eternity. Amen.

(There is an indulgence of one hundred days attached to the following prayer, for each time of reciting it.)

Angele Dei,	O Angel of God,
Qui custos es mei,	Who art my guard,
Me tibi commissum pietate superna,	Committed by heavenly care to thy ward.
Hodie illumina custodi, rege, et guberna.	Rule, govern, enlighten and keep me this day.
Amen.	*Amen.*

Prayers to the Holy Apostles.

ST. PETER AND ST. PAUL.

Pope Pius VI., by a rescript of July 28, 1778, issued through the *Segretaria* of the memorials, granted:

I. The Indulgence of one hundred days to all the faithful, who, being contrite, shall say at least once a day the following prayer, with one *Pater, Ave* and *Gloria,* in honor of the blessed Apostles Peter and Paul.

II. The Plenary Indulgence, on all Feasts of SS. Peter and Paul, provided that, after having Confessed and Communicated, they shall on such feast-day itself, or one of the nine days preceding it, or eight days following it, visit a church or altar dedicated to those Saints, saying there the following prayer, and remembering the Holy Church and its Sovereign Pontiff.

THE PRAYER.

O blessed Apostles Peter and Paul, I, N N , take you this day for my special protectors and advocates with God. In all humility I rejoice with thee, blessed Peter, Prince of the Apostles, because thou art the rock whereon God hath built His Church; and I rejoice with thee, too, blessed Paul, because thou wast chosen of God for a vessel of election, and preacher of the truth throughout the world. Ask for me, I pray you both, a lively faith, firm hope, and perfect charity, entire detachment from myself, contempt of the world, patience in adversity, humility in prosperity, attention in prayer, purity of heart, right intention in my works, diligence in the fulfilment of all the duties of my state of life, constancy in my good resolutions, resignation to the holy will of God, perseverance in His grace even unto death; that by your joint intercession and your glorious merits I may overcome the temptations of the world, the flesh, and the devil, and be made worthy to stand before the face of the chief and eternal Bishop of Souls, Jesus Christ our Lord, to enjoy Him and to love Him for all eternity, Who, with the Father and the Holy Ghost, liveth and reigneth ever world without end. Amen.

Pater, Ave, and Gloria.

PRAYERS TO ST. PATRICK.

O blessed apostle of Ireland! glorious St. Patrick! who didst become the father and benefactor of that land long before my birth, receive my prayers, and accept the sentiments of gratitude and veneration with which my heart is filled towards thee. Thou wast the channel of the greatest graces; deign then to become also the channel of my grateful thanksgivings to God for having granted, through thee, that precious gift of faith which is dearer to us than life. O most blessed father and patron of that country! do not, I beseech thee, despise my weakness. Remember that the cries of little children were the mysterious invitation that thou didst receive to go thither. Listen then to my most humble supplications; I unite them to the praises and blessings which will ever follow thy name and thy memory throughout the Church; I unite them to the prayers of the multitude of our ancestors, who now enjoy eternal bliss, and owe their salvation, under God, to thy zeal and charity. They will eternally share thy glory, because they listened to thy word and followed thy example. Ah! since I am descended from saints, may I blush to differ from them; may I begin from this moment to love God with all my heart, and serve Him with all my strength. For this end I most humbly beg thy blessing, O great St. Patrick! and thy particular intercession, for obtaining whatever grace thou seest to be most necessary for me. Amen.

O God, Who wast pleased to send blessed Patrick, Thy bishop and confessor, to preach Thy glory to the Gentiles, grant that, by his merits and intercession, we may through Thy grace, be enabled to keep Thy commandments. Through Christ our Lord. Amen.

Our Father, Hail Mary, and *Glory be to the Father*, three times, in union with St. Patrick, to obtain the gift of faith, a lively hope, and perfect charity; also, to thank the adorable Trinity for the graces and privileges bestowed on this great Saint.

PRAYER TO ST. ALOYSIUS GONZAGA.

Pope Pius VII., at the prayer of many bishops, the more to increase devotion towards St. Aloysius Gonzaga, who from the time of his canonization was given by Benedict XIII. as the special protector of the young, granted, by a decree of the S. Congr. of Indulgences, March 6, 1802:

The Indulgence of one hundred days, once a day, to all the faithful, who, being contrite, shall devoutly say the following prayer with one *Pater noster* and one *Ave Maria*.

THE PRAYER.

O blessed Aloysius, adorned with angelic graces, I thy most unworthy suppliant recommend specially to thee the chastity of my soul and body, praying thee by thy angelic purity to plead for me with Jesus Christ the Immaculate Lamb, and His most holy Mother, Virgin of virgins, that they would vouchsafe to keep me from all grievous sin. O never let me be defiled with any stain of fleshly sin; but when thou dost see me in temptation, or in danger of falling, then far from my heart remove all bad thoughts and unclean desires, and awaken in me the memory of eternity to come and of Jesus crucified: impress deeply in my heart a sense of the holy fear of God; and thus kindling in me the fire of divine love, enable me so to follow Thy footsteps here on earth, that in heaven with thee I may be made worthy to enjoy the vision of our God for ever. Amen.

One Pater noster and one Ave Maria.

PRAYER OF A SOUL IN DESOLATION.

By St. Alphonsus.

My Jesus, because I love Thee, all the pain arising from the troubles of my conscience consists in the fear of displeasing and losing Thee, Who art an infinite Good. There was a time (and Oh! that it had never been) when I did not love Thee, and cared but little to be loved by Thee. But now I desire nothing but to love Thee, and to be loved by Thee, my dear Redeemer. I do not wish ever more to displease Thee. Thou knowest my wish to love Thee at any cost; do not abandon me. If I have hitherto offended Thee I now feel more pain at the offences I have offered to Thee than if I lost all things, property, relatives, and life. Thou hast died for me, to Thee I consign my soul, into Thy hands I recommend it. *In manus tuas Domine commendo spiritum meum.* Thou lovest me, and therefore I abandon myself entirely into Thy hands, and hope never to see myself confounded, and in enmity with Thee. "In Thee, O Lord, have I hoped; let me never be confounded." My Jesus, I wish always to love Thee. This I repeat, and hope to repeat during life, at death, and for all eternity. My Jesus I love Thee, and wish always to love Thee. Mary, my hope, Mother of mercy, assist me, have pity on me.

A PRAYER TO OUR HOLY PATRON OF BAPTISM.

Glorious St. N.! whose name I have the honor to bear, who wast given in baptism as a protector and pattern, and who, although secure of thy own immortal bliss, art nevertheless solicitous about my happiness; assist me by thy powerful intercession, as thou instructest me by the examples of thy holy life. For I truly can behold in thy life, as in a bright mirror, what I am to correct in myself, and what I am to practice. Thou hast been like me, subject to suffering, encompassed with infirmities, assaulted with temptations: but being rooted and founded in charity, thou hast spurned the rage and persecutions of the world, despised its allurements, and triumphed over its malignity. Obtain by thy prayers, that I may be endued with thy spirit, and become a follower of thee, as thou hast been of Christ. Draw me, that I may run after thee in the odor of thy ointments; that is, of thy virtues. On the day in which I was buried together with Christ by baptism unto death, thou wast given me for a witness and a guardian of my engagements. I beseech thee, therefore, that thou assist me in thy prayers for me to God, that I may hold fast the confession of my hope without wavering, and that laboring to make sure by good works my vocation and election, I may pursue towards the mark for the prize of the celestial vocation of God, in Christ Jesus. Amen.

A PRAYER FOR RENEWING THE PROMISES OF BAPTISM.

Most holy Trinity! Father, Son, and Holy Ghost, one God in three persons! I present myself before Thy sovereign Majesty, to pay

Thee the tribute of my adoration and thanksgiving, for the innumerable graces and blessings which Thou hast so liberally bestowed upon me, from my first coming into the world, until now. I thank Thee particularly, O my God! for the inestimable grace of my baptism. What gratitude can bear proportion to such a favor? By baptism, I have been delivered from the power of darkness, and translated into the kingdom of Thy beloved Son; by baptism, I have been cleansed from the stain of that sin, in which I was born; by baptism, I have been made a member of the body of Jesus Christ, to live of His life, to be animated and guided by His spirit, to be fed with His sacred flesh, to enter into His designs, to imitate His virtues; finally, to be a living image of what He has been during His mortal life. These are the obligations of my baptism, these are the conditions of the alliance, which Thou wouldst have me to contract with Thee: and although I was at that time ignorant of them, and my will had no part in this sacred contract, far from wishing to be released from them, or appealing, in any manner, from my vows and professions, I ratify them now, and renew them in Thy presence from the bottom of my heart, with a profound sorrow for having hitherto led a life so little conformable to my promises, and proved myself, by repeated transgressions, so unworthy of the glorious quality of Thy child. But now, relying on the promised assistance of Thy grace, it is my firm determination to labor all my life in fulfilling the sacred engagements which my sponsors have contracted in my name.

Yes, O my God! I renounce, for ever, Satan and all his suggestions, the world and all its pomps, sin and all its concupiscences. I am resolved, as it was promised in my behalf, to unite and attach myself more and more to Jesus Christ, my Saviour, and to make His divine laws and maxims the object of my earnest study, and the invariable rule of all my actions.

O Eternal Father! Who wast pleased to adopt me in Thy Son Jesus Christ, as one of Thy children, and to call me to Thy celestial inheritance, revive in me the grace of this divine adoption; and since I am regenerated by Thee alone, in order to be a citizen of heaven, grant that I may live for Thee alone, and that all my desires and labors may be directed to the acquisition of heavenly goods.

O Jesus, the only begotten Son of the Father! Who hast made me a member of Thy mystical body, washed me in Thy blood, and sanctified me by Thy holy sacraments, perfect Thy work in me. Purify my heart from the remains of the pride and corruption of Adam; and form Thy precious image in my soul, by engraving in Thy charity, Thy humility, Thy purity, and all Thy other virtues, which are the glorious features of that image.

O Holy Spirit! adorable principle of the divine adoption! be also the principle of my life, of my actions, of my desires, and of all the motions of my heart, that they may be worthy of a child of God, and member of Jesus Christ.

O Holy Trinity! Who, in consecrating me to Thy service by baptism, hast made me the adorer of the Unity of Thy name, and of the Trinity of Thy persons, mercifully grant, that I may adore Thee in spirit and in truth during my life, and love, praise, and enjoy Thee during eternity. Amen.

A PRAYER IN SICKNESS OR AFFLICTION.

O Lord Jesus Christ, I receive this sickness (or this affliction,) with which Thou art pleased to visit me, as coming from Thy fatherly hand. It is Thy will, and therefore I submit; "not my will, but Thine be done." May it be to the honor of Thy holy name, and for the good of my soul. I here offer myself with an entire submission to all Thine appointments; to suffer whatever Thou pleasest, as long as Thou pleasest, and in what manner Thou pleasest: for I am a creature, O Lord, Who hast often and most ungratefully offended Thee, and whom Thou mightst justly have visited with Thy severest punishments. Oh, let Thy justice be tempered with mercy, and let Thy heavenly grace come to my assistance, to support me under this affliction! Confirm my soul with strength from above, that I may bear with true Christian patience all the uneasiness, pains, disquiets and troubles under which I labor; preserve me from all temptations and murmuring thoughts, that in this time of affliction I may in no way offend Thee; and grant that this and all other earthly trials may be the means of preparing my soul for its passage into eternity, that, being purified from all my sins, I may believe in Thee, hope in Thee, love Thee above all things and finally, through Thy infinite merits, be admitted into the company of the blessed in heaven, there to praise Thee for ever and ever.— Amen.

O God, Who hast doomed all men to die, but hast concealed from all the hour of their death, grant that I may pass my days in the practice of holiness and justice, and that I may deserve to quit this world in the peace of a good conscience, and in the embrace of Thy love, through Christ our Lord. Amen.

PRAYER BEFORE EXTREME UNCTION.

Most merciful Lord and loving Saviour, Jesus Christ, what a consoling promise Thou hast attached to the reception of this sacrament: "*Is any one sick among you, let him bring in the Priests of the Church, and let him pray over him, anointing him with oil, in the name of the Lord, and the prayer of faith shall save the sick man; and the Lord will lift him up, and if he be in sin, his sins shall be forgiven him.*" (St. James, v.)

By Thy infinite goodness, O Jesus, through which Thou hast established this Holy Sacrament, I beseech Thee to purify me from my sins, defend me from the enemy, strengthen me in temptation, and give me a happy end; or, if it be profitable for my soul's salvation, restore me to my former health. This I ask, through Thy infinite merits, Who, with God the Father, and the Holy Ghost, livest and reignest, one only God forever! Amen.

During the anointing of each of the five senses of your body, pray, in the silence of your heart, that God may pardon the sins which you have committed with each, and offer up for your sins those sufferings which Christ endured in this same sense for your sins.

PRAYER AFTER EXTREME UNCTION.

Most merciful Jesus, I have now received this Sacred Unction, which Thou didst institute for the consolation and benefit of the sick. I thank Thee for this powerful remedy of my soul and my body. Enable me to enjoy the full benefits of this Holy Sacrament, upon which I place my hope and confidence. Amen.

Protestation for Death.

By St. Alphonsus.

My God, prostrate in Thy presence, I adore Thee; and I intend to make the following protestation, as if I were on the point of passing from this life into eternity:

My Lord, because Thou art the Infallible Truth, and hast revealed it to the Holy Church, I believe in the mystery of the Most Holy Trinity, Father, Son, and Holy Ghost; three Persons, but only one God; Who for all Eternity rewards the just in heaven, and punishes the wicked in hell. I believe that the second Person, that is, the Son of God, became man, and died for the salvation of mankind; and I believe all that the Holy Church believes. I thank Thee for having made me a Christian, and I protest that I will live and die in this holy Faith.

My God, my Hope, trusting in Thy promises, I hope from Thy mercy, not through my own merits, but through the merits of Jesus Christ, for the pardon of my sins, perseverance, and, after this miserable life, the glory of Paradise. And should the devil at death tempt me to despair at the sight of my sins, I protest that I will always hope in Thee, O Lord, and that I desire to die in the loving arms of Thy goodness.

O God! worthy of infinite love, I love Thee with my whole heart, more than I love myself; and I protest that I desire to die making an act of love, that I may thus continue to love Thee eternally in heaven, which for this end I desire and ask of Thee.

And if hitherto, O Lord, instead of loving Thee, I have despised Thy infinite goodness, I repent of it with all my heart, and I protest that I wish to die, always weeping over and detesting the offences I have committed against Thee. I purpose for the future rather to die than ever to sin again; and for the love of Thee I pardon all who have offended me.

O God, I accept of death, and of all the sufferings which will accompany it; I unite it with the sufferings and death of Jesus Christ, and offer it in acknowledgment of Thy supreme dominion, and in satisfaction for my sins. Do Thou, O Lord, accept of this sacrifice which I make of my life, for the love of that great sacrifice which Thy divine Son made of Himself upon the altar of the Cross. I resign myself entirely to Thy divine will, as though I were now on my death-bed, and protest that I wish to die, saying: " O Lord, always Thy will be done!"

Most Holy Virgin, my Advocate and my Mother, Mary, you are and will always be, after God, my hope and my consolation at the hour of death. From this moment, I have recourse to you, and beg of you to assist me in that passage. O my dear Queen, do not abandon me in that last moment; come then to take my soul and present it to your Son. Henceforward I shall expect you; and I hope to die under your mantle and clinging to your feet.— My Protector Saint Joseph, St. Michael Archangel, my Angel Guardian, my Holy Patrons, do you all assist me in that last combat with hell.

And Thou my Crucified Love, Thou, my Jesus, Who wert pleased to choose for Thyself so bitter a death to obtain for me a good death, remember at that hour that I am one of those dear sheep Thou didst purchase with

Thy blood. Thou Who, when all the world shall have forsaken me, and not one shall be able to assist me, canst alone console me and save me, do Thou make me worthy then to receive Thee in the Viaticum, and suffer me not to lose Thee forever, and to be banished forever to a distance from Thee. No, my beloved Saviour, receive me then into Thy sacred wounds, for I now embrace Thee. At my last breath, I intend to breathe forth my soul into the loving wound in Thy side, saying now, for that moment: Jesus and Mary, I give you my heart and my soul. Jesus and Mary, I give you my heart and my soul.

O happy suffering, to suffer for God! Happy death, to die in the Lord!

I embrace Thee now, my good Redeemer, that I may die in Thy embraces. If, O my soul, Mary assists you at your departure, and Jesus receives your last breath, it will not be death, but a sweet repose.

The Words of a Dying Man to Jesus Crucified.

By St. Alphonsus.

O Jesus, my Redeemer, Who within a few moments wilt be my Judge, have mercy upon me before the moment comes when Thou wilt judge me. No, my sins do not terrify me, nor the rigors of Thy judgment, while I see Thee dead upon this cross to save me.

Yet, cease not to comfort me in the agony to which I am come: my enemies would terrify me by saying that there is no salvation for me; "Many say unto my soul, there is no salvation for him in his God." But I will never cease to trust in Thy goodness, and say, "Thou, oh, Lord, art my lifter up." Do Thou comfort me; do Thou make me feel that Thou art my salvation; "Say unto my soul, I am Thy salvation." O, let not all those pangs, those insults endured, that blood poured forth by Thee, be lost unto me. "Thou hast redeemed me, dying upon the cross; let not so great labor be in vain." Especially, I pray Thee, through that bitterness Thou didst feel when Thy blessed soul was separated from Thy most holy body, have mercy upon my soul when it departs from my body.

It is true that through my sins I have continually despised Thee; but now I love Thee above everything, I love Thee more than myself; and I grieve with all my heart for all the offences I have committed against Thee; I detest them, I hate them above every evil. I see that through the offences I have been guilty of, I have deserved a thousand hells: but the bitter death which Thou hast been willing to endure for me, and the great mercies Thou hast already shown me, make me confidently hope, that when I appear before Thee, Thou wilt welcome me with the kiss of peace.

Trusting all in Thy goodness, oh my God, I abandon myself into Thy loving arms. "In Thee, oh Lord, I have hoped; I shall not be confounded forever." Through the sins I have committed, I have again and again deserved hell; but I hope in Thy blood, that Thou hast now pardoned me; and I hope that I shall come to heaven to praise Thy mercies forever: "the mercies of God I will sing forever."

I willingly accept all the pains Thou dost destine for me in purgatory: it is just that the fire should purge away the wrongs I have done Thee. O holy prison, when shall I find myself shut up in thee, secure from being able ever to lose my God! O holy fire, when wilt thou purge away my vileness, and make me worthy to enter the kingdom of the blessed!

O eternal Father, through the merits of the death of Thy Son, Jesus Christ, make me to die in Thy grace, and in Thy love, that I may come to love Thee throughout eternity. I thank Thee for all the graces Thou hast given me through my life, and especially for the great grace of Thy holy faith, and for having caused me to receive, in these my last days, all the holy Sacraments. Thou willest that I should die, and I desire to die to please Thee. It is little, oh Jesus, my Saviour, that I should die for Thee, Who hast died for me. I am satisfied to say to Thee, with St. Francis, "Let me die for love of Thee, Who hast vouchsafed to die for love of me."

I receive death with peace, and also the pains which I must endure so long as I breathe; give me strength to suffer with a perfect uniformity to Thy will. I offer them all to Thy glory, uniting them to the pains which Thou didst suffer in Thy passion. O eternal Father, I sacrifice to Thee my life, and all my being; and I pray Thee to accept this my sacrifice, through the merits of that great sacrifice which Jesus Thy Son offered up of Himself upon the cross.

O Mother of God, and my mother Mary, thou hast obtained many graces from God for me during my life; I thank thee with all my heart. O abandon me not in this hour of my death, in which I have greater need of thy prayers. Pray to Jesus for me, and increase thy prayers; obtain for me sorrow for my sins, and more love for God, that I may come to love Him forever, in company with thee, and with all my powers, in heaven. "In thee, oh Lady, I have hoped: I shall not be confounded forever." Mary, my hope, in thee I trust.

Acts of Devotion for the Time of Death.

By St. Alphonsus.

It was revealed to St. Liduvina by an angel, that the crown of merits and glory which awaited her in heaven could only be completed through the sufferings which she was to endure in the days which would immediately precede her death. The same thing happens to all devout souls when they depart from this world. It is certain that all good acts, and especially those of resignation in accepting death, performed with the view of pleasing God, are of great merit to every one who dies in the grace of God. Let us here set down certain acts of devotion, which may be very acceptable to the Lord at the time of death.

O my God, I offer Thee my life, and I am prepared to die at any hour which may be pleasing to Thy holy will. "Thy will be done;" ever, ever, may Thy will be done.

O Lord, if Thou willest to leave me in life for some time longer, blessed be Thy name; but I desire not life, except to spend it all in loving Thee and giving Thee pleasure. If Thou wilt that I should die of this sickness, still blessed art Thou. I embrace death to do Thy will, and I repeat, "Thy will, Thy will be done;" I only beg Thee to help me all through this hour. "Have mercy on me, oh God, according to Thy great mercy." If, then, Thou wilt that I should leave this earth, I declare that I desire to die, because thus Thou wilt have it.

I desire also to die, in order that, by the pain and bitterness of my death, I may satisfy Thy Divine justice for all my sins, through which I have offended Thee and deserved hell.

I desire also to die, that I may never more offend Thee, or cause Thee displeasure in this life.

I also desire to die in acknowledgment of the gratitude which I owe Thee for all the benefits and gifts that Thou hast given me, contrary to all my own deserts.

I desire to die, that I may show that I love Thy will more than my life.

I desire, if it pleases Thee, to die now, at a time when I trust I am in Thy grace, in order to be assured that I shall praise and bless Thee forever.

I desire, above all, to die, in order that I may come to love Thee eternally, and with all my powers, in heaven; where through Thy blood, oh my Redeemer, I hope to come, and to be safe from ceasing to love Thee through all eternity. O my Jesus, Thou didst accept the death of the cross through love of me; I accept death, and all the pains which await me, through love of Thee. Therefore I say with St. Francis, "May I die, oh Lord, through love of Thee, Who, through love of me, didst not disdain to die."

I pray Thee, oh my Saviour, my love, and my only good, by Thy holy wounds and Thy bitter death make me to die in Thy grace, and through Thy blood suffer me not to perish. O sweetest Jesus, suffer me not to be separated from Thee; suffer me not to be separated from Thee.

O Lord, drive me not away from Thy face. I confess that, through my sins, I have deserved hell, and I mourn for them more than for any evil; and I hope to come to heaven to praise forever the great mercies Thou hast shown to me. "The mercies of the Lord I shall sing forever."

I adore Thee, oh my God, Who hast created me. I believe in Thee, oh Eternal Truth. I hope in Thee, oh Infinite Mercy. I love Thee, oh Supreme Goodness; I love Thee above everything; I love Thee more than myself, for Thou art worthy of being loved: And because I love Thee, I repent with all my heart for having despised Thy grace. I promise Thee to suffer every kind of death, and a thousand deaths, rather than displease Thee.

O Jesus, Son of God, Who didst die for me, have pity upon me! My Saviour, save me; and let it be my salvation to praise Thee through eternity.

O Mary, Mother of God, pray to Jesus for me; now it is the time for thee to aid me. — Mary, Mother of grace, Mother of mercy, do thou defend us from the enemy, and receive us in the hour of death. To thy protection we fly, oh holy Mother of God! O Mary, Holy Mother of God, pray for us sinners!

St. Joseph, my patron and father, help me in this hour. St. Michael the Archangel, deliver me from the devils who lie in wait for my soul. O my holy advocates, and ye Saints of paradise, pray to God for me.

And Thou, my Jesus crucified, at the moment when I must breathe my last breath, receive my soul in Thy arms; to Thee I recommend it; remember that Thou hast redeemed me with Thy blood. "We therefore pray Thee, help Thy servants Whom Thou hast redeemed with Thy precious blood." O my crucified Jesus, my love, and my hope, whether I live or die, I declare that I desire Thee alone, and nothing more. Thou art my God and my all, and what else can I desire but Thee! What have I in heaven or upon earth! Thou art the God of my heart and my portion forever! Thou art the love of my heart; Thou art all my riches!

To Thee, then, I recommend my soul: to Thee, Who hast redeemed it with Thy death. Into Thy hands, oh Lord, I commend my spirit: Thou hast redeemed me, oh Lord God of truth. Trusting in Thy mercy, I therefore say, in Thee, oh Lord, have I hoped; I shall not be confounded forever. O Mary, thou art my hope; to thee, therefore, I say again, in thee, oh Lady, have I hoped; I shall not be confounded forever.

The Recommendation of a Departing Soul.

(From the Roman Breviary.)

Lord, have mercy on him (or her.)
Christ, have mercy upon him.
Lord, have mercy on him.
Holy Mary,
All ye holy Angels and Archangels,
Holy Abel,
All ye Choirs of the Just,
Holy Abraham,
St. John Baptist,
St. Joseph,
All ye holy Patriarchs and Prophets,
St. Peter,
St. Paul,
St. Andrew,
St. John,
All ye holy Apostles and Evangelists,
All ye holy Disciples of our Lord,
St. Stephen,
St. Lawrence,
All ye holy Martyrs,
All ye holy Innocents,
St. Sylvester,
St. Gregory,
St. Augustine,
All ye holy Bishops and Confessors,
St. Benedict,
St. Francis,
All ye holy Monks and Hermits,
St. Mary Magdalen,
St. Lucy,
All ye holy Virgins and Widows,
All ye Men and Women, Saints of God,
} *Pray for him (or her)*

Be merciful unto him, }
Be merciful unto him, } *Spare him (or her,) O Lord.*
Be merciful unto him, }
From Thy wrath,
From the Danger of eternal death,
From an evil death,
From the pains of hell,
From all evil,
From the power of the devil,
By Thy nativity,
By Thy cross and passion,
By Thy death and burial,
By Thy glorious resurrection,
By Thy wonderful ascension,
By the grace of the Holy Ghost the Comforter,

Deliver him (or her,) O Lord.

      Deliver him (or her,) O Lord.
In the Day of Judgment, *Deliver him (or her,) O Lord.*
We sinners, *Beseech Thee hear us.*
That Thou spare him, *We beseech Thee hear us.*
Lord, have mercy on him.
Christ, have mercy on him.
Lord, have mercy on him.

PRAYER.

Go forth, O Christian soul, from this world, in the name of God the Father Almighty, Who created thee; in the name of Jesus Christ, the Son of the living God, Who suffered for thee; in the name of the Holy Ghost, Who has sanctified thee; in the name of the Angels and Archangels; in the name of the heavenly Thrones and Dominations; in the name of the Principalities and Powers; in the name of the Cherubim and Seraphim; in the name of the Patriarchs and Prophets; in the name of the Holy

Apostles and Evangelists; in the name of the Holy Martyrs and Confessors; in the name of the Holy Monks and Hermits; in the name of the Holy Virgins and all the Saints of God; let thy place be this day in peace and thy abode in the Holy Sion. Through the same Jesus Christ our Lord. *R. Amen.*

O most merciful and good God! Thou Who by the multitude of Thy mercies dost blot out the sins of the penitent, and dost remit the punishment of their past sins; graciously look down upon this Thy servant (Thy handmaid,) and hear his (her) supplication, since he (she) with his (her) whole heart confesses and begs Thy forgiveness of his (her) sins. Renew in him (her,) O most merciful Father, every thing that has been deformed through human frailty, or through the cunning of the devil, and receive this member, redeemed by the blood of Thy Son, to the unity of the body of the Church. Have compassion, O Lord, upon his (her) sighs, have compassion on his (her) tears, and admit him (her,) because he (she) has no hope but in Thy mercy, to the grace of reconciliation to Thee. *R. Amen.*

I commend thee, dear brother (dear sister,) to Almighty God, and commit thee to the hands of thy Creator, that then when thou, by death, hast paid the debt of nature, thou mayest return to thy Maker, Who formed thee from the clay of the earth. When thy soul leaves the body, may the bright host of Angels come to meet thee; the company of the Apostles who are to judge the world, receive thee; the triumphant army of Martyrs meet thee; the multitude of Confessors surround thee, with their lilies in their hands; the choir of joyful Virgins welcome thee; and may the Patriarchs with loving embrace receive thee into their rest. May Jesus appear to thee with a mild and radiant face, and may he give a place among those who are ever near him.— Mayest thou never know the dreadful darkness, the crackling flames, and the torments of the damned. May the devil, with his evil spirits, depart from thee trembling and flying into the horrid confusion of eternal night, when he sees thee accompanied by the angels. Let God arise, and His enemies be put to flight, and all who hate Him flee before His presence! Let them be driven away as smoke; as wax melts before the fire, so may sinners disappear before His countenance. But may the just rejoice and be glad in the presence of God. Let all the hosts of hell be confounded and put to shame, and may the servants of satan place no hindrance in the way. May Christ, Who was crucified for thee, deliver thee from all torments. May Christ, Who vouchsafed to die for thee, deliver thee from eternal death. May Christ, the Son of the living God, conduct thee to the possession of the eternal joys of Paradise. May He, the true Shepherd, receive thee as His sheep. May He absolve thee from all thy sins, and place thee at His right hand among the number of His elect.— Mayest thou see thy Redeemer face to face, and always in His presence behold, with happy eyes, the purest truth. Mayest thou, in the company of the blessed, eternally enjoy the sweetness of the Divine presence. *R. Amen.*

PRAYER.

Receive, O Lord, thy servant (handmaid) into the place of salvation, which he (she) hopes to obtain through Thy mercy. *R. Amen.*

Deliver, O Lord, the soul of thy servant (handmaid) from all dangers of hell, and from all pain and tribulation. *R. Amen.*

Deliver, O Lord, the soul of thy servant (handmaid) as Thou didst deliver Enoch and Elias from the common death of the world. *R. Amen.*

Deliver, O Lord, the soul of thy servant (handmaid) as Thou didst deliver Noe from the flood. *R. Amen.*

Deliver, O Lord, the soul of thy servant (handmaid) as Thou didst deliver Abraham from the midst of the Chaldeans. *R. Amen.*

Deliver, O Lord, the soul of thy servant (handmaid) as Thou didst deliver Isaac from the hand of Abraham his father. R. Amen.

Deliver, O Lord, the soul of thy servant (handmaid) as Thou didst deliver Lot from being destroyed in the flames of Sodom. R. Amen.

Deliver, O Lord, the soul of thy servant (handmaid) as Thou didst deliver Moses from the hands of Pharoah, king of Egypt. R. Amen.

Deliver, O Lord, the soul of thy servant (handmaid) as Thou didst deliver Daniel from the lions' den. R. Amen.

Deliver, O Lord, the soul of thy servant (handmaid) as Thou didst deliver the three children from the fiery furnace, and from the hands of an unmerciful king. R. Amen.

Deliver, O Lord, the soul of thy servant (handmaid) as Thou didst deliver Susanna from her false accusers. R. Amen.

Deliver, O Lord, the soul of thy servant (handmaid) as Thou didst deliver David from the hand of king Saul and Goliath. R. Amen.

Deliver, O Lord, the soul of thy servant (handmaid) as Thou didst deliver Peter and Paul out of prison. R. Amen.

And, finally, as Thou didst deliver, O Lord, the blessed virgin and martyr, Thecla, from three most cruel torments, so vouchsafe to deliver the soul of this thy servant, and bring him (her) to share Thy heavenly joys. R. Amen.

We commend to Thee, O Lord! the soul of Thy servant N. (Thy handmaid N.,) and beseech Thee, O Lord Jesus Christ, the Saviour of the world! that Thou wouldst admit into the bosom of Thy Patriarchs this soul, for which, in Thy mercy, Thou didst come into the world. Acknowledge, O Lord, this Thy creature; not made by any strange gods, but by Thee, the only living and true God; for there is no other God but Thee, and nothing equals Thy works. Fill him (her,) O Lord, with the joy of Thy presence. Remember no more those sins and errors into which he (she) was led by the power of evil desires. He (she) has indeed sinned, but has never renounced his (her) faith in the Father, Son and Holy Ghost, and has had a zeal for the glory of God, and faithfully worshipped Thee, the God and the Creator of all things.

Remember not, O Lord, the sins of his (her) youth and his (her) ignorance, but according to Thy great mercy be mindful of him (her) in the brightness of Thy glory. May the heavens be opened to him (her,) and may the angels rejoice in him (her.) Receive, O Lord, Thy servant (Thy handmaid) into Thy kingdom. May St. Michael, the Archangel of God, who has merited to be the chief of the heavenly host, conduct him (her.) May the holy Angels of God come to meet him (her,) and take him (her) to the city of the heavenly Jerusalem. May St. Peter, to whom God committed the keys of the kingdom of heaven, receive him (her.) May St. Paul, who was worthy to be a vessel of election, assist him (her.) May St. John, the chosen Apostle of God, to whom the secrets of heaven were revealed, intercede for him (her.) May all the holy Apostles, to whom the Lord has intrusted the power of loosing and binding, pray for him (her.) May all the Saints and chosen servants of God, who for the name of Christ in this world have suffered martyrdom, intercede for him (her,) that he (she) being delivered from the bonds of the flesh, may merit to be received into the glory of the kingdom of heaven; by the mercy of our Lord Jesus Christ, Who, with the Father and the Holy Ghost, liveth and reigneth forever. Amen.

AFTER THE SOUL HAS DEPARTED.

Come to his (her) assistance, ye Saints of God! Come to meet him (her,) ye Angels of the Lord! Receive his (her) soul, and bring it into the presence of the Most High. May Jesus Christ, Who has called Thee, receive Thee, and His Angels bear Thee to Abraham's bosom

Lord, have mercy on him (her.)
Christ have mercy on him (her.)
Lord, have mercy on him (her.) Our Father, &c.

V. Eternal rest give to him (her,) O Lord.

R. *And let perpetual light shine upon him (her.)*

V. From the gates of hell,

R. *Deliver him (her,) O Lord.*

V. May he (she) rest in peace.

R. *Amen.*

V. O Lord, hear my prayer,

R. *And let my cry come unto Thee.*

PRAYER.

To Thee, O Lord, we commend the soul of Thy servant (handmaid,) that, having departed from this world, he (she) may live to Thee alone, and that in Thy infinite goodness and mercy Thou wilt pardon him (her) whatever sins he (she) may have committed in this world, through human frailty. This we ask through Jesus Christ our Lord. Amen.

The body is then decently laid out, and a light placed before it. A small crucifix is placed in the hands of the deceased, upon his breast, or the hands are themselves placed crosswise; and the body is sprinkled with holy water.

Occasional Prayers.

FOR THE HOLY CATHOLIC CHURCH.

Defend, O Lord, Thy servants, we beseech Thee, from all dangers both of body and soul; and, by the intercession of the blessed and glorious Virgin Mary, Mother of God, of the blessed Apostles Peter and Paul, of blessed N., and of all Thy saints, mercifully grant us the blessings of peace and safety; that all adversities and errors being removed, Thy Church may freely and securely serve Thee; through our Lord, &c.

FOR ALL DEGREES OF MEN IN THE CHURCH.

Almighty and everlasting God, by Whose Spirit the whole body of the Church is sanctified and governed; mercifully hear our humble supplications for all degrees and orders therein; that, by the gift of Thy grace, all in their several stations may faithfully serve Thee; through, &c,

FOR THE POPE.

O God, the Pastor and Governor of all the faithful, mercifully look upon Thy servant N., whom Thou has been pleased to appoint the pastor of Thy Church; grant, we beseech Thee, that both by word and example he may edify those over whom he is set, and, together with the flock committed to his care, may attain everlasting life; through, &c.

FOR BISHOPS, AND THE PEOPLE COMMITTED TO THEM.

Almighty and everlasting God, Who alone dost great marvels, send down upon Thy servants, the Bishops of Thy Church, (especially N., our Bishop,) and all congregations committed unto them, the spirit of Thy saving grace; and that they may truly please Thee, pour upon them the continual dew of Thy blessing; through, &c.

FOR A CONGREGATION OR FAMILY.

Defend, we beseech Thee, O Lord, by the intercession of the blessed Mary ever Virgin, this Thy family from all adversity; and mercifully protect us, now prostrate before Thee with our whole hearts, from all the snares of our enemies; through, &c.

IN ANY TRIBULATION.

O Almighty God, despise not Thy people who cry unto Thee in their affliction; but for the glory of Thy name, turn away Thine anger, and help us in our tribulations; through, &c.

IN TIMES OF CALAMITY.

O Lord Jesus Christ, holy, immortal God! have mercy upon us and upon all men: purify us by Thy holy blood, forgive us by Thy holy blood, save us by Thy holy blood, now and for ever. Amen.

IN TIME OF FAMINE OR PESTILENCE.

Grant, we beseech Thee, O Lord, an answer to our hearty supplications; and, Thy wrath being appeased, turn away from us this famine (or pestilence,) that the hearts of men may know that these scourges proceed from Thine anger, and cease by Thy mercy; through, &c.

IN TIMES OF GREAT MORTALITY.

(Deus qui non mortem, &c.)

O God, Who desirest not the death, but the penance of sinners, mercifully look upon Thy people returning to Thee; and grant that they being devoted unto Thee, may by Thy clemency, be delivered from the scourges of Thine anger; through, &c.

(Exaudi nos, Deus, &c.)

Hear us, O God of our salvation; and deliver Thy people from the terrors of divine anger, and make them secure by the bountifulness of Thy mercy; through, &c.

FOR HERETICS AND SCHISMATICS.

O Almighty and everlasting God, Who hast compassion on all, and wouldst not that any should perish; favorably look down upon all those who are seduced by the deceit of Satan; that all heretical impiety being removed, the hearts of such as err may repent, and return to the unity of Thy truth; through, &c.

FOR JEWS.

O Almighty and Everlasting God, Who repellest not from Thy mercy even the perfidious Jews; hear the prayer which we offer for the blindness of that people; that the light of Thy truth, Christ our Lord, being known to them, they may be delivered from their darkness; through, &c.

FOR PAGANS.

O Almighty and Everlasting God, Who desirest not the death but the life of sinners; mercifully accept our prayers, and, delivering pagans from the worship of idols, unite them to Thy Church, to the praise and honor of Thy glorious name; through, &c.

FOR OUR FRIENDS.

O God, Who, by the grace of Thy Holy Spirit, hast poured into the hearts of Thy faithful the gifts of charity; grant to Thy servants, for whom we implore Thy mercy, health both of body and soul; that they may love Thee with all their strength, and cheerfully perform those things which are pleasing unto Thee; through, &c.

PRAYER FOR A FRIEND OR FRIENDS.

Preserve, O Lord, Thy servants (servant) N. N., for whose health, happiness, and prosperity I humbly offer up these my prayers to Thy sacred majesty, beseeching Thee to grant them a persevering constancy in the Catholic faith, and a safe passage through this life's dangerous pilgrimage; that no worldly, carnal, or diabolical temptation may have the power to separate them from Thee their first and only good. Give them grace to correspond to that state and condition of life in which Thou hast placed them; direct them in all their ways; defend them against all their enemies; and finally grant them a happy death and departure out of this world, and a speedy passage after death to the fruition of Thy eternal felicity. Amen.

FOR A FRIEND IN DISTRESS.

Vouchsafe, O merciful Lord, to afford the sweetness of Thy comfort to Thy afflicted servant N., and to remove, according to Thy accustomed mercy, the heavy burden of his calamities. Give him, I humbly beseech Thee, patience in his sufferings, resignation to Thy good pleasure, perseverance in Thy service, and a happy translation from this afflicting life to Thy eternal felicity. Amen.

FOR ANOTHER'S CONVERSION.

O divine and adorable Saviour, Thou Who art the way, the truth, and the life, I beseech Thee to have mercy upon N., and bring him (or her) to the knowledge and love of Thy truth. Thou, O Lord, knowest all his darkness, his weakness, and his doubts; have pity upon him, O merciful Saviour; let the bright beams of Thy eternal truth shine upon his mind; clear away the cloud of error and prejudice from before his eyes, and may he humbly submit to and embrace with his whole heart the teaching of Thy Church. Oh, let not the soul for whom I pray be shut out from Thy blessed fold! Unite him to Thyself in the sacraments of Thy love, and grant that, partaking of the blessings of Thy grace in this life, he may come at last to the possession of those eternal rewards which Thou hast promised to all those who believe in Thee and who do Thy will. Hear this my petition, O merciful Jesus, Who with the Father and the Holy Ghost, livest and reignest ever and ever. Amen.

FOR THE SICK.

V. Heal Thy servants, O Lord, who are sick, and who put their trust in Thee.

R. Send them help, O Lord, and comfort them from Thy holy place.

O Almighty and Everlasting God, the eternal salvation of them that believe in Thee, hear us in behalf of Thy servants who are sick; for whom we humbly crave the help of Thy mercy; that, their health being restored to them, they may render thanks to Thee in Thy Church; through, &c.

FOR THE DEAD.

O Almighty and Eternal God, Who hast dominion over the living and the dead, and art merciful to all whom Thou foreknowest shall be Thine by faith and good works; we humbly beseech Thee, that they for whom we have determined to offer up our prayers, whether this present world still detain them in the flesh, or the world to come hath already received them out of their bodies, may, by the clemency of Thy goodness (all Thy saints interceding for them,) obtain pardon and full remission of their sins; through our Lord Jesus Christ, Thy Son, Who with Thee and the Holy Ghost, liveth and reigneth one God, world without end. Amen.

A PRAYER BEFORE STUDY OR INSTRUCTIONS.

O incomprehensible Creator, the true Fountain of light, and only Author of all knowledge; vouchsafe, we beseech Thee, to enlighten our understandings, and to remove from us all darkness of sin and ignorance. (Thou, Who makest eloquent the tongues of those that want utterance, direct our tongues, and pour on our lips the grace of Thy blessing.) Give us a diligent and obedient spirit, quickness of apprehension, capacity of retaining, and the powerful assistance of Thy holy grace; that what we hear or learn, we may apply to Thy honor and the eternal salvation of our own souls, through Jesus Christ our Lord. Amen.

A PRAYER FOR PARENTS, FOR THEMSELVES AND FOR THEIR CHILDREN.

O Father of mankind, Who hast given unto me these my children, and committed them to my charge, to bring them up for Thee, and to prepare them for everlasting life; assist me with Thy heavenly grace, that I may be able to fulfil this most sacred duty and stewardship. Teach me both what to give and what to withhold; when to reprove, and when to forbear: make me to be gentle, yet firm; considerate and watchful; deliver me equally from the weakness of indulgence and excess of severity; and grant that, both by word and example, I may be careful to lead them in the ways of wisdom and true piety; so that at last I may, with them, be admitted to the unspeakable joys of our true home in heaven, in the unity of the blessed angels and saints, where Thou, O Father, with Jesus, Thy only begotten Son, in the unity of the Holy Ghost, livest and reignest one God, for ever and ever.

O heavenly Father, I commend my children unto Thee. Be Thou their God and Father; and mercifully supply whatever is wanting in me, through frailty or negligence. Strenghten them to overcome the corruptions of the world, to resist the solicitations of evil, whether from within or without; and deliver them from the secret snares of the enemy. Pour Thy grace into their hearts, and confirm and multiply in them the gifts of Thy Holy Spirit, that they may daily grow in grace, and in the knowledge of our Lord Jesus Christ; and so faithfully serving Thee here, may come to rejoice before Thee hereafter; through the merits of the same our Lord Jesus Christ, Who with Thee and the Holy Ghost livest and reignest. Amen.

A Practical Method of Meditation.

By St. Alphonsus.

In the preparation, say: 1. *My God, I believe that Thou art really present, and I adore Thee with all my heart.* 2. *O Lord, I ought to be at this moment in hell; I am sorry for having offended Thee: grant me pardon.* 3. *O Eternal Father, for the love of Jesus and Mary, enlighten me.* Then recommend yourself to the most Holy Virgin, to St. Joseph, to your Angel Guardian, and to your Patron Saint; for this purpose say a *Hail Mary*, and then pass on to the Meditation.

Read the Meditation, and pause whenever you find food for reflection. After, this be careful to make affections of humility, gratitude, and, above all, of sorrow and of love, resigning yourself in every thing to the divine will, and make an offering of yourself, saying, *O Lord, do with me whatever Thou pleasest, and tell me what Thou wilt have me to do, for I wish to do Thy will in all things.*

Be also very careful to ask for particular blessings and graces, for example begging of God the grace of Holy Perseverance, His divine Love, and the light and strength to do always the divine will, and always to pray.

Before concluding your Meditation make a special resolution to avoid some defect into which you fall most frequently, and then finish with an *Our Father* and *Hail Mary;* and remember always to recommend to God the souls in purgatory, and poor sinners.

LIVE JESUS OUR LOVE,
AND MARY OUR HOPE.

Prayers for the Faithful Departed.

I. Method of Hearing Mass for the Dead.

MAKE YOUR INTENTION.

O God of all mercy, I come to offer Thee the blood of the Lamb without spot for the souls which Thou lovest, and which sigh only after the blessedness of seeing Thee and glorifying Thee. Just as are the punishments which Thou inflictest, open to them this day, I beseech Thee, the boundless treasure of the satisfaction of Thy divine Son; and bestow upon them in this holy sacrifice wherewithal to discharge the debt which they still owe to Thy sovereign justice.

If you are intending to communicate, and wish to offer your Communion for particular Souls, say:

I beseech Thee, O Lord, to apply to the souls of N. N. the indulgences which I shall be able to obtain by the communion I am about to make.

WHILST THE PRIEST IS AT THE FOOT OF THE ALTAR.

We confess our sins, O God; and we acknowledge that, if Thou hadst regard only to our iniquities, no man could be justified in Thy sight, and endure the severity of Thy countenance. Woe to us if Thou judgest us without mercy! To appease Thy justice, we have recourse, after the example of Thy saints, to the unbloody sacrifice of Him Who was pleased to be nailed to the cross for us, and Who never ceaseth to make intercession with Thee in our behalf. Forgive us our sins; forgive also our brethren departed the sins which they committed against Thee, whilst they abode in this land of exile. Let Thy mercy prevail over Thy justice, since Thou hast promised graciously to hear those who shew mercy, and be Thou faithful to Thy promises.

INTROIT.

Requiem æternam dona eis, Domine; et lux perpetua luceat eis. *Ps.* 64. Te decet hymnus, Deus, in Sion; et tibi reddetur votum in Jerusalem. Exaudi orationem meam: ad te omnis caro veniet. Requiem.

Eternal rest give unto them, O Lord; and let perpetual light shine upon them. *Ps.* To Thee is due the hymn, O God, in Sion; and to Thee shall the vow be paid in Jerusalem. Oh, hear my prayer: to thee all flesh shall come. Eternal, &c.

AT THE KYRIE.

O Jesus, shew Thyself a God of mercy; have pity on the souls that groan in the place of suffering and expiation.

COLLECT.

Fidelium Deus omnium Conditor et Redemptor, animabus famulorum famularumque tuarum remissionem cunctorum tribue peccatorum; ut indulgentiam, quam semper optaverunt, piis supplicationibus consequenter. Qui vivis et regnas, &c.

O God, the Creator and Redeemer of all the faithful, give to the souls of Thy servants departed the remission of all their sins; that through pious supplications, they may obtain the pardon which they have always desired. Who livest and reignest, &c.

EPISTLE.

"Brethren, we will not have you ignorant concerning them that are asleep, that you be not sorrowful even as others who have no hope. For if we believe that Jesus died and rose again, even so them who have slept through Jesus, will God bring with Him. For this we say unto you in the word of the Lord, that we who are alive, who remain unto the coming of the Lord, shall not prevent them who have slept. For the Lord Himself shall come down from heaven with commandment, and with the voice of an archangel, and with the trumpet of God; and the dead who are in Christ shall rise first. Then we who are alive, who are left, shall be taken up together with them in the clouds to meet Christ, into the air, and so shall we be always with the Lord. Wherefore, comfort ye one another with these words." 1 Thes. iv. 12-17.

GRADUAL.

Requiem æternam dona eis, Domine; et lux perpetua luceat eis. *V. Ps.* 111. In memoria æterna erit justus: ab auditione mala non timebit.

Eternal rest give unto them, O Lord; and let perpetual light shine upon them. *V.* The just shall be in everlasting remembrance: he shall not be afraid for any evil report.

Absolve, Domine, animas omnium fidelium defunctorum ab omni vinculo delictorum. *V.* Et gratia tua illis succurrente, mereantur evadere judicium ultionis. *V.* Et lucis æterne beatitudine perfrui.

Release, O Lord, the souls of all the faithful departed from the bonds of their sins. *V.* And by the assistance of Thy grace, may they merit to escape the sentence of condemnation. *V.* And enjoy the bliss of eternal light.

THE SEQUENCE.

Dies iræ, dies illa,

The day of wrath, that dreadful day,

Solvet sæclum in favilla:

Shall the whole world in ashes lay,

Teste David cum Sybilla.

As David and the Sybil say.

Quantus tremor est futurus,

What horror must invade the mind,

Quando Judex est venturus,

When the approaching Judge shall find,

Cuncta stricte discussurus!

Few venial faults in all mankind!

Mass for the Dead.

Tuba mirum spargens sonum	The last loud trumpet's wondrous sound
Per sepulchra regionum,	Shall through the rending tombs rebound,
Coget omnes ante thronum.	And wake the nations under ground.
Mors stupebit, et natura,	Nature and death shall with surprise
Cum resurget creatura,	Behold the trembling sinner rise,
Judicanti responsura.	To view his Judge with conscious eyes.
Liber scriptus proferetur,	Then shall with universal fear,
In quo totum continetur,	The seven-seal'd judgment book appear,
Unde mundus judicetur.	To scan the whole of life's career.
Judex ergo cum sedebit,	The Judge ascends His awful throne,
Quidquid latet, apparebit:	Each secret sin shall here be known.
Nil inultum remanebit.	All must with shame confess their own.
Quid sum, miser! tunc dicturus,	Ah, wretched! what shall I then say,
Quem patronum rogaturus.	What patron find, my fears t' allay,
Cum vix justus sit securus?	When even the just shall dread that day?
Rex tremendæ majestatis!	Thou mighty, formidable King!
Qui salvandos salvas gratis	Of mercy unexhausted spring!

Salva me, fons pietatis.	Save me! O save! and comfort bring.
Recordare, Jesu pie,	Remember what my ransom cost;
Quod sum causa tuæ viæ,	Let not my dear-bought soul be lost,
Ne me perdas illa die.	In storms of guilty terrors tost.
Quærens me, sedisti lassus:	In search of me why feel such pain;
Redemisti, crucem passus:	Why on Thy cross such pangs sustain,
Tantus labor non sit cassus.	If now those sufferings must be vain?
Juste Judex ultionis,	Avenging Judge, Whom all obey,
Donum fac remissionis	Cancel my debt, too great to pay,
Ante diem rationis.	Before the sad accounting day.
Ingemisco tanquam reus,	O'erwhelmed, oppressed with doubts and fears,
Culpa rubet vultus meus:	Their load my soul in anguish bears;
Supplicanti parce, Deus.	I sigh, I weep—accept my tears.
Qui Mariam absolvisti,	Thou, Who wast moved at Mary's grief,
Et latronem exaudisti,	Who didst absolve the dying thief,
Mihi quoque spem dedisti.	Dost bid me hope, O grant relief.

Preces meæ non sunt dignæ,	Reject not my unworthy prayer,
Sed tu bonus fac benigne,	Preserve me from the dangerous snare,
Ne perenni cremer igne.	Which death and gaping hell prepare.
Inter oves locum præsta,	Give my immortal soul a place
Et ab hœdis me sequestra,	Among Thy chosen right-hand race,
Statuens in parte dextra.	The sons of God, and heirs of grace.
Confutatis maledictis,	From that insatiate abyss,
Flammis acribus addictis,	Where flames devour and serpents hiss,
Voca me cum benedictis.	Deliver me, and raise to bliss.
Oro supplex et acclinis,	Prostrate my contrite heart I rend,
Cor contritum quasi cinis,	My God, my Father and my Friend!
Gere curam mei finis.	Do not forsake me in the end.
Lacrymosa dies illa,	Well may they curse their second birth,
Qua resurget ex favilla Judicandus homo reus.	Who rise to a surviving death.
Huic ergo parce Deus:	Thou great Creator of mankind,
Pie Jesu Domine, dona eis requiem. Amen.	Let all Thy faithful mercy find. Amen.

GOSPEL.

"At that time, Martha said to Jesus: Lord, if Thou hadst been here, my brother had not died. But now, also, I know that whatsoever Thou wilt ask of God, God will give it Thee. Jesus saith to her: Thy brother shall rise again. Martha saith to Him: I know that he shall rise again in the resurrection at the last day. Jesus said to her: I am the resurrection and the life: He that believeth in Me, although he be dead, shall live. And every one that liveth, and believeth in Me, shall not die for ever. Believest thou this? She saith to Him: Yea, Lord, I have believed that Thou art Christ, the Son of the living God, Who art come into this world." John xi. 21-28.

OFFERTORY.

Domine Jesu Christe, Rex gloriæ, libera animas omnium fidelium defunctorum de pœnis inferni, et de profundo lacu: libera eas de ore leonis, ne absorbeat eas tartarus, ne cadant in obscurum; sed signifer sanctus Michael repræsentet eas in lucem sanctam: *quam olim Abrahæ promisisti, et semini ejus. *V.* Hostias et

Lord Jesus Christ, King of glory, deliver the souls of all the faithful departed from the pains of hell, and from the deep pit: deliver them from the lion's mouth, lest hell swallow them up, lest they fall into darkness: and let the standard bearer, St. Michael, bring them into the holy light: * as Thou promisedst of old to

preces tibi, Domine, laudis offerimus; tu suscipe pro animabus illis, quarum hodie memoriam facimus: faceas, Domine, de morte transire ad vitam. *Quam, &c. Abraham and to his seed. *V.* We offer Thee, O Lord, a sacrifice of praise and prayers: accept them in behalf of the souls we commemorate this day; and make them pass, O Lord, from death to life. *As, &c.

AT THE SECRETA.

I will go down, O just Judge of the living and the dead, I will go down in spirit to that dread place where Thy hand is heavy on Thy children, the heirs of Thy glory. There I will sigh and lament, I will unite my prayers to the sacrifice of Thy dear Son, that Thou mayest shorten their pains, and change their sufferings into consolation, their humiliation into glory. Lord, in the grief that oppresses them, their soul cries unto Thee. Have mercy on me, for I acknowledge that I have sinned in Thy sight. One thing have I asked of Thee, this will I seek after; that I may dwell in Thy house for ever, to behold the fair beauty of Thy temple. I believe verily to see Thy face in the land of the living.

DURING THE PREFACE.

It is just and reasonable, right and salutary, to give Thee thanks at all times and in all places, Father almighty, eternal God, through Jesus Christ our Lord; through Whom Thou hast given us the hope of a blessed resurrection, to the end that, if the recollection of the sentence of death passed upon all men comes to sadden us, the promise of immortality may encourage and console our faith; for to those who are faithful to Thee, O Lord, to die is to lose a mortal life to pass into a better, and when this their earthly tabernacle is dissolved, they obtain one in the heavens, which shall endure eternally. And therefore, with all the heavenly host, we sing a hymn to Thy glory, saying, without ceasing: Holy, holy, holy Lord God of Sabaoth; heaven and earth are full of Thy glory. Blessed is He that cometh in the name of the Lord; His blood cries aloud for pardon, and its voice reacheth even to the throne of mercy.

DURING THE CANON.

O almighty God, Whose providence extendeth over all Thy creatures, for Thou art their Father, cast an eye of pity on the souls that love Thee, and whose bitterest pain is to be separated from Thee. Remember, O my God, that they are the work of Thine hands, and the price of the sufferings, the death, and the infinite merits of Thy divine Son, Jesus. Wilt Thou not relent towards them for His name's sake? We offer Thee, in their behalf, the precious blood which was shed for them on the Cross; the powerful intercession of the blessed Virgin Mary, St. Joseph, St. Peter and St. Paul, and all the Saints; the humble supplications of Thy Church, and the prayers and meritorious works of all the faithful. Having this confidence, we hope all from Thy mercy, O my God, for the souls which were dear unto us, and which Thou hast made it our duty to love and succor. Let Thy paternal tenderness disarm at length Thy justice. Open to them Thy heart; manifest to them Thy glory; shew Thyself to them as Thou art, and let flow into their souls that torrent of delights of which Thou art the everlasting source.

AT THE ELEVATION.

O holy Victim, immolated for the salvation of the world, listen favorably to our prayers. O precious Blood of our Saviour, which wast shed to take away our sins, sanctify us, and cry for mercy on the souls of the faithful departed.

CONTINUANCE OF THE CANON.

O Jesus, Who didst go down into Limbo to deliver thence the souls of the patriarchs and prophets who awaited Thy coming, visit the souls of Thy servants in their place of suffering. Moderate the heat of the furnace in which they are tried, with the dew of Thy grace. Thou hast said that Thou wilt consider as done unto Thyself, the least good which we shall do unto our brethren: I may hope, then, that the relief which I shall procure for the souls of the faithful will be as acceptable to Thee as if I had procured it for Thyself. Cease from Thy anger, O my God, through the intercession of her who is the comforter of the afflicted, and through the prayers of all the heavenly host, who plead for the blessedness of the souls in purgatory. Grant, I beseech Thee, eternal rest to these our brethren in whose behalf we prostrate ourselves before Thee.

AT THE PATER.

O Jesus, O Thou at Whose name every knee doth bow in heaven, on earth, and under the earth; O Thou, Who art the sovereign Judge of the living and the dead; let Thy name be hallowed by the deliverance of the souls for whom we pray. Let the gate of Thy tabernacles be opened to them, and Thy will to save them be done this day. Grant that, after having eaten the bread of affliction, they may be nourished with the living bread which is the fruition of Thyself. We beseech Thee in Thy mercy to forgive the sins of *our parents, friends and benefactors*, ———, and the sins which we have caused them to commit, that Thou mayest not impute the guilt to them in the rigor of Thy justice. Preserve us from those avenging flames, which, alas! we have too justly merited by the abuse of Thy graces, our tepidity in Thy service, and our unfaithfulness in resisting temptation. Deliver us from sin, the greatest of all evils, for we know that it is a fearful thing to fall into the hands of the living God.

AT THE AGNUS DEI.

O Jesus, how great is the love which led Thee to offer Thyself, as a lamb to the sacrifice, for the expiation of the sins of the world! What tongue can worthily extol that charity which leads Thee to become surety for our debts, even after our death! What ought not our gratitude to be for so great a benefit!

Lamb of God, Who, by Thy death, didst overcome the roaring lion that goeth about seeking whom he may devour, have mercy on the faithful departed.

Lamb without spot, Who wast immolated to the justice of Thy divine Father, to the end that He might forgive us our sins, have mercy on those who have died united by love to Thy sacred heart.

Lamb of God, Who wast offered in sacrifice, that Thou mightest lead us out of this land of perdition to the true land of promise: Thou Who hast said: *I am the resurrection and the life; he that believeth in me, although he be dead, shall live,*—give to the souls of the faithful departed that life, the principle of which was imparted to them by the grace of the holy sacraments; bestow upon them the happiness of which they have so often received the precious pledge in Thy heavenly banquet. I desire to have part therein (*spiritually,*) that I may obtain for them, as much as in me lies, the society of Thine elect for ever; I offer to Thee in their behalf, and especially for N., all the devotions and good works which I may be enabled to perform. Despise not my humble prayer; but be Thou Thyself my consolation in my loss, and grant relief to those souls which were so dear to me, and especially N.

Communion.

Let shine upon them, O Lord, Thy eternal light, that they may dwell for ever with Thy saints: grant this favor to them, I beseech Thee, O God of mercy.

Post-Communion.

O my God, Who hast constituted prayer for the souls in purgatory one of the most essential of our duties, grant that I may find, in Thy infinite merits and charity, the pardon of all my past tepidity and sloth. Let the remembrance of Thy justice, which keeps them fast bound in prison for faults which I myself so commonly commit, excite in me a firm resolution of entering on the way of penance to expiate my sins, and cause me to walk with more circumspection, that I may not relapse into my former errors.— I will no longer delay to do penance. Henceforth I will labor thereat whilst there is yet time. I will pray most humbly for the souls of the faithful departed; I will deprive myself even of allowable pleasures and enjoyments, to quench the flames in which they suffer; I will pour my alms into the lap of the poor, to make interest in their behalf. Bless these resolutions, O my God, and grant me grace to fulfil them.

THE LAST GOSPEL.

I know that my Redeemer liveth, and in the last day I shall rise out of the earth, and I shall be clothed again with my skin, and in my flesh I shall see my God my Saviour; my eyes shall behold him; this my hope is laid up in my bosom. Job xix. 25-27.

I will look towards the Lord, I will wait for God my Saviour; my God will hear my voice. I shall arise when I sit in darkness, the Lord is my light. . . . He will bring me forth into the light, I shall behold His justice. Mich. vii. 7-9.

II. The Office for the Dead.

St. Pius V., in a Bull dated July 9, 1568, granted:

I. The Indulgence of one hundred days to all the faithful, as often as they shall devoutly say of obligation, the Office of the Dead, on the days prescribed by the rubrics of the Roman Breviary.

II. Fifty days' Indulgence to all the faithful, every time they say it out of their own devotion.

VESPERS.

Antiphona. Placebo.   *Ant.* I will please.

PSALM CXIV.

Dilexi quoniam exaudiet Dominus: vocem orationis meæ.	I have loved, because the Lord will hear the voice of my prayer.
Quia inclinavit aurem suam mihi: et in diebus meis invocabo.	Because He has inclined His ear to me, and in my days I will call to Him.

Circumdederunt me dolores mortis; et pericula inferni invenerunt me.

Tribulationem et dolorem inveni; et nomen Domini invocavi.

O Domine, libera animam meam: misericors Dominus, et justus: et Deus noster miseretur.

Custodiens parvulos Dominus; humiliatus sum, et liberavit me.

Convertere anima mea in requiem tuam; quia Dominus benefecit tibi.

Quia eripuit animam meam de morte: oculos meos a lacrymis, pedes meos a lapsu.

Placebo Domino in regione vivorum.

Requiem æternam dona eis Domine:

Et lux perpetua luceat eis.

Ant. Placebo Domino in regione vivorum.

Ant. Heu mihi, Domine, quia incolatus meus prolongatus est.

The sorrows of death have surrounded me; and the dangers of hell are come upon me.

I have found tribulation and sorrow; and I have invoked the name of the Lord.

O Lord deliver my soul; the Lord is merciful and just: and our God shows mercy.

The Lord keeps the little ones; I was humbled and He delivered me.

Return, my soul, into thy rest; because the Lord has done good to thee.

Because He has delivered my soul from death; my eyes from tears, and my feet from slipping.

I will please the Lord in the land of the living.

Grant them eternal rest, O Lord:

And let perpetual light shine on them.

Ant. I will please the Lord in the land of the living.

Ant. Woe is me, O Lord, that my abode is prolonged.

PSALM CXIX.

Ad Dominum, cum tribularer, clamavi: et exaudivit me.

Domine libera animam meam a labiis iniquis: et a lingua dolosa.

Quid detur tibi, aut quid apponatur tibi; ad linguam dolosam?

Sagittæ potentis acutæ; cum carbonibus desolatoriis.

Heu mihi, quia incolatus meus prolongatus est, habitavi cum habitantibus Cedar; multum incola fuit anima mea.

Cum his qui oderunt pacem, eram pacificus; cum loquebar illis, impugnabant me gratis.

Requiem æternam, &c.

Ant. Heu, mihi, Domine, quia incolatus meus prolongatus est.

Ant. Dominus custodit te ab omni malo; custodiat animam tuam Dominus.

When I was in tribulation, I cried to the Lord; and He heard me.

O Lord, deliver my soul from unjust lips, and from a deceitful tongue.

What is to be given to thee, or what is to be added to thee: to a deceitful tongue?

The sharp arrows of the mighty: with coals of desolation.

Woe is me, that my abode is prolonged. I have dwelt with the inhabitants of Cedar; my soul has been long a sojourner.

I was peaceable with those that hated peace; when I spoke to them, they insulted me for no reason.

Grant them eternal rest, &c.

Anth. Woe is me, O Lord, that my abode is prolonged.

Anth. The Lord preserve thee from all evil; may the Lord keep thy soul.

PSALM CXX.

Levavi oculos meos in montes: unde veniet auxilium mihi.

I lifted up my eyes to the mountains; from whence my help will come.

Auxilium meum á Domino: qui fecit cœlum et terram.

Non det in commotionem pedem tuum; neque dormitet, qui custodit te.

Ecce non dormitabit, neque dormiet: qui custodit Israel.

Dominus custodit te, Dominus protectio tua; super manum dexteram tuam.

Per diem sol non uret te; neque luna per noctem.

Dominus custodit te ab omni malo: custodiat animam tuam Dominus.

Dominus custodiat introitum tuum, et exitum tuum; ex hoc nunc, et usque in sæculum.

Requiem æternam, &c.

Ant. Dominus custodit te ab omni malo; custodiat animam tuam Dominus.

Ant. Si iniquitates observaveris Domine; Domine, quis sustinebit?

My help is from the Lord; Who made heaven and earth.

May He not suffer thy foot to stagger; and may He not slumber that keeps thee.

Lo, He will not slumber nor sleep; that keeps Israel.

Our Lord keeps thee, our Lord is thy protection; on thy right hand.

The sun shall not burn thee by day; nor the moon by night.

The Lord preserveth thee from all evil; may the Lord keep thy soul.

May the Lord keep thy coming in, and thy going out; from henceforth, now, and for ever.

Grant them eternal rest, &c.

Anth. The Lord preserve thee from all evil, may the Lord keep thy soul.

Anth. If Thou wilt observe iniquities, O Lord: Lord, who shall bear it?

PSALM CXXIX.

De profundis clamavi ad te Domine, Domine exaudi vocem meam.

From the depths I have cried unto Thee, O Lord, Lord hear my voice.

Fiant aures tuæ intendentes; in vocem deprecationis meæ.

Si iniquitates observaveris Domine; Domine, quis sustinebit?

Quia apud te propitiatio est: et propter legem tuam sustinui te, Domine.

Sustinuit anima mea in verbo ejus; speravit anima mea in Domino.

A custodia matutina usque ad noctem; speret Israel in Domino.

Quia apud Dominum misericordia; et copiosa apud eum redemptio.

Et ipse redimet Israel ex omnibus iniquitatibus ejus.

Requiem æternam, &c.

Ant. Si iniquitates observaveris Domine; Domine, quis sustinebit?

Ant. Opera manuum tuarum, Domine, ne despicias.

Let Thy ears be attentive; to the voice of my petition.

If Thou wilt observe iniquities, O Lord; Lord, who shall sustain it?

Because with Thee is propitiation; and for Thy law I have expected Thee, O Lord.

My soul has relied on His word; my soul has hoped in the Lord.

From the morning watch even until night; let Israel hope in the Lord.

Because with the Lord there is mercy; and with Him plentiful redemption.

And He will redeem Israel, from all his iniquities.

Grant them eternal rest, &c.

Anth. If Thou wilt observe iniquities, Lord; Lord, who shall bear it?

Anth. Despise not, O Lord, the works of Thy hands.

PSALM CXXXVII.

Confitebor tibi Domine in toto corde meo; quoniam audisti verba oris mei.

I will confess Thee, O Lord, with all my heart; because Thou hast heard the words of my mouth.

In conspectu angelorum psallam tibi; adorabo ad templum sanctum tuum, et confitebor nomini tuo.

Super misericordia tua, et veritate tua; quoniam magnificasti super omne, nomen sanctum tuum.

In quacumque die invocavero te, exaudi me; multiplicabis in anima mea virtutem.

Confiteantur tibi, Domine, omnes reges terræ; quia audierunt omnia verba oris tui.

Et cantent in viis Domini; quoniam magna est gloria Domini.

Quoniam excelsus Dominus, et humilia respicit: et alta a longe cognoscit.

Si ambulavero in medio tribulationis vivificabis me; et super iram inimicorum meorum extendisti manum tuam et salvum me fecit dextera tua.

Dominus retribuet pro me; Domine misericordia tua in sæculum; opera manuum tuarum ne despicias.

Requiem æternam, &c.

In the sight of angels I will sing to Thee; I will adore in Thy holy temple, and confess Thy name.

For Thy mercy, and Thy truth; because Thou hast magnified Thy holy name above every thing.

In what day soever I shall call to Thee, hear me; Thou wilt increase strength in my soul.

Let all kings of the earth confess Thee, O Lord, for they have heard all the words of Thy mouth.

And let them sing in the ways of our Lord; because the glory of the Lord is great.

Because the Lord is high, and He beholds the low things; and the high things He knows afar off.

If I shall walk in the midst of trouble, Thou wilt enliven me; and upon the wrath of my enemies Thou hast stretched Thy hand, and Thy right hand has saved me.

The Lord will repay for me; Thy mercy, O Lord, is for ever; despise not the works of Thy hands.

Grant them eternal rest, &c.

Ant. Opera manuum tuarum, Domine, ne despicias.

V. Audivi vocem de cœlo dicentem mihi;

R. Beati mortui qui in Domino moriuntur.

Ant. Omne quod dat mihi pater ad me veniet et eum qui venit ad me non ejiciam foras.

Ant. Despise not, O Lord, the works of Thy hands.

V. I heard a voice from heaven saying to me:

R. Blessed are the dead that die in the Lord.

Anth. All that My Father gives Me shall come to Me, and him that comes to Me I will not cast out.

For the MAGNIFICAT, *see page* 49.

PSALM CXLV.

Lauda, anima mea, Dominum; laudabo Dominum in vita mea; psallam Deo meo quamdiu fuero.

Nolite confidere in principibus; in filiis hominum, in quibus non est salus.

Exibit spiritus ejus, et revertetur in terram suam; in illa die peribunt omnes cogitationes eorum.

Beatus cujus Deus Jacob adjutor ejus, spes ejus in Domino Deo ipsius; qui fecit cœlum et terram, mare, et omnia quæ in eis sunt.

Qui custodit veritatem in sæculum, facit judicium injuriam patientibus; dat escam esurientibus.

Praise the Lord, O my soul; I will praise the Lord while I live; I will sing to my God as long as I have being.

Trust not in princes; in the sons of men, in whom there is no salvation.

His spirit shall go forth, and He shall return into His earth; in that day all their thoughts shall perish.

Blessed is he whose helper is the God of Jacob; his hope is in the Lord his God. Who made heaven and earth, the sea, and all that are in them.

Who keeps truth for ever, does justice for them that suffer wrong; gives food to the hungry.

Dominus solvit compeditos: Dominus illuminat cæcos.

The Lord looses the fettered; the Lord enlightens the blind.

Dominus erigit elisos; Dominus diligit justos.

The Lord lifts up the bruised; the Lord loves the just.

Dominus custodit advenas, pupillum et viduam suscipiet; et vias peccatorum disperdet.

The Lord keeps the strangers; He will receive the orphan and widow; and the ways of sinners he will destroy.

Regnabit Dominus in sæcula, Deus tuus, Sion; in generationem et generationem.

The Lord will reign for ever; thy God, O Sion, from generation to generation.

Requiem æternam, &c.

Grant them eternal rest, &c.

V. A porta inferi.
R. Erue Domine animas eorum!
V. Requiescant in pace.
R. Amen.
V. Domine, exaudi orationem meam.
R. Et clamor meus ad te veniat.
V. Dominus vobiscum.
R. Et cum spiritu tuo.

V. From the gates of hell.
R. Deliver their souls, O Lord.
V. May they rest in peace.
R. Amen.
V. O Lord hear my prayer.
R. And let my cry come to Thee.
V. The Lord be with you.
R. And with Thy spirit.

A PRAYER SAID AFTER THE DEPARTURE OF A SODALIST.

Absolve, quæsumus, Domine, animam famuli tui (*vel* famulæ tuæ) N. ut de-

Absolve, we beseech Thee, O Lord, the soul of Thy servant N., that being dead

functus (*vel* defuncta) sæculo tibi vivat: et quæ per fragilitatem carnis humana conversatione commisit, tu venia misericordissimæ pietatis absterge; per Dominum nostrum Jesum Christum Filium tuum, qui tecum vivit et regnat in unitate Spiritus Sancti Deus per omnia sæcula sæculorum.

R. Amen.

to the world he (*or* she) may live to thee; and whatever he (*or* she) has committed through human frailty, do Thou wipe away by the pardon of Thy most merciful goodness; thro' our Lord Jesus Christ Thy Son, Who livest and reignest with Thee in the unity of the Holy Ghost, one God, world without end.

R. Amen.

FOR A FATHER AND MOTHER DECEASED.

Deus, qui nos patrem et matrem honorare præcipisti, miserere clementer animabus patris et matris meæ, eorumque peccata dimitte, meque eos in æternæ claritatis gaudio fac videre; per Dominum nostrum, &c.

O God, Who hast commanded us to honor our father and mother, have compassion, in Thy mercy, on the souls of my father and mother, and forgive them their sins, and that we may meet in the joy of eternal bliss; thro', &c.

FOR SODALISTS DEPARTED.

Inclina, Domine, aurem tuam ad preces nostras, quibus misericordiam tuam supplices deprecamur; ut animas famulorum tuorum, quas de hoc sæculo migrare jussisti, in pacis ac lucis regione constituas; et sanc-

Incline, O Lord, Thy ear to my prayers, in which we humbly beseech Thy mercy; that Thou wouldst place the souls of Thy servants, which Thou hast caused to depart from this world into the region of

FOR BRETHREN, RELATIONS AND BENEFACTORS.

torum tuorum jubeas esse consortes; per Dominum nostrum, &c.

peace and light; and unite them in the fellowship of Thy saints; thro', &c.

Deus veniæ largitor et humanæ salutis amator; quæsumus clementiam tuam, ut nostræ congregationis fratres, propinquos, et benefactores, qui ex hoc sæculo transierunt, beata Maria semper virgine intercedente, cum omnibus sanctis tuis, ad perpetuæ beatitudinis consortium pervenire concedas: per Dominum nostrum, &c.

O God, the giver of pardon, and lover of human salvation, we beseech Thy clemency to grant that the brethren, relations, and benefactors of our congregation, who are departed this world, may, by the intercession of the blessed Mary, ever virgin, and of all Thy saints, attain to the fellowship of eternal beatitude; thro', &c.

FOR THE DEAD IN GENERAL.

Fidelium Deus omnium conditor et redemptor, animabus famulorum famularumque tuarum remissionem cunctorum tribue peccatorum; ut indulgentiam, quam semper optaverunt, piis supplicationibus consequantur. Qui vivis et regnas cum Deo Patre in unitate Spiritus Sancti Deus, per omnia sæcula sæculorum.

R. Amen.

O God, the Creator and Redeemer of all the faithful, give to the souls of Thy servants, men and women, the remission of all their sins; that by pious supplications they may obtain the pardon which they have always desired. Who livest and reignest with God the Father, in the unity of the Holy Ghost, one God, world without end.

R. Amen.

V. Requiem æternam dona eis, Domine.

R. Et lux perpetua luceat eis.

R. Requiescant in pace.

V. Amen.

V. Grant them eternal rest, O Lord.

R. And let perpetual light shine on them.

V. May they rest in peace.

R. Amen.

At Matins.

The following Invitatory *is recited on* All-Souls Day, *and as often as the* Three Nocturns *are said. At other times it is omitted, and the Office begins with the Anthem of the* Psalms *of the* Nocturn.

THE INVITATORY.

Regem cui omnia vivant, venite adoremus.

Regem cui omnia vivunt, venite adoremus.

Come, let us adore the King, to Whom all things live.

Come, let us adore the King, to Whom all things live.

Psalm XCIV.

Venite exultemus Domino, jubilemus Deo salutari nostro; præoccupemus faciem ejus in confessione, et in psalmis jubilemus ei.

Come, let us rejoice in the Lord, let us make a joyful noise to God our Saviour; let us approach His presence in confession, and let us sing joyfully in psalms to Him.

Regem cui omnia vivunt, venite adoremus.

Quoniam Deus magnus Dominus, et Rex magnus super omnes deos; quoniam non repellet Dominus plebem suam, qua in manu ejus sunt omnes fines terræ; et altitudines montium ipse conspicit.

Venite adoremus.

Quoniam ipsius est mare, et ipse fecit illud, et aridam fundaverunt manus ejus; Venite adoremus, et procidamus ante Deum; ploremus coram Domino, qui fecit nos, quia ipse est Dominus Deus noster; nos autem populus ejus, et oves pascuæ ejus.

Regem cui omnia vivunt, venite adoremus.

Hodie si vocem ejus audieritis, nolite obdurare corda vestra, sicut in exacerbatione secundum diem tentationis in deserto; ubi tentaverunt me patres vestri, probaverunt, et viderunt opera mea.

Venite adoremus.

Quadraginta annis proximus fui generationi huic, et

Come, let us adore the King, to Whom all things live.

Because the Lord is a great God, and a great King above all gods; because the Lord repels not His people, for in His hands are all the bounds of the earth; and He beholds the heights of the mountains,

Come, let us adore.

Because the sea is His, and He made it, and His hands formed the dry land; come let us adore, and fall down before God; let us lament before the Lord that made us; because He is the Lord our God; and we are His people, and the sheep of His pasture.

Come, let us adore the King, to Whom all things live.

To-day, if you will hear His voice harden not your hearts, as in the provocation, according to the day of temptation in the wilderness; where your fathers tempted Me, they proved and saw My works.

Come, let us adore.

Forty years was I nigh to this generation, and said

dixi, semper hi errant corde; ipsi vero non cognoverunt vias meas, quibus juravi, in ira mea, si introibunt in requiem meam.

Regem cui omnia vivunt, venite adoremus.

Requiem æternam dona eis, Domine, et lux perpetua luceat eis.
Venite adoremus.
Regem cui omnia vivunt, venite adoremus.

they always err in their hearts; and have not known My ways, to whom I swore in My wrath, that they should not enter into My rest.

Come, let us adore the King, to Whom all things live.

Grant them eternal rest, O Lord, and let perpetual light shine on them.
Come, let us adore.
Come, let us adore the King, to Whom all things live.

In the First Nocturn.

On Monday and Thursday.

Ant. Dirige, Domine, &c.   *Anth.* Direct, O Lord, &c.

PSALM V.

Verba mea auribus percipe, Domine; intellige clamorem meum.

Intende voci orationis meæ; Rex meus, et Deus meus.

Quoniam ad te orabo; Domine, mane exaudies vocem meum

Give ear, O Lord, to my words; hearken to my cry.

Attend to the voice of my prayer; my King and my God.

Because I will pray to Thee; O Lord, in the morning Thou wilt hear my voice.

Mane astabo tibi et videbo; quoniam non Deus volens iniquitatem tu es.

Neque habitabit juxta te malignus; neque permanebunt injusti ante oculos tuos.

Odisti omnes qui operantur iniquitatem; perdes omnes, qui loquuntur mendacium.

Virum sanguinum, et dolosum abominabitur Dominus; ego autem in multitudine misericordiæ tuæ.

Introibo in domum tuam, adorabo ad templum sanctum tuum, in timore tuo.

Domine deduc me in justitia tua; propter inimicos meos dirige in conspectu tuo viam meam.

Quoniam non est in ore eorum veritas; cor eorum vanum est.

Sepulchrum patens est guttur eorum, linguis suis dolose agebant, judica illos, Deus.

Decidant à cogitionibus suis, secundum multitudinem impietatum eorum expelle eos, quoniam irritaverunt te, Domine.

Et lætentur omnes qui sperant in te, æternum ex-

In the morning I will stand by Thee and will see; for Thou art not a God that willest iniquity.

Neither shall the wicked dwell near Thee nor the unjust abide before Thy eyes.

Thou hatest all that work iniquity; Thou wilt destroy all those that speak lies.

The bloody and deceitful man our Lord will abhor; but I, in the multitude of Thy mercies,

Will enter into Thy house; I will adore at Thy holy temple, in Thy fear.

Conduct me, O Lord, in Thy justice; because of my enemies, direct my way in Thy sight.

Because there is no truth in their mouth: their heart is vain.

Their throat is a gaping sepulchre, they dealt deceitfully with their tongues, judge them, O God.

Let them fail in their designs, according to the multitude of their impieties expel them, for they have provoked Thee, O Lord.

And let all be glad that hope in Thee, they shall

ultabunt; et habitabis in eis.

Et gloriabuntur in te omnes, qui diligunt nomen tuum, quoniam tu benedices justo.

Domine, ut scuto bonæ voluntatis tuæ, coronasti, nos.

Requiem æternam, &c.

Ant. Dirige, Domine Deus meus, in conspectu tuo, viam meam.

Ant. Convertere Domine.

rejoice for ever: and Thou wilt dwell in them.

And all that love Thy name shall glory in Thee, because Thou wilt bless the just.

Lord, as with a shield of Thy good-will, Thou hast crowned us.

Grant them eternal rest, &c.

Anth. Direct, O Lord my God, my steps in Thy sight.

Anth. Turn, O Lord.

PSALM VI.

Domine, ne in furore tuo arguas me, neque in ira tua corripias me.

Miserere mei Domine, quoniam infirmus sum; sana me Domine quoniam conturbata sunt ossa mea.

Et anima mea turbata est valde: sed tu Domine usquequo?

Convertere Domine, et eripe animam meam; salvum me fac propter misericordiam tuam.

Quoniam non est in morte, qui memor sit tui; in inferno autem quis confitebitur tibi?

Lord, rebuke me not in Thy fury, nor chastise me in Thy wrath.

Have mercy on me, O Lord, because I am infirm; heal me, O Lord, because my bones are disordered.

And my soul is very much troubled; but Thou, O Lord, how long?

Turn, O Lord, and deliver my soul; save me for Thy mercies sake.

Because there is none in death, that is mindful of Thee: and in hell who will confess Thee?

Laboravi in gemitu meo, lavabo per singulas noctes lectum meum; lacrymis meis stratum meum rigabo.	I have labored in my sighing, every night I will wash my bed; I will water my couch with my tears.
Turbatus est à furore oculos meus; inveteravi inter omnes inimicos meos.	My eye is troubled with fury; I am grown old among all enemies.
Discedite à me omnes qui operamini iniquitatem quoniam exaudivit Dominus vocem fletus mei.	Depart from me, all ye workers of iniquity: because the Lord has heard the voice of my weeping.
Exaudivit Dominus deprecationem meam, Dominus, orationem meam suscepit.	The Lord has heard my petition; the Lord has received my prayer.
Erubescant et conturbentur vehementer omnes inimici mei: convertantur et erubescant valde velociter.	Let all my enemies blush, and be troubled exceedingly; let them be turned back and ashamed very speedily.
Requiem æternam, &c.	Grant them eternal rest, &c.

Ant. Convertere Domine, et eripe animam meam; quoniam non est in morte, qui memor sit tui.

Anth. Turn O Lord, and deliver my soul; for there is none in death who will be mindful of Thee.

Ant. Nequando rapiat.

Anth. Lest at any time.

PSALM VII.

Domine Deus meus in te speravi; salvum me fac ex omnibus persequentibus me, et libera me.	O Lord my God, I have hoped in Thee: save me from all that persecute me, and deliver me.
Nequando rapiat ut leo animam meam; dum non	Lest at any time he snatch away my soul as a

est qui redimat, neque qui salvum faciat.

Domine Deus meus si feci istud; si est iniquitas in manibus meis;

Si reddidi retribuentibus mihi mala; decidam merito ab inimicis meis inanis.

Persequatur inimicus animam meam, et comprehendat, et conculcet in terra vitam meam; et gloriam meam in pulverem deducat.

Exurge Domine in ira tua; et exaltare in finibus inimicorum meorum.

Et exurge, Domine, Deus meus in precepto quod mandasti; et synagoga populorum circumbabit te.

Et propter hanc in altum regredere; Dominus judicat populos.

Judica me, Domine, secundum justitiam meam; et secundum innocentiam meam super me.

Consumetur nequitia peccatorum, et diriges justum: scrutans corda et renes, Deus.

lion; whilst there is none to redeem, nor to save it.

O Lord my God, if I have done this; if there be iniquity in my hands;

If I have repaid to them that returned the evils; let me deservedly fall empty before my enemies.

Let the enemy persecute my soul, and seize it and tread down my life on the earth; and bring down my glory into dust.

Arise, O Lord, in Thy wrath; and be exalted in the borders of my enemies.

And arise, O Lord my God, in the precept which Thou hast commanded; and an assembly of people shall encompass Thee.

And for this return on high: the Lord judges the people.

Judge me, O Lord, according to my justice; and according to my innocence upon me.

The wickedness of sinners shall be consumed, and Thou wilt direct the just; Who searchest the hearts and reins, O God.

Justum adjutorium meum à Domino; qui salvos facit rectos corde.

Deus judex justus, fortis et patiens; numquid irascitur per singulos dies?

Nisi conversi fueritis gladium suum vibrabit; arcum suum tetendit, et paravit illum.

Et in eo paravit vasa mortis sagittas suas ardentibus effecit.

Ecce parturiit injustitiam; concepit dolorem, et peperit iniquitatem.

Lacum aperuit et effodit eum; et incidit in foveam quam fecit.

Convertetur dolor ejus in caput ejus; et in verticem ipsius iniquitas ejus descendet.

Confitebor Domino secundum justitiam ejus; et psallam nomini Domini altissimi.

Requiem æternam, &c.

Ant. Ne quando rapiat ut leo animam meam, dum non est qui redimat, neque qui salvum faciat.

My just help is from the Lord; Who saves the right of heart.

God is a just judge, strong and patient; is He angry every day?

Except ye be converted, He will shake His sword; He has bent His bow, and prepared it.

And in it He has prepared weapons of death; He has made His arrows with fiery points.

Behold He has bred with injustice; He has conceived sorrow, and brought forth iniquity.

He has opened a pit and and digged it up; and He is fallen into the ditch which He made.

His sorrow shall be turned upon His head, and His iniquity shall descend upon His crown.

I will confess our Lord according to His justice; and will sing to the name of the most high Lord.

Grant them eternal rest, &c.

Anth. Lest at any time the enemy snatch my soul as a lion, whilst there is none to redeem, nor to save it.

V. A porta inferi.

R. Erue Domine animas eorum.

Pater noster, &c., *secreto.*

V. From the gates of hell.

R. Deliver my soul, O Lord.

Our Father, &c. *in secret.*

THE FIRST LESSON. JOB VII.

Parce mihi, Domine, nihil enim sunt dies mei.— Quid est homo, quia magnificas eum? aut quid apponis erga eum cor tuum? Visitas cum diliculo, et subito probas illum. Usquequo non parcis mihi, nec dimittis me ut glutiam salivam meam? Peccavi; quid faciam tibi, O custos hominum? Quare posuisti me contrarium tibi, et factus sum mihimet ipsi gravis? Cur non tollis peccatum meum? et quare non aufers iniquitatem meam? Ecce nunc in pulvere dormiam, et si mane me quæsieris, non subsistam.

Spare me, O Lord, for my days are nothing. What is man that Thou magnifiest him? or why settest Thou Thy heart towards him? Thou dost visit him early, and suddenly Thou provest him; how long dost Thou not spare me, nor suffer me to swallow my spittle? I have sinned; what shall I do to Thee, O keeper of men? Why hast Thou set me contrary to Thee, and I am become burthensome to myself? Why dost Thou not take away my sin, and why dost Thou not take away my iniquity! Behold now I shall sleep in the dust, and if Thou seek me in the morning, I shall not be.

R. Credo quod Redemptor meus vivit; et in novissimo die de terra surrecturus sum;* et in carne mea videbo Deum salvatorem meum.

R. I believe my Redeemer liveth, and that in the last day I shall rise from the earth,* and in my flesh I shall see God my Saviour.

V. Quem visurus sum ego ipse, et non alius, et oculi mei conspecturi sunt. *Et in carne mea.

V. Whom I myself shall see, and not another, and my eyes shall behold. *And in my flesh.

THE SECOND LESSON. JOB X.

Tædet animam meam vitæ meæ, dimittam adversum me eloquium meum, loquar in amaritudine animæ meæ. Dicam Deo; noli me condemnare; indica mihi, cur me ita judices. Numquid bonum tibi videtur, si calumnieris me, et opprimas me opus manuum tuarum, et consilium impiorum adjuves? Numquid oculi carnei tibi sunt; aut sicut videt homo, et tu videbis? Numquid sicut dies hominis dies tui: et anni tui sicut humana sunt tempora, ut quæras iniquitatem meam, et peccatum meum scruteris? Et scias quia nihil impium fecerim, cum sit nemo qui de manu tua possit eruere.

My soul is weary of life, I will let my speech loose against myself, I will speak in the bitterness of my soul. I will say to God condemn me not; shew me, why Thou judgest me so. Does it seem good to Thee, if Thou calumniate me, and oppress me, the work of Thy hands, and help the design of the impious? Hast Thou eyes of flesh: or as a man sees, shalt Thou also see? Are Thy days as the days of man; and are Thy years as the times of men, that Thou shouldst seek my iniquity, and search my sin. And Thou mayest know that I have done no impious thing; whereas there is no man that can escape out of Thy hand.

R. Qui Lazarum resuscitasti a monumento fœtidum. *Tu eis Domine dona requiem, et locum indulgentiæ.

R. Thou didst raise Lazarus stinking from the grave. *Thou, O Lord, give them rest, and a place of pardon.

V. Qui venturus es judicare vivos et mortuos, et sæcula per ignem. * Tu eis, Domine.

V. Who art to come to judge the living and the dead, and the world by fire. *Thou, O Lord.

THE THIRD LESSON.

Manus tuæ fecerunt me, et plasmaverunt me totum in circuitu; et sic repente præcipitas me? Memento quæso quod sicut lutum feceris me, et in pulverem reduces me. Nonne sicut lac mulsisti me, et sicut caseum me coagulasti? Pelle et carnibus vestisti me; ossibus, et nervis compegisti me. Vitam et misericordiam tribuisti mihi, et visitatio tua custodibit spiritum meum.

Thy hands have made me, and framed me wholly round about; and dost Thou so suddenly cast me down headlong? Remember, I beseech Thee, that as the clay Thou didst make me, and into dust Thou wilt bring me again. Hast Thou not milked me like milk, and curdled me like cheese? With skin and flesh hast Thou clothed me; with bones and sinews hast Thou bound me. Life and mercy Thou hast given me, and Thy visitation has kept my spirit.

R. Domine quando veneris judicare terram, ubi me abscondam a vultu iræ tuæ? Quia peccavi nimis in vita mea.

R. O Lord, when Thou shalt come to judge the earth, where shall I hide myself from the face of Thy wrath. For I have sinned exceedingly in my life.

V. Commissa mea pavesco, et ante te erubesco; dum veneris judicare, noli me condemnare. * Quia peccavi nimis in vita mea.

V. I dread my misdeeds, and blush before Thee; do not condemn me, when Thou shalt come to judge. *For I have sinned exceedingly in my life.

Second Nocturn.

V. Requiem æternam dona eis, Domine, et lux perpetua luceat eis. *Quia peccavi nimis in vita.

V. Grant them eternal rest, O Lord, and let perpetual light shine on them. * For I have.

Here the Lauds *are recited when the First Nocturn only is said.*

At the Second Nocturn.

On Tuesday and Friday.

Ant. In loco pascuæ.

Anth. In a place of pasture, &c.

Psalm XXII.

Dominus regit me, et nihil mihi deerit; in loco pascuæ, ibi me collocavit.

Super aquam refectionis educavit me; animam meam convertit.

Deduxit me super semitas justitiæ, propter nomen suum.

Nam, et si ambulavero in medio umbræ mortis, non timebo mala; quoniam tu mecum es.

The Lord rules me, and I shall want nothing; in a place of pasture, He has put me there.

Near the refreshing waters He has brought me up; and has converted my soul.

He has conducted me in the paths of justice, for His name's sake.

For though I shall walk in the midst of the shadow of death, I will not fear evils; because Thou art with me.

Virga tua, et baculus tuus; ipsa me consolata sunt.

Parasti in conspectu meo mensam; adversus eos qui tribulant me.

Impinguasti in oleo caput meum; et calix meus inebrians quam præclatus est.

Et misericordia tua subsequetur me; omnibus diebus vitæ meæ.

Et ut inhabitem in domo Domini; in longitudinem dierum.

Requiem æternam, &c.

Ant. In loco pascuæ ibi me collocavit.

Ant. Delicta.

Thy rod and Thy staff; they have comforted me.

Thou hast prepared in my sight a table; against them that afflict me.

Thou hast anointed my head with oil; and my inebriating cup how excellent is it?

And Thy mercy shall follow me; all the days of my life.

And that I may dwell in the house of the Lord; for length of days.

Grant them eternal rest, &c.

Anth. in a place of pasture He hath set me.

Anth. The offences.

PSALM XXIV.

Ad te, Domine, levavi animam meam; Deus meus in te confido, non erubescam.

Neque irrideant me inimici mei; etenim universi, qui sustinent te, non confundentur.

Confundantur omnes niqua agentes supervacue.

To Thee, O Lord, I have lifted up my soul; my God, in Thee I put my trust, let me not be ashamed.

Neither let my enemies insult over me; for all that hope in Thee shall not be confounded.

Let all be confounded; who vainly do unjust things.

Second Nocturn.

Vias tuas, Domine, demonstra mihi; et semitas tuas edoce me.

Dirige me in veritate tua, et doce me; quia tu es Deus Salvator meus, et te sustinui tota die.

Reminiscere miserationum tuarum, Domine; et misericordiarum tuarum quæ a sæculo sunt.

Delicta juventutis meæ; et ignorantias meas ne memineris.

Secundum misericordiam tuam, memento mei tu; propter bonitatem tuam, Domine.

Dulcis et rectus Dominus; propter hoc legem dabit delinquentibus in via.

Diriget mansuetos in judicio; docebit mites vias suas.

Universæ viæ Domini misericordia et veritas, requirentibus testamentum ejus et testimonia ejus;

Propter nomen tuum, Domine, propitiaberis peccato meo; multum est enim.

Quis est homo qui timet Dominum? Legem statuit ei in via, quam elegit.

Show me Thy ways, O Lord; and teach me Thy paths.

Direct me in Thy truth, and teach me; because Thou art God my Saviour, and Thee I have expected all the day.

Remember Thy compassion, O Lord; and Thy mercies that are from the beginning of the world.

The sins of my youth; and my ignorances, remember not.

According to Thy mercy do Thou remember me; for Thy goodness sake, O Lord.

The Lord is sweet and righteous; for this cause He will give a law to them that sin in the way.

He will direct the mild in judgment; He will teach the meek His ways.

All the ways of the Lord are mercy and truth; to them that seek His testament and His testimonies.

For Thy name, O Lord, Thou wilt be propitious to my sin; for it is great.

Who is the man that fears the Lord? He appoints him a law in the way He has chosen.

Anima ejus in bonis demorabitur; et semen ejus hæreditabit terram.

Firmamentum est Dominus timentibus cum; testamentum ipsius ut manifestetur illis.

Oculi mei semper ad Dominum; quoniam ipse evellet de laqueo pedes meos.

Respice in me, et miserere mei; quia unicus et pauper sum ego.

Tribulationes cordis mei multiplicatæ sunt; de necessisatibus meis erue me.

Vide humilitatem meam et laborem meum; et dimitte universa delicta mea.

Respice inimicos meos, quoniam multiplicati sunt; et odio iniquo oderunt me.

Custodi animam meam, et erue me; non erubescam quoniam speravi in te.

Innocentes et recti adhæserunt mihi; quia sustinui te.

Libera, Deus, Israel; ex omnibus tribulaţionibus suis.

His soul shall abide in good things; and his seed shall inherit the land.

The Lord is a support to them that fear Him; and that His testament may be manifested to them.

My eyes are always towards the Lord: because He will deliver my feet out of the snare.

Look upon me, and have mercy on me; because I am alone and poor.

The tribulations of my heart are multiplied; deliver me from my necessities.

See my humiliation and my labor; and remit all my sins.

Look upon my enemies, for they are multiplied; and with unjust hatred they hated me.

Keep my soul, and deliver me; I shall not be ashamed, because I have hoped in Thee.

The innocent and righteous have adhered to me; because I have expected Thee.

Deliver Israel, O God, out of all his tribulations.

SECOND NOCTURN.

Requiem æternam, &c.

Ant. Delicta juventutis meæ, et ignorantias meas, ne memineris, Domine.

Ant. Credo videre.

Grant them eternal rest &c.

Anth. The offences of my youth, and my ignorances, remember not, O Lord.

Anth. I think to see.

PSALM XXVI.

Dominus illuminatio mea, et salus mea; quem timebo?

Dominus protector vitæ meæ; a quo trepidabo.

Dum appropriant super me nocentes; ut edant carnes meas.

Qui tribulant me inimici mei; ipsi infirmati sunt, et ceciderunt.

Si consistant adversum me castra; non timebit cor meum.

Si exurgat adversum me prælium; in hoc ego sperabo.

Unam petii a Domino, hanc requiram; ut inhabitem in domo Domini omnibus diebus vitæ meæ.

Ut videam voluptatem Domini; et visitem templum ejus.

The Lord is my light and my salvation; whom shall I fear. ?

The Lord is the protector of my life; who shall make me tremble?

Whilst the wicked approach to me; to devour my flesh.

My enemies that afflict me; themselves are weakened, and are fallen.

If camps stand against me; my heart shall not fear.

If battle rise up against me; in this will I hope.

One thing have I asked for of the Lord, this will I seek; that I may dwell in the house of the Lord all the days of my life.

That I may see the delight of the Lord; and visit His temple.

Quoniam abscondit me in tabernaculo suo; in die malorum protexit me in abscondito tabernaculi sui.

In petra exaltavit me; et nunc exaltavit caput meum super inimicos meos.

Circuivi, et immolavi in tabernaculo ejus hostiam vociferationis; cantabo et psalmum dicam Domino.

Exaudi Domine vocem meam, qua clamavi ad te; miserere mei, et exaudi me.

Tibi dixit cor meum, exquisivit te facies mea; faciem tuam Domine requiram.

Ne avertas faciem tuam a me; ne declines in ira a servo tuo.

Adjutor meus esto; ne derelinquas me, neque despicias me, Deus salutaris meus.

Quoniam pater meus et mater mea dereliquerunt me; Dominus autem assumpsit me.

Legem pone mihi Domine in via tua; et dirige me in semitam rectam propter inimicos meos.

Because He has hid me in His tabernacle; in the day of evils He has protected me in the secret of His tabernacle.

On a rock He has exalted me: and now He hath exalted my head above my enemies.

I have gone round, and have immolated in His tabernacle an host of loud acclamation; I will sing, and say a psalm to the Lord.

Hear my voice, O Lord, wherewith I have cried to Thee; have mercy on me, and hear me.

My heart has spoken to Thee: my face has sought Thee out; Thy face, O Lord, I will seek.

Hide not Thy face from me; turn not away in wrath from Thy servant.

Be Thou my helper; forsake me not, nor despise me, O God my Saviour.

Because my father and my mother have forsaken me; but the Lord has received me.

Set me a law; O Lord, in Thy way; and direct me in the right paths because of Thy enemies.

SECOND NOCTURN.

Ne tradideris me in animas tribulantium me; quoniam insurrexerunt in me testes iniqui, et mentita est iniquitas sibi.

Credo videre bona Domini in terra viventium.

Expecta Dominum, viriliter age; et confortetur cor tuum, et sustine Dominum.

Requiem æternam, &c.

Ant. Credo videre bona Domini in terra viventium.

V. Collocet eos Dominus cum principibus.

R. Cum principibus populi sui.

Pater noster, *secreto.*

Deliver me not to the will of them that afflict me; because unjust witnesses have risen up against me, and iniquity has lied to itself.

I believe I shall see the good things of the Lord in the land of the living.

Expect the Lord, do manfully; and let Thy heart take courage, and expect thou the Lord.

Grant them eternal rest, &c.

Anth. I think to see the good things of the Lord in the land of the living.

V. May the Lord place them with the princes.

R. With the princes of His people.

Our Father, &c., *in secret.*

THE FOURTH LESSON. JOB XIII.

Responde mihi quantas habeo iniquitates, et peccata; scelera mea, atque delicta ostende mihi. Cur faciem tuam abscondis, et arbitraris me inimicum tuum? Contra folium, quod vento rapitur, ostendis potentiam tuam et stipulam siccam persequeris. Scribis enim contra me amaritu-

Answer me; how many iniquities and sins I have; my crimes and my offences show me. Why dost Thou hide Thy face, and esteem me Thy enemy? Against the leaf that is carried away with the wind, Thou showest Thy power, and pursuest a dry straw. For Thou writest bitter things

dines, et consumere me vis peccatis adolescentiæ meæ. Posuisti in nervo pedem mum, et observasti omnes semitas meas, et vestigia pedum meorum considerasti. Qui quasi putredo consumendus sum, et quasi vestimentum quod comeditur a tinea.

R. Memento mei, Deus, quia ventus est vita mea; * nec aspiciat me visus hominis.

V. De profundis clamavi ad te, Domine; Domine exaudi vocem meam. * Nec aspiciat.

against me, and hast a mind to consume me for the sins of my youth. Thou hast put my feet in the stocks, and hast observed all my paths and hast considered the steps of my feet. Who as rottenness am to be consumed, and as a garment that is eaten by the moth.

R. Remember me, O God, because my life is but wind; * nor may the sight of man behold me.

V. From the depths I have cried to Thee, O Lord: Lord hear my voice. *Nor may.

THE FIFTH LESSON. JOB XIV.

Homo natus de muliere, brevi vivens tempore, repletur multis miseriis. Qui quasi flos egreditur et fugit velut umbra, et nunquam in eodem statu permanet. Et dignum ducis super hujuscemodi aperire oculos tuos, et adducere eum tecum in judicium? Quis potest facere mundum de immundo conceptum semine? Nonne tu qui solus es? Breves dies hominis sunt, numerus mensium ejus apud

Man born of a woman, living a short time, is filled with many miseries. Who as a flower comes forth, and is destroyed, and flies away as a shaddow, and never abides in the same state. And dost Thou count it a worthy thing, to open Thy eyes on such a one, and to bring him with Thee into judgment? Who can make him clean that is conceived of unclean seed? Is it not Thou Who only art? The

SECOND NOCTURN.

te est. Constituisti terminos ejus, qui præteriri non poterunt. Recede paululum ab eo, ut quiescat, donec optata veniat, sicut mercenarii dies ejus.

days of man are short, the number of his months is with Thee; Thou hast appointed his limits, which cannot be passed. Depart a little from him, that he may rest, till his wished-for day comes, even as that of the hired man.

R. Hei mihi, Domine, quia peccavi nimis in vita mea: quid faciam, miser ubi fugiam, nisi ad te, Deus meus? *Miserere mei dum veneris in novissimo die.

R. Woe is me, O Lord, because I have sinned exceedingly in my life; O wretch, what shall I do, whither shall I fly to Thee my God? * Have mercy on me when Thou comest at the latter day.

V. Anima mea turbata est valde; sed tu, Domine, succurre ei. *Miserere mei.

V. My soul is greatly troubled; but Thou, O Lord, succor it. * Have mercy on me.

THE SIXTH LESSON. JOB XIV.

Quis mihi hoc tribuat, ut in inferno protegas me, et abscondas me, donec pertranseat furor tuus, et constituas mihi tempus, in quo recorderis mei? Putasne mortuus homo rursum vivat? Cunctis diebus, quibus nunc milito; expecto donec venit immutatio mea. Vocabis me, et ego respondebo tibi: operi manuum

Who will grant me this, that in hell Thou protect me, and hide me till Thy fury pass away, and appoint me a time wherein Thou wilt remember me? Shall a man that is dead, thinkest Thou, live again? All the days, in which I am now in warfare; I expect till my change comes. Thou shalt call me, and I shall

tuarum porriges dexteram. Tu quidem gressus meos dinumerasti, sed parce peccatis meis.

R. Ne recorderis peccata mea, Domine, dum veneris judicare sæculum per ignem.
V. Dirige, Domine, Deus meus, in conspectu tuo viam meam. * Dum veneris judicare sæculum per ignem.
V. Requiem æternam dona eis, Domine, et lux perpetua luceat eis; * Dum veneris.

answer Thee; to the work of Thy hands, Thou shalt stretch out Thy right hand. Thou indeed hast numbered my steps, but spare my sins.
R. Remember not my sins, O Lord, when Thou shalt come to judge the world by fire.
V. Direct, O Lord my God, my way in Thy sight. * When Thou shalt come to judge the world by fire.
V. Grant them eternal rest, O Lord, and let perpetual light shine on them; * When.

Here the Lauds *are recited when the Second Nocturn only is said.*

In the Third Nocturn.

On Wednesdays and Saturdays.

Ant. Complaceat. *Anth.* May it please Thee.

PSALM XXXIX.

Expectans expectavi Dominum; et intendit mihi.
Et exaudivit preces meas; et eduxit me de lacu miseriæ, et de luto fæcis.

Expecting I expected the Lord; and He has heard me.
He heard my prayers; and brought me out of the lake of misery, and from the mire of dregs.

Third Nocturn.

Et statuit supra petram pedes meos; et direxit gressus meos.

Et immisit in os meum canticum novum, carmen Deo nostro.

Videbunt multi, et timebunt; et sperabunt in Domino.

Beatus vir, cujus est nomen Domini spes ejus; et non respexit in vanitates, et insanias falsas.

Multa fecisti tu, Domine, Deus meus, mirabilia tua; et cogitationibus tuis non est qui similis sit tibi.

Annuntiavi, et locutus sum; multiplicati sunt super numerum.

Sacrificium, et oblationem noluisti; aures autem perfecisti mihi.

Holocaustum, et pro peccato non pastulasti; tunc dixi: ecce venio.

In capito libri scriptum est de me, ut facerem voluntatem tuam; Deus meus, volui, et legem tuam in medio cordis mei.

Annuntiavi justitiam tuam in ecclesia magna; ecce

And He has set my feet upon a rock; and has directed my steps.

And He has put a new song into my mouth; a song to our God.

Many shall see, and shall fear; and they shall hope in the Lord.

Blessed is the man, whose hope is the name of the Lord; and has not regarded vanities, and false madness.

Thou hast done many wonderful things, O Lord my God; and in Thy thoughts there is none like to Thee.

I have declared, and have spoken; they are multiplied above number.

Sacrifice, and oblation Thou wouldst not; but ears Thou hast perfected to me.

Holocaust, and for sin Thou didst not require; then said I: behold I come.

In the head of the book it is written of me, that I shall do Thy will; my God, I am willing, and have Thy law in the midst of my heart.

I have declared Thy justice in the church; behold

labia mea non prohibebo, Domine, tu scisti.

Justitiam tuam non abscondi in corde meo: veritatem tuam salutare tuum dixi.

Non abscondi misericordiam tuam et veritatem tuam; a concilio multo.

Tu autem, Domine, ne longe facias miserationes tuas a me; misericordia tua et veritas tua semper susceperunt me.

Quoniam circumdederunt me mala, quorum non est numerus; comprehenderunt me iniquitates meæ, et non potui ut viderem.

Multiplicatæ sunt super capillos capitis mei; et cor meum dereliquit me.

Complaceat tibi Domine, ut eruas me; Domine, ad adjuvandum me respice.

Confundantur et revereantur simul, qui quærunt animam meam, ut auferant eam.

Convertantur retrorsum, et revereantur; qui volunt mihi mala.

Ferant confestim confusionem suam; qui dicunt mihi; Euge, Euge.

I will not stay my lips, Lord, Thou hast known it.

Thy justice I have not hid in my heart; Thy truth and Thy salvation I have spoken.

I have not hidden Thy mercy and truth; from the great council.

But Thou, O Lord, remove not Thy compassion far from me; Thy mercy and Thy truth have always received me.

Because evils without number have encompassed me; my iniquities have overtaken me, and I was not able to see.

They are multiplied above the hairs of my head: and my heart has forsaken me.

May it please Thee, O Lord, to deliver me; Lord, have regard to help me.

Let them be confounded, and ashamed together, who seek my soul; to take it away.

Let them be turned backward, and be ashamed; who desire evils to me.

Let them forthwith receive their confusion; who say to me, Well, Well.

Exultent, et lætentur super te omnes quærentes te; et dicant semper; magnificetur Dominus, qui diligunt salutare tuum.

Ego autem mendicus sum et pauper; Dominus sollicitus est mei.

Adjutor meus et protector meus tu es; Deus meus, ne tardaveris.

Requiem æternam, &c.

Ant. Complaceat tibi, Domine, ut eripias me; Domine, ad adjuvandum me respice.

Ant. Sana, Domine, animam meam.

Let all that seek Thee, rejoice and be glad in Thee; and let them that love Thy salvation, say always, the Lord be magnified.

But I am needy, and poor; the Lord is careful of me.

Thou art my helper and my protector; my God do not delay.

Grant them eternal rest, &c.

Anth. May it please Thee, O Lord, to deliver me; Lord, have regard to help me.

Anth. Heal my soul, O Lord.

PSALM XL.

Beatus qui intelligit super egenum, et pauperem; in die mala liberabit eum Dominus.

Dominus conservet eum, et vivificet eum, et beatum faciat eum in terra; et non tradat eum in animam inimicorum ejus.

Dominus opem ferat illi super lectum doloris ejus; universum stratum ejus versasti in infirmitate ejus.

Blessed is the man that thinks on the needy and poor; in the evil day the Lord will deliver him.

May the Lord preserve him and give him life, and make him blessed in the land; and deliver him not to the will of his enemies.

May the Lord help him on his bed of sorrow; Thou hast turned all his couch to his infirmity.

Ego dixi; Domine, miserere mei; sana animam meam; quia peccavi tibi.

Inimici mei dixerunt mala mihi quando morietur et peribit nomen ejus.

Et si ingrediebatur, ut videret, vana loquebatur; cor ejus congregavit iniquitatem sibi.

Egrediebatur foras, et loquebatur in idipsum.

Adversum me susurrabant omnes inimici mei; adversum me cogitabant mala mihi.

Verbum iniquum constituerunt adversum me; numquid qui dormit, non adjiciet ut resurgat?

Etenim homo pacis meæ, in quo speravi: qui edebat panes meos, magnificavit super me supplantationem.

Tu autem, Domine, miserere mei, et resuscita me; et retribuam eis.

In hoc cognovi quoniam voluisti me; quoniam non gaudebit inimicus meus super me.

Me autem propter innocentiam suscepisti; et con-

I said: Lord, have mercy on me; heal my soul, because I have sinned against Thee.

My enemies have said evil things to me; when shall he die, and his name perish?

And if he came in to see, he spoke vain things; his heart assembled iniquity to himself.

He went forth; and spoke to the same purpose.

All my enemies whisper against me; they thought evil against me.

They have made an unjust decree against me; but he that sleeps, shall not rise again!

For the man of my peace, in whom I hoped; who did eat my bread, has gloried in supplanting me.

But Thou, O Lord, have mercy on me, and raise me up again; and I will repay them.

In this I have known that Thou hast consented to me; because my enemy shall not rejoice over me.

But Thou hast received me, because of my inno-

firmasti me in conspectu tuo in æternum.

Benedictus Dominus Deus Israel a sæculo, et usque in sæculum; fiat, fiat.

Requiem æternam, &c.

Ant. Sana, Domine, animam meam; quia peccavi tibi.

Ant. Sitivit.

cence; and Thou hast confirmed me in Thy sight for ever.

Blessed be the Lord God of Israel, from eternity to eternity; so be it, so be it.

Grant them eternal rest, &c.

Anth. Heal my soul, O Lord, because I have sinned against Thee.

Anth. My soul.

PSALM XLI.

Quemadmodum desiderat cervus ad fontes aquarum; ita desiderat anima mea ad te, Deus.

Sitivit anima mea ad Deum fortem vivum;— quando veniam, et apparebo ante faciem Dei.

Fuerunt mihi lacrymæ meæ panes die ac nocte; dum dicitur mihi quotidie; ubi est Deus tuus:

Hæc recordatus sum, et effudi in me animam meam; quoniam transibo in locum tabernaculi admirabilis, usque ad domum Dei.

Even as the heart thirsts after the fountains of waters; so does my soul thirst after Thee, O God.

My soul has thirsted after the mighty living God; when shall I come, and appear before the face of God?

My tears have been my bread day and night; whilst it is said to me daily; Where is thy God?

These things I remembered, and have poured out my soul within me; because I shall pass to the place of a wonderful tabernacle, even to the house of God.

In voce exultationis, et confessionis; sonus epulantis.

Quare tristis es anima mea; et quare conturbas me?

Spera in Deo, quoniam adhuc confitebor illi; salutare vultus mei, et Deus meus.

Ad meipsum anima mea conturbata est; propterea memor ero tui de terra Jordanis, et Hermoniim a monte modico.

Abyssus abyssum invocat; in voce cataractarum tuarum.

Omnia excelsa tua et fluctus tui; super me transierunt.

In die mandavit Dominus misericordiam, suam; et nocte canticum ejus.

Apud me oratio Deo vitæ meæ; dicam Deo, susceptor meus es.

Quare oblitus es mei, et quare contristatus incedo; dum affligit me inimicus.

Dum confringuntur ossa mea; exprobraverunt mihi,

In the voice of joyfulness and confession; the sound of one who feasts.

Why art thou sorrowful, my soul; and why dost thou trouble me?

Hope in God, for I will still confess Him; the salvation of my countenance and my God.

My soul is troubled within myself; therefore will I be mindful of Thee, from the land of Jordan and Hermon, from the little mountain.

Abyss calls upon abyss, in the noise of Thy waterfalls.

All Thy high things and Thy waves have passed over me.

In the day the Lord hath commanded His mercy; and in the night His song.

With me is prayer to the God of my life; I will say to God Thou art my defender.

Why hast Thou forgot me, and why go I sorrowful; whilst my enemy afflicts me?

Whilst my bones are broken; my enemies that

Third Nocturn.

qui tribulant me inimici mei.

Dum dicunt mihi per singulos dies; ubi est Deus tuus? Quare tristis es anima mea, et quare conturbas me?

Spera in Deo, quoniam adhuc confitebor illi; salutare vultus mei et Deus meus.

Requiem æternam, &c.

Ant. Sitivit anima mea ad Deum vivum; quando veniam, et apparebo ante faciem Domini?

V. Ne tradas bestiis animas confitentes tibi.

R. Et animas pauperum tuorum ne obliviscaris in finem

Pater noster, &c.
Totum secreto.

afflict me, have upbraided me.

Whilst they said to me every day: Where is thy God? Why art thou sorrowful, O my soul, and why dost thou trouble me?

Hope in God, for I will still confess Him; the salvation of my countenance, and my God.

Grant them eternal rest, &c.

Anth. My soul has thirsted after the living God; when shall I come and appear before the face of the Lord?

V. Deliver not to beasts the souls that confess Thee.

R. And the souls of Thy poor forget not to the end.

Our Father, &c.
All in secret.

THE SEVENTH LESSON. JOB XVII.

Spiritus meus attenuabitur, dies mei breviabuntur, et solum mihi super est sepulchrum. Non peccavi; et in amaritudinibus moratur oculos meos. Libera me, Domine, et pone me juxta te, cujusvis manus

My spirit shall be humbled; my days shall be shortened, and the grave only remains for me. I have not sinned, and my eye abides in bitterness. Deliver me, O Lord, and set me beside Thee, and

pugnet contra me. Dies mei transierunt, cogitationes meæ dissipatæ sunt, torquentes cor meum. Noctem verterunt in diem, et rursum post tenebras spero lucem. Si sustinuero infernus domus mea est, et in tenebris stravi lectulum meum. Putredini dixi; pater meus es; mater mea, et soror mea vermibus. Ubi est ergo nunc præstolatio mea, et patientiam meam, quis considerat?

R. Peccantem me quotidie, et non me pœnitentem timor mortis conturbat me; * quia in inferno nulla est redemptio, miserere mei, Deus, et salva me.

V. Deus in nomine tuo salvum me fac, et in virtute tua libera me; * quia in inferno.

let any man's hand fight against me. My days are passed, my thoughts are dissipated, tormenting my heart. Night they have turned into day, and again after darkness I hope for light. If I shall expect hell is my house, and in darkness I have made my bed. I have said to rottenness: thou art my father; my mother and sister, to the worms. Where then is now my expectation, and my patience who considers?

R. The fear of death troubles me; sinning daily and not repenting; *because in hell there is no redemption, have mercy on me, O God, and save me.

V. O God, in Thy name save me, and in Thy strength deliver me; *because in hell.

THE EIGHTH LESSON. JOB XIX.

Pelli meæ, consumptis carnibus, adhæsit os meum; et derelicta sunt tantummodo labia circa dentes meos. Miseremini mei, miseremini mei, saltem vos

My flesh being consumed my bone has cleaved to my skin, and there are left only lips about my teeth. Have mercy on me, have mercy on me, at least you my

amici mei, quia manus Domini tetigit me. Quare persequimini me sicut Deus, et carnibus meis saturamini? Quis mihi tribuat, ut scribantur sermones mei? Quis mihi det, ut exarentur in libro stylo ferreo, et plumbi lamina, vel scelte sculpantur in silice? Scio enim quia redemptor meus vivit, et in novissimo die de terra surrecturus sum; et rursum circumdabor pelle mea, et in carne mea videbo Deum salvatorem meum; quem visurus sum ego ipse, et oculi mei conspecturi sunt, et non alius; resposita est hæc spes mea in sinu meo.

R. Domine, secundum actum meum noli me judicare; nihil dignum in conspectu tuo egi; ideo deprecor majestatem tuam, * ut tu, Deus, deleas iniquitatem meam.

V. Amplius lava me, Domine ab injustitia mea; et a dilecto meo munda me. * Ut tu, Deus.

friends, because the hand of the Lord has touched me. Why do you persecute me as God, and are glutted with my flesh? Who will grant me that my words may be written? Who will grant that they may be drawn in a book, with an iron pen, and on a plate of lead, or else be graven with steel on a flint stone? For I know that my Redeemer lives, and that in the last day I shall rise out of the earth; and I shall be encompassed again with my skin, and in my flesh I shall see God my Saviour, whom I myself shall see, and my eyes shall behold and not another; this my hope is laid up in my bosom.

R. Judge me not, O Lord, according to my deeds, for I have done nothing worthy in Thy sight; therefore I beseech Thy majesty, *that Thou, O God, mayest blot out my iniquity.

V. Wash me, O Lord, yet more from my injustice and cleanse me from my sin. *That.

THE NINTH LESSON. JOB X.

Quare de vulva eduxisti me? Qui utinam consumptus essem; ne oculus me videret. Fuissem quasi non essem, de utero translatus ad tumulum. Numquid non paucitas dierum meorum finietur brevi? Dimitte ergo me, ut plangam paululum dolorem meum; antequam vadam, et non revertar, ad terram tenebrosam, et opertam mortis caligne; terram miseriæ et tenebrarum, ubi umbra mortis, et nullus ordo, sed sempiternus horror inhabitat.

℟. Libera me Domine, de viis inferni, qui portas æreas confregisti; et visitasti infernum, et dedisti eis lumen, ut viderent te *qui erant in pœnis tenebrarum.

℣. Clamantes et dicentes: advenisti Redemptor noster. *Qui erant.

℣. Requiem æternam dona eis, Domine, et lux perpetua luceat eis. *Qui erant.

Why didst Thou bring me forth out of the womb? Who would to God I had been consumed, that eye might not see me. I had been as if I were not, translated from the womb to the grave. Shall not the fewness of my days be shortly ended? Suffer me then that I may a little lament my sorrow; before I go, and return not, unto the dark land, that is covered with the mist of death, a land of misery and darkness, where the shadow of death and no order, but everlasting horror, inhabits.

℟. Deliver me, O Lord, from the ways of hell, Who hast broken the brazen gates, and hast visited hell, and hast given light to them, that they may behold Thee *who were in the pains of darkness.

℣. Crying, and saying: Thou art come, O our Redeemer. *Who were.

℣. Grant them eternal rest, O Lord, and let perpetual light shine on them. *Who were.

This is always said in the Week Day Office. But the following RESPONSORY *is said only on* ALL-SOULS DAY, *and when the* THREE NOCTURNS *are said together.*

R. Libera me Domine, de morte æterna, in die illa tremenda, † quando cœli movendi sunt et terra: * cum veneris judicare sæculum per ignem.

V. Tremens factus sum ego, et timeo, dum discussio venerit atque ventura ira. †Quando cœli movendi sunt et terra; * dum veneris judicare.

V. Dies illa, dies iræ, calamitatis et miseriæ, dies magna et amara valde. * Dum veneris judicare.

V. Requiem æternam dona eis Domine, et lux perpetua luceat eis.

R. Libera me Domine, de morte æterna, in die illa tremenda, † quando cœli movendi sunt et terra, * dum veneris judicare.

R. Deliver me, O Lord, from eternal death, in that dreadful day †when the heavens and earth are to be moved, * when Thou shalt come to judge the world by fire.

V. I tremble and do fear when the examination is to be, and Thy wrath to come. †When the heavens and earth are to be moved; *when Thou.

V. That day is the day of anger, of calamity, and of misery, a great day and very bitter. *When Thou.

V. Grant them eternal rest, O Lord, and let perpetual light shine on them.

R. Deliver me, O Lord, from eternal death, in that dreadful day, †when the heavens and earth are to be moved, *when Thou.

AT LAUDS.

Ant. Exultabunt Domino ossa humiliata.

Anth. The humbled bones shall rejoice in our Lord.

PSALM L.

Miserere mei, Deus; secundum magnam misericordiam tuam.

Et secundum multitudinem miserationum tuarum; dele iniquitatem meam.

Amplius lava me ab iniquitate mea; et à peccato meo munda me.

Quoniam iniquitatem meam ego cognosco; et peccatum meum contra me est semper.

Tibi soli peccavi, et malum coram te feci; ut justificeris in sermonibus tuis, et vincas cum judicaris.

Ecce enim iniquitatibus conceptus sum; et in peccatis concepit me mater mea.

Ecce enim veritatem dilexisti; incerta et occulta

Have mercy on me, O God; according to Thy great mercy.

And according to the multitude of Thy tender mercies blot out my iniquities.

Wash me yet more from my iniquity, and cleanse me from my sin.

Because I know my iniquity; and my sin is always against me.

To Thee only have I sinned, and have done evil before Thee, that Thou mayest be justified in Thy words, and overcome when Thou art judged.

For behold I was conceived in iniquities; and in sins my mother conceived me.

For behold Thou hast loved truth; the uncertain

sapientiæ tuæ manifestasti mihi.

Asperges me hyssopo, et mundabor; lavabis me, et super nivem dealbabor.

Auditui meo dabis gaudium et lætitiam; et exultabunt ossa humiliata.

Averte faciem tuam a peccatis meis; et omnes iniquitates meas dele.

Cor mundum crea in me Deus; et spiritum rectum innova in visceribus meis.

Ne projicias me a facie tua; et spiritum sanctum tuum ne auferas a me.

Redde mihi lætitiam salutaris tui; et spiritu principali confirma me.

Docebo iniquos vias tuas; et impii ad te convertentur.

Libera me de sanguinibus Deus, Deus salutis meæ; et exultabit lingua mea justitiam tuam.

Domine, labia mea aperies; et os meum annuntiabit laudem tuam.

and hidden things of Thy wisdom Thou hast manifested to me.

Thou wilt sprinkle me with hyssop, and I shall be cleansed; Thou shalt wash me and I shall be made whiter than snow.

To my hearing Thou wilt give joy and gladness; and the humbled bones shall rejoice.

Turn away Thy face from my sins; and blot out all my iniquities.

Create a clean heart in me, O God; and renew a right spirit within my bowels.

Cast me not away from Thy face; and take not away Thy holy spirit from me.

Restore to me the joy of Thy salvation; and confirm me with a perfect spirit.

I will teach Thy ways to the unjust; and the impious shall be converted to Thee.

Deliver me from blood, O God, the God of my salvation; and my tongue shall extol Thy justice.

Lord, Thou wilt open my lips; and my mouth shall declare Thy praise.

Quoniam si voluisses, sacrificium dedissem utique; holocaustis non delectaberis.

Sacrificium Deo spiritus contribulatus; cor contritum et humiliatum Deus non despicies.

Benigne fac Domine in bona voluntate tua Sion; ut ædificentur muri Jerusalem.

Tunc acceptabis sacrificium justitiæ, oblationes, et holocausta: tunc imponent super altare tuum vitulos.

Requiem æternam, &c.

Ant. Exultabunt Domino ossa humiliata.

Ant. Exaudi.

Because if Thou wouldst have had sacrifice, I had verily given it; with holocausts Thou wilt not be delighted.

An afflicted spirit is a sacrifice to God; a contrite and humble heart, O God, Thou wilt not despise.

Deal favorably, O Lord, in Thy good will with Sion; that the walls of Jerusalem may be built up.

Then wilt Thou accept a sacrifice of justice, oblations and holocausts; then shall they lay calves on Thy altar.

Grant them eternal rest, &c.

Anth. The humbled bones shall rejoice in the Lord.

Anth. Hear.

PSALM LXIV.

Te decet hymnus Deus in Sion; et tibi reddetur votum in Jerusalem.

Exaudi orationem meam; ad te omnis caro veniet.

Verba iniquorum prævaluerunt super nos: et im-

A hymn, O God, becomes Thee in Sion: and a vow shall be rendered to Thee in Jerusalem.

Hear my prayer: all flesh shall come to Thee.

The words of the wicked have prevailed over us;

pietatibus nostris tu propitiaberis.

Beatus, quem elegisti, et assumpsisti; inhabitabit in atriis tuis.

Replebimur in bonis domus tuæ; sanctum est templum tuum, mirabile æquitate.

Exaudi nos Deus, salutaris noster; spes omnium finium terræ, et in mari longe.

Præparans montes in virtute tua, accinctus potentia, qui conturbas profundum maris, sonum fluctuum ejus.

Turbabuntur gentes, et timebunt qui habitant terminos a signis tuis; exitus matutini, et vespere delectabis.

Visitasti terram, et inebriasti eam; multiplicasti locupletare eam.

Flumen Dei repletum est aquis, parasti cibum illorum; quoniam ita est præparatio ejus.

Rivos ejus inebria, multiplica, genimina ejus; in

and Thou wilt be propitious to our impieties.

Blessed is he whom Thou hast chosen and taken; he shall dwell in Thy courts.

We shall be filled with the good things of Thy house; holy is Thy temple; wonderful in equity.

Hear us, O God, our Saviour; the hope of all the bounds of the earth, and in the sea afar off.

Preparing mountains in Thy strength, girded with power; Who troublest the depth of the sea, the sound of its waves.

The nations shall be troubled, and they that inhabit the borders shall be afraid of Thy signs; the end of the morning and evening Thou shalt delight.

Thou hast visited the earth, and hast inebriated it; Thou hast greatly enriched it.

The river of God, is replenished with waters, Thou hast prepared their meat; because so is the preparation thereof.

Inebriate its rivers, multiply its fruits; in its drops

stillicidiis ejus lætabitur germinans.

Benedices coronæ anni benignitatis tuæ; et campi tui replebuntur ubertate.

Pinguescent speciosa deserti; et exultatione colles accingentur.

Induti sunt arietes ovium et valles abundabunt frumento; clamabunt, etenim hymnum dicent.

Requiem æternam dona eis, Domine.

Ant. Exaudi, Domine, orationem meam; ad te omnis caro veniet.

Ant. Me suscepit.

it shall rejoice springing.

Thou wilt bless the circle of the year of Thy goodness; and Thy fields shall be filled with plenty.

The beautiful places of the desert shall be fat; and the little hills encompassed with joy.

The rams of the sheep are clothed, and the valleys shall abound with corn; they shall cry out, yes they shall sing a hymn.

Grant them eternal rest, &c.

Anth. Hear my prayer, O Lord, all flesh shall come to Thee.

Anth. Thy right hand.

PSALM LXII.

Deus Deus meus, * ad te de luce vigilo.

Sitivit in te anima mea, * quam multipliciter tibi caro mea.

In terra deserta, et invia, et inaquosa:* sic in sancto apparui tibi, ut viderem virtutem tuam et gloriam tuam.

O God, my God, to Thee I watch from the morning light.

My soul has thirsted after Thee; my flesh also very many ways!

As in the desert land, and inaccessible and without water: so in the holy place have I appeared to Thee, that I might behold Thy strength and Thy glory.

Quoniam melior est misericordia tua super vitas: *labia mea laudabunt te.

Sic benedicam te in vita mea :* et in nomine tuo levabo manus meas.

Sicut adipe et pinguedine repleatur anima mea ; et labiis exultationis laudabit os meum.

Si memor fui tui super stratum meum, in matutinis meditabor in te ; * quia fuisti adjutor meus.

Et in velamento alarum tuarum exultabo, adhæsit anima mea post te : * me suscepit dextera tua.

Ipsi vero in vanum quæsierunt animam meam, introibunt in inferiora terræ ; * tradentur in manus gladii, partes vulpium erunt.

Rex vero lætabitur in Deo, laudabuntur omnes qui jurant in eo ; * quia obstructum est os loquentium iniqua.

Because Thy mercy is better than life, my lips shall praise Thee.

So will I bless Thee in my life, and in Thy name I will lift up my hands.

As with marrow and fatness let my soul be filled, and my mouth shall praise with lips of joy.

If I have been mindful of Thee on my bed, in the morning I will meditate on Thee: because Thou hast been my helper.

And under the cover of Thy wings I will rejoice, my soul has cleaved after Thee ; Thy right hand has taken me under its protection.

But they in vain have sought my soul, they shall enter into the lowest parts of the earth; they shall be delivered into the power of the sword; they shall be the portions of foxes.

But the king shall rejoice in God, all shall be praised that swear by Him; because the mouth of those that speak wicked things is stopped.

PSALM LXVI.

Deus misereatur nostri, et benedicat nobis;* illuminet vultum suum super nos, et misereatur nostri.

Ut cognoscamus in terra viam tuam;* in omnibus gentibus salutare tuum.

Confiteantur tibi populi Deus;* confiteantur tibi populi omnes.

Lætentur et exultent Gentes;* quoniam judicas populos in æquitate, et Gentes in terra dirigis.

Confiteantur tibi populi Deas; confiteantur tibi populi omnes;* terra dedit fuctum suum.

Benedicat nos Deus, Deus noster, benedicat nos Deus;* et metuant eum omnes fines terræ.

Requiem æternam, &c.

Ant. Me suscepit dextera tua, Domine.

Ant. A porta inferi.

God have mercy on us and bless us, cause His countenance to shine on us, and have mercy on us.

That we may know Thy way on earth, Thy salvation in all nations.

Let people, O God, confess to Thee, let all people praise Thee.

Let nations be glad, and rejoice, because Thou judgest people with equity, and directest the nations on the earth.

Let people, O God, confess to Thee, let all people praise Thee; the earth has yielded her fruit.

May God, our God, bless us; may God bless us, and may all the ends of the earth fear Him.

Grant them eternal rest, &c.

Anth. Thy right hand, O Lord, has received me.

Anth. From the gate.

THE SONG OF EZECHIAS. ISAIAS XXXVIII.

Ego dixi; in dimidio dierum meorum vadam ad portas inferi.

I have said; in the midst of my days I shall go to the gates of hell.

Quæsivi residuum annorum meorum; dixi, non videbo Dominum Deum in terra viventium.

Non aspiciam hominem ultra; et habitatorem quietis.

Generatio mea ablata est, et convoluta est a me; quasi tabernaculum pastorum.

Præcisa est velut a texente, vita mea; dum adhuc ordirer, succidit me; de mane usque ad vesperum finies me.

Sperabam usque ad mane; quasi leo sic contrivit omnia ossa mea.

De mane usque ad vesperam finies me; sicut pullus hirundinis sic clamabo, meditabor ut columba.

Attenuati sunt oculi mei: suspicientes in excelsum.

Domine, vim patior, responde pro me: quid dicam aut quid respondebit mihi, cum ipse fecerit?

Recogitabo tibi omnes annos meos; in amaritudine animæ meæ.

I have sought the residue of my years; I have said, I shall not see the Lord God in the land of the living.

I shall behold man no more; and the inhabitant of my rest.

My generation is taken away, and is folded up for me; as the tent of shepherds.

My life is cut off as by a weaver; whilst I yet began, he cut me off, between morning and night Thou wilt make an end of me.

I hoped until the morning; as a lion so has he broken all my bones.

Between morning and evening Thou wilt make an end of me; as a young swallow so will I cry, I will meditate as a dove.

My eyes are weakened; looking up on high.

Lord, I suffer violence, answer for me; what shall I say, or what shall He answer me, whereas Himself has done it?

I will relate to Thee all my years; in the bitterness of my soul.

Domine, si sic vivitur et in talibus vita spiritus mei, corripies me, et vivificabis me; ecce in pace amaritudo mea amarissima.

Tu autem eruisti animam meam, ut non periret; projecisti post tergum tuum omnia peccata mea.

Quia non infernus confitebitur tibi, neque mors laudabit te; non expectabunt, qui descendunt in lacum veritatem tuam.

Vivens, vivens ipse confitebitur tibi, sicut et ego hodie; pater filiis notam faciet veritatem tuam.

Domine, salvum me fac; et psalmos nostros cantabimus cunctis diebus vitæ nostræ, in domo Domini.

Requiem æternam, &c.

Ant. A porta inferi, erue, Domine animam meam.

Ant. Omnis spiritus.

Lord, if man's life be such, and the life of my spirit in such things, Thou shalt chastise me, and enliven me; behold in peace is my bitterness most bitter.

But Thou hast delivered my soul, that it should not perish; Thou hast cast all my sins behind Thy back.

Because hell shall not confess Thee, neither shall death praise Thee; they that go down into the lake, shall not expect Thy truth.

He that lives, he that lives shall confess Thee, as I do this day; the father shall make Thy truth known to the children.

Lord save me; and we will sing our psalms all the days of our life in the house of our Lord.

Grant them eternal rest, &c.

Anth. From the gate of hell, deliver my soul, O Lord.

Anth. Let every spirit.

PSALM CXLVIII.

Laudate Dominum de cœlis; * laudate eum in excelsis.

Praise the Lord from the heavens, praise Him in the high places.

Laudate eum omnes Angeli ejus;* laudate eum omnes virtutes ejus.	Praise Him all His angels; praise Him all His powers.
Laudate eum sol et luna;* laudate eum omnes stellæ, et lumen.	Praise Him sun and moon, praise Him all ye stars and light.
Laudate eum cœli cœlorum;* et æquæ omnes, quæ super cœlos sunt, laudent nomen Domini.	Praise Him, O heavens of heavens, and let the waters that are above the heavens, praise the name of the Lord.
Quia ipse dixit, et facta sunt;* ipse mandavit, et creata sunt.	Because He spoke, and they were made; He commanded, and they were created.
Statuit ea in æternum, et in sæculum sæculi:* præceptum posuit, et non præteribit.	He established them for ever, world without end; He made a precept and it shall not be annulled.
Laudate Deum de terra;* dracones, et omnes abyssi.	Praise the Lord from the earth, ye dragons and all depths.
Ignis, grando, nix, glacies, spiritus procellarum;* quæ faciunt verbum ejus;	Fire, hail, snow, ice, tempestuous winds, which obey His word.
Montes, et omnes colles;* ligna fructifera, et omnes cedri;	Mountains and all hills, trees that bear fruit, and all cedars.
Bestiæ, et universa pecora;* serpentes, et volucres pennatæ.	Beasts and all cattle; serpents and winged fowls.
Reges terræ, et omnes populi;* principes, et omnes judices terræ.	Kings of the earth, and all people, princes and all judges of the earth.
Juvenes, et virgines; senes cum junioribus lau-	Young men and virgins, the old with the young; let

dent nomen Domini; * quia exaltatum est nomen ejus solius.

Confessio ejus super cœlum et terram; * et exaltavit cornu populi sui.

Hymnus omnibus sanctis ejus; * filiis Israel, populo appropinquanti sibi.

them praise the name of the Lord, because His name alone is exalted.

The confession of Him is above heaven and earth, and He has exalted the horn of His people.

A hymn to all His saints, to the sons of Israel, a people that approaches to Him

PSALM CXLIX.

Cantate Domino canticum novum; * laus ejus in ecclesia sanctorum.

Lætetur Israel in eo, qui fecit eum; * et filii Sion exultent in rege suo.

Laudent nomen ejus in choro; * in tympano, et psalterio psallant ei;

Quia beneplacitum est Domino in populo suo; * et exaltabit mansuetos in salutem.

Exultabunt sancti in gloria; * lætauntur in cubilibus suis.

Exaltationes Dei gutture eorum; * et gladii ancipites in moniqus eorum;

Sing to the Lord, a new song, let His praise be in the church of saints.

Let Israel be joyful in Him that made Him, and the children of Sion rejoice in their King.

Let them praise His name in choir; on timbrel and psalter let them sing to Him.

Because the Lord is well pleased with His people, and He will exalt the meek to salvation.

The saints shall rejoice in glory, they shall be joyful in their beds.

The praise of God shall be in their mouths, and two edged swords in their hands.

Ad faciendam vindictam in nationibus, * increpationes in populis.	To execute revenge on the nations, chastisements among the people.
Ad alligandos reges eorum in compedibus; * et nobiles eorum in manicis ferreis.	To bind their kings in fetters, and their nobles in chains of iron.
Ut faciant in eis judicium conscriptum; * gloria hæc est omnibus sanctis ejus.	That they may execute on them the judgment that is written; this glory is to all His saints.

PSALM CL.

Laudate Dominum in sanctis ejus; * laudate eum in firmamento virtutis ejus.	Praise the Lord in His saints; praise Him in the firmament of His strength.
Laudate eum in virtutibus ejus; * laudate eum secundum multitudinem magnitudinis ejus.	Praise Him in His power; praise Him according to the multitude of His greatness.
Laudate eum in sono tubæ; * laudate eum in psalterio, et cithara.	Praise Him in the sound of trumpet; praise Him on the psalter and harp.
Laudate eum in tympano et choro; * laudate eum in chordis, et organo.	Praise Him on the timbrel and in choir; praise Him on strings and organs.
Laudate eum in cymbalis benesonantibus; laudate eum in symbalis jubilationis; * omnis spiritus laudet Dominum.	Praise Him on well sounding cymbals; praise him on cymbals of joy; let every spirit praise our Lord.
Requiem æternam, &c.	Grant them eternal rest, &c.
Ant. Omnis spiritus laudet Dominum.	*Anth.* Let every spirit praise the Lord.

V. Audivi vocem de cœlo dicentem mihi:

R. Beati mortui qui in Domino moriuntur.

Ant. Ego sum resurrectio.

V. I heard a voice from heaven saying to me:

R. Blessed are the dead that die in the Lord.

Anth. I am the resurrection.

THE SONG OF ZACHARIAS. LUKE I.

Benedictus Dominus Deus Israel,* quia visitavit, et fecit redemptionem plebis suæ:

Et erexit cornu salutis nobis;* in domo David pueri sui.

Sicut locutus est per os sanctorum,* qui a sæculo sunt, prophetarum ejus:

Salutem ex inimicis nostris;* et de manu omnium qui oderunt nos;

Ad faciendam misericordiam cum patribus nostris;* et memorari testamenti sui sancti.

Jusjurandum, quod juravit ad Abraham patrem nostrum,* daturam se nobis:

Ut sine timore de manu inimicorum nostrorum liberati* serviamus illi,

Blessed be the Lord God of Israel, because He has visited and wrought the redemption of His people.

And raised up a kingdom of salvation to us, in the house of David His servant.

As He spoke by the mouth of His holy prophets that are from the beginning.

Salvation from our enemies, and from the hand of all that hate us.

To work mercy with our fathers, and to remember His holy covenant.

The oath which He swore to Abraham our father that He would grant Himself to us.

That without fear, being delivered from the hands of our enemies, we may serve Him.

In sanctitate, et justitia coram ipso,* omnibus diebus nostris.

Et tu puer, Propheta Altimissi vacaberis;* præibis enim ante faciem Domini parare vias ejus:

Ad dandam scientiam salutis plebi ejus :* in remissionem peccatorum eorum;

Per viscera misericordiæ Dei nostri :* in quibus visitavit nos, oriens ex alto.

Illuminare his qui in tenebris, et in umbra mortis sedent ;* ad dirigendos pedes nostros in viam pacis.

Requiem æternam, &c.

Ant. Ego sum resurrectio, et vita; qui credit in me, etiam si mortuus fuerit, vivet; et omnis qui vivit, et credit in me, non morietur in æternum.

In holiness and justice before Him all our days.

And thou, child, shalt be called the Prophet of the Highest; for thou shalt go before the face of our Lord, to prepare His ways.

To give knowledge of salvation to His people, for remission of their sins.

Through the bowels of the mercy of our God; in which the rising sun from on high has visited us.

To enlighten them that sit in darkness, and in the shadow of death ; to direct our feet in the way of peace.

Grant them eternal rest, &c.

Anth. I am the resurrection, and the life; he that believes in Me, though he be dead, shall live; and every one that lives, and believes in Me, shall never die.

The following Prayers are said kneeling.

Pater noster, &c., *secreto.*

V. Et ne nos inducas in tentationem.

Our Father, &c. *in secret.*

V. And lead us not into temptation.

De profundis, &c., or, *Out of the depths,* &c., page 239.

R. Sed libera nos à malo.

R. But deliver us from evil.

V. A porta inferi.
R. Erue Domine animas eorum.
V. Requiescant in pace.
R. Amen.
V. Domine, exaudi orationem meam.
R. Et clamor meus ad te veniat.
V. Dominus vobiscum.
R. Et cum spiritu tuo.
Oremus.

V. From the gates of hell.
R. Deliver their soul, O Lord.
V. May they rest in peace.
R. Amen.
V. O Lord hear my prayer.
R. And let my cry come to Thee.
V. The Lord be with you.
R. And with Thy spirit.
Let us pray.

A PRAYER SAID AFTER THE DEPARTURE OF A SODALIST.

Absolve, quæsumus, Domine, animam famuli tui (*vel* famulæ tuæ) N. ut defunctus (*vel* defuncta) sæculo tibi vivat: et quæ per fragilitatem carnis humana conversatione commisit, tu venia misericordissimæ pietatis absterge; per Dominum nostrum Jesum Christum Filium tuum, qui tecum vivit et regnat in unitate Spiritus Sancti Deus per omnia sæcula sæculorum.
R. Amen.

Absolve, we beseech Thee, O Lord, the soul of Thy servant N., that being dead to the world he (*or* she) may live to thee; and whatever he (*or* she) has committed through human frailty, do Thou wipe away by the pardon of Thy most merciful goodness; thro' our Lord Jesus Christ Thy Son, Who livest and reignest with Thee in the unity of the Holy Ghost, one God, world without end.
R. Amen.

For the other Prayers, see page 244.

V. Requiem, &c.
V. Requiescant, &c.
R. Amen.

V. Grant them, &c.
V. And let perpetual, &c.
R. Amen.

III. The Psalm 129, De Profundis, or Out of the Depths, after the Angelus at Night.

Pope Clement XII, granted by a Brief of Ausust 14, 1736:

I. The Indulgence of one hundred days to all the faithful, every time that, after the Angelus at night, they say devoutly on their knees the Psalm "Out of the Depths," with a "Eternal Rest" at the end of it.

II. The Plenary Indulgence to those who perform this pious exercise at the time appointed for a whole year, once in the year, on any one day after having Confessed and Communicated. Those who do not know by heart the above Psalm, may gain these Indulgences by saying, in the way already mentioned for this Psalm, one *Our Father* and one *Hail Mary*, with *Eternal Rest, etc.*

PSALM 129.

Out of the depths, I have cried unto Thee, O Lord: Lord, hear my voice.

Let thine ears hearken, to the voice of my supplication.

If Thou, O Lord, shalt mark our iniquities, O Lord, who can abide it?

For with Thee there is mercy; and by reason of Thy law I have waited on Thee, O Lord.

My soul has waited on His word: my soul hath hoped in the Lord.

From the morning watch even unto night, let Israel hope in the Lord.

For with the Lord there is mercy; and with Him plenteous redemption.

And He shall redeem Israel, from all his iniquities.

Eternal rest give to them, O Lord.

And let perpetual light shine upon them.

May they rest in peace.

Amen.

V. Lord, hear my prayer.

R. And let my cry come unto Thee.

LET US PRAY.

O God, the Creator and Redeemer of all the faithful, grant to the souls of Thy servants, and Thy handmaids departed, the remission of all their sins, that through the devout prayers of Thy Church on earth they may obtain that remission of pain which they have ever desired. Who livest and reignest world without end. Amen.

V. Eternal rest give to them, O Lord.

R. And let everlasting light enlighten them.

V. May they rest in peace.

R. Amen.

IV.

1. The Indulgence of three hundred days to all the faithful who, being contrite in heart, and devoutly meditating on the Passion of our Lord Jesus Christ, shall say in suffrage for

the faithful departed the *Our Father* and *Hail Mary* five times, with the versicle.

"Eternal Father, we pray Thee help the souls of Thy servants, whom Thou hast redeemed with the blood of Jesus Christ."

And afterwards the ETERNAL REST, ETC., as above.

2. The Plenary Indulgence and remission of all sins to all who shall have practised this pious exercise every day for a month, on any one day in each month when, being truly penitent, having Confessed and Communicated, they shall pray for our holy Mother, the Church, etc., and for the eternal repose of the departed.—*Brief of Pius VII, Feb. 7, 1817.*

V. Prayers for the Whole Week.

The Indulgence of one hundred days is granted to all who say with contrite heart and devotion one of the following prayers on the day appointed.—*Leo XII. Nov. 18, 1826.*

FOR SUNDAY.

O Lord God Almighty, I pray Thee by the precious blood which Thy divine Son Jesus shed in the garden, deliver the souls in purgatory, and specially amongst them all that soul which is most destitute of aid; and bring it to Thy glory, there to praise and bless Thee for ever. Amen.

Pater, Ave and *De Profundis, Out of the Depths*, p. 293.

FOR MONDAY.

O Lord God Almighty, I pray Thee, by the precious blood which Thy divine Son Jesus shed in His cruel scourging, deliver the souls in purgatory, and amongst them all that soul specially which is nearest to its entrance into Thy glory; that so it may soon begin to praise and bless Thee for ever. Amen.

Pater, Ave and *De Profundis, p.* 293.

FOR TUESDAY.

O Lord God Almighty, I pray Thee, by the precious blood which Thy divine Son Jesus shed in His bitter crowning with thorns, deliver the souls in purgatory, and in particular amongst them all deliver that one which would be the last to issue out of those pains, that it tarry not so long a time before it come to praise Thee in Thy glory and bless Thee for ever. Amen.

Pater, Ave and *De Profundis, p.* 293.

FOR WEDNESDAY.

O Lord God Almighty, I pray Thee, by the precious blood which Thy divine Son Jesus shed through the streets of Jerusalem when He carried the cross upon His sacred shoulders, deliver the souls in purgaory, and specially that soul which is richest in merits before Thee; that so, in that throne of glory which awaits it, it may magnify Thee and bless Thee for ever. Amen.

Pater, Ave and *De Profundis, p.* 293.

FOR THURSDAY.

O Lord God Almighty, I beseech Thee, by the precious body and blood of Thy divine Son Jesus, which He gave with His own hand upon the eve of His passion to His beloved apostles to be their meat and drink, and which He left to His whole Church to be a perpetual sacrifice and life-giving food of His own faithful people, deliver the souls in purgatory, and specially that one which was most devoted to this Mystery of infinite love; that with the same Thy divine Son, and with Thy holy Spirit, it may ever praise Thee for this Thy wondrous love in Thy eternal glory. Amen.

Pater, Ave and *De Profundis, p.* 293.

FOR FRIDAY.

O Lord God Almighty, I pray Thee, by the precious blood which Thy divine Son shed on this day upon the wood of the cross from His most sacred hands and feet, deliver the souls in purgatory, and specially that soul for which I am bound to pray ; that the blame rest not with me that Thou bringest it not forthwith to praise Thee in Thy glory and to bless Thee for ever. Amen

Pater, Ave and *De Profundis, p.* 293.

FOR SATURDAY.

O Lord God Almighty, I beseech Thee, by the precious blood which burst forth from the side of Thy divine Son Jesus, in the sight of, and to the extreme pain of His Most Holy Mother, deliver the souls in purgatory, and specially that one amongst them all which was ever the most devout to this great lady ; that it may soon attain unto Thy glory, there to praise Thee in her and her in Thee world without end.— Amen.

Pater, Ave and *De Profundis, p.* 293.

VI. Devout Exercise for the Nine Days preceding All Soul's Day, for the Repose of the Holy Souls in Purgatory.

By St. Alphonsus.

FIRST DAY.

O Jesus, my Saviour, I have so often merited hell: if I were now among the damned, how great would be the pain which I should feel in thinking that I was the cause of my own damnation? I thank Thee for the patience with which Thou hast borne me. My God, because Thou art infinite goodness, I love Thee above all things and I am sorry from my heart for having offended Thee. I promise Thee rather to die than ever to offend Thee again. Have pity on me, and have pity also on those blessed souls who burn in that fire. Mary, mother of God, succor them by Thy powerful prayers.

Let us here say a Pater and Ave for these souls. Then all the people shall say the following prayer:

"O Jesus, for mercy's sake console these souls, these spouses whom Thou lovest so tenderly, and who are so severely tormented."

SECOND DAY.

Ah, unhappy me, who have lived so long, and have acquired merits only for hell! I thank Thee, O Lord, for having given me time to repair the evil which I have done. I am sorry for having offended so good a God. Help me to spend the remainder of my life in loving and serving Thee. Have pity on me, and have pity also on those holy souls who burn in that fire. O Mary, mother of God, succor them by Thy powerful prayers.

Pater. Ave. O Jesus, for mercy's sake, &c., as above.

THIRD DAY.

O my God, because Thou art infinite goodness, I love Thee above all things, and I am sorry, from the bottom of my heart for having offended Thee, I promise Thee to die rather than ever to offend Thee again. Give me holy perseverance; have pity on me, and have pity also on those holy souls who burn in that fire. O mother of God, assist them by thy powerful prayers.

Pater. Ave. O Jesus, for mercy's sake, &c.

FOURTH DAY.

O my God, because Thou art infinite goodness, I am sorry, with my whole heart, for having offended Thee. I promise to die rather than ever to offend Thee again. Give me holy perseverance: have pity on me, and have pity on all those holy souls who burn in that fire, and love Thee with all their hearts. O Mary, mother of God, assist them by thy powerful prayers.

Pater. Ave. O Jesus, for mercy's sake, &c.

FIFTH DAY.

Unhappy me! O Lord, if Thou hadst sent me to hell I should be certain of never leaving that prison of torture. I love Thee above all things, O infinite goodness, and I am sorry, with my whole heart, for having offended Thee. Give me holy perseverance; have pity on me, and have pity also on those holy souls who burn in that fire. O Mary, mother of God, assist them by thy powerful prayers.

Pater. Ave. O Jesus, for mercy's sake, &c.

SIXTH DAY.

O my God, Thou hast died also for me, and hast given Thyself so often to me in the holy communion. And I have always repaid Thee with ingratitude! But now, I love Thee above all things, O my sovereign good, and I am sorry, with my whole heart, for having offended Thee.

I promise to die rather than ever to offend Thee again. Give me holy perseverance; have pity on me, and have pity also on all those holy souls who burn in that fire. O Mary, mother of God, assist them by thy powerful prayers.

Pater. *Ave.* *O Jesus, for mercy's sake, &c.*

SEVENTH DAY.

Who, O Lord, more ungrateful than I have been? Thou hast waited for me with so much patience, Thou hast often pardoned me with so much love, and I, after so many promises, have again offended Thee! Ah, do not send me to hell. I am sorry, O infinite goodness, for having offended Thee; I promise to die rather than ever to offend Thee again. Give me holy perseverance; have mercy on me, and have mercy also on those holy souls who burn in that fire. O Mary, mother of God, assist them by thy powerful prayers.

Pater. *Ave.* *O Jesus, for mercy's sake, &c.*

EIGHTH DAY.

Behold, O my God, I am one of those ungrateful souls, who, after having received from Thee such great favors, have despised Thy love, and have forced Thee to condemn me to hell. O infinite goodness, I now love Thee above all things, and I am sorry, with my whole heart, for having offended Thee. I promise Thee to die rather than ever to offend Thee again. Give me holy perseverance; have mercy on me, and have mercy also on those holy souls who burn in that fire. O Mary, mother of God, assist them by thy powerful prayers.

Pater. Ave. O Jesus, for mercy's sake, &c.

NINTH DAY.

O my God, how have I been able to live so many years at a distance from Thee, and bereft of Thy grace? O infinite goodness, I love Thee above all things, and I am sorry, with my whole heart, for having offended Thee. Give me holy perseverance, and do not permit me ever again to see myself Thy enemy. Have mercy, I entreat Thee, on these blessed souls; alleviate their pains, and abridge the time of their exile, by calling them soon to love Thee face to face in paradise. O Mary, mother of God, assist them by thy powerful prayers: pray also for us, who are still in danger of being lost for ever.

Pater. Ave. O Jesus, for mercy's sake, &c.

PRAYERS TO JESUS CHRIST,

For these souls, through the pains which He suffered during His passion.

O most sweet Jesus, through the bloody sweat which Thou didst suffer in the garden of Gethsemani, have mercy on these blessed souls.

The People shall answer:

Have mercy on them, O Lord, have mercy on them.

O most sweet Jesus, through the pains which Thou didst suffer during Thy most cruel scourging, have mercy on them.

R. *Have mercy on them, &c.*

O most sweet Jesus, through the pains which Thou didst suffer in Thy most painful crowning with thorns, have mercy on them.

R. *Have mercy on them, &c.*

O most sweet Jesus, through the pains which Thou didst suffer in carrying Thy cross to Calvary, have mercy on them.

R. *Have mercy on them, &c.*

O most sweet Jesus, through the pains which Thou didst suffer during Thy most cruel crucifixion, have mercy on them, &c.

R. *Have mercy on them, &c.*

O most sweet Jesus, through the pains which Thou didst suffer in Thy most bitter agony on the cross, have mercy on them.

R. *Have mercy on them, &c.*

O most sweet Jesus, through that immense pain which Thou didst suffer in breathing forth Thy blessed soul, have mercy on them.

R. *Have mercy on them, &c.*

Let us recommend ourselves to the souls in Purgatory, and say:

Blessed souls, we have prayed for you: we entreat you, who are so dear to God, and who are secure of never losing Him, to pray for us miserable sinners, who are in danger of being damned, and of losing God for ever.

LET US PRAY.

O God, the author of mercy, the lover of the salvation of mankind; we address Thy clemency, in behalf of our brethren, relations, and benefactors, who are departed this life, that by the intercession of blessed Mary, ever a virgin, and of all the saints, Thou wouldst receive them into the enjoyment of eternal happiness; through Christ our Lord. Amen.

Prayers of St. Gertrude for the Souls in Purgatory.

First, we must kneel to ask pardon of our sins, saying:

"O most sweet Lord Jesus, in union with the celestial praises which the ever blessed Trinity renders to itself as alone worthy of praise, and which it imparts to Thy blessed humanity, Thy glorious mother, Thy angels and saints, and then returns to the abyss of Thy divinity, from whence it had flowed forth, I offer my prayers and good works to Thy praise and glory. I adore Thee, praise Thee, bless Thee, and give Thee thanks, for the love of Thy incarnation, Thy birth, the hunger, thirst, labors, and griefs of Thy three-and-thirty years on earth, and for Thy love in giving Thyself to us in the Sacrament of the Altar; and I beseech Thee to unite my prayers and good works to the merit of Thy most holy life and conversation, which I offer for the living and for the dead, for the souls of —— and of ——; and I pray Thee to supply for and repair all that they have neglected or omitted in praise, in thanksgiving, in prayer, in devotion, in good works, which by Thy grace, they might have accomplished, and in which they have failed by their negligence."

Secondly, having again implored pardon, repeat this prayer:

"O most sweet Lord Jesus Christ, I adore Thee and bless Thee, giving thanks to Thee for Thy love in redeeming us by Thy cruel sufferings, and because Thou, the Creator of the universe, wert taken prisoner, bound, betrayed, defamed, cast upon the ground, scourged, crowned with thorns, condemned, crucified, slain cruelly, and transfixed with a lance, for love of us. I offer Thee my petitions in union with the love with which Thou didst bear these outrages and indignities; beseeching Thee, by the merit of Thy most holy passion and death, to pardon the sins of those for whom I pray, whether they have offended against Thee by thought, word or deed; and I implore Thee to offer to God, the Father, all Thy pains and griefs of body and soul, and the merit of each pain, for those who are still indebted to Thy justice."

Thirdly, repeat the following prayer, standing up:

"I adore Thee, praise Thee, and bless Thee, O most sweet Lord Jesus Christ, giving Thee thanks for the victorious love by which Thou didst elevate our nature to the right hand of God, the Father, after raising it up victoriously from the tomb; and I beseech Thee to grant the souls for whom I pray a participation in Thy victory and triumphs."

Fourthly, after imploring the mercy of God, say:

"Saviour of the world, save us all; Mary, holy mother of God, and ever Virgin, pray for us. We beseech Thee, by the intercession of all Thy holy apostles, martyrs, confessors and holy virgins, to keep us from evil, and to lead us to the perfection of all good. O most sweet Lord Jesus, I adore Thee, praise Thee, and bless Thee, for all the favors Thou hast conferred on Thy blessed mother and on Thy elect, in union with that gratitude with which Thy saints rejoice in Thy blessed incarnation, passion and resurrection; beseeching Thee, by the prayers of Thy glorious virgin mother and all the saints, to supply the needs of these souls."

Fifthly, recite the hundred and fifty Psalms of the Psalter devoutly and consecutively, saying after each verse:

"Hail, Jesus Christ, Splendor of the Father, Prince of peace, Gate of heaven, Bread of life, Son of a virgin, Vessel of the divinity!" At the conclusion of each Psalm, repeat the following words, kneeling: "Eternal rest give to them, O Lord, and let perpetual light shine upon them." Then say a hundred and fifty Masses, or have them said, or offer as many Communions, or at least fifty or thirty. Give alms also a hundred and fifty times, or, if this is impossible, say the *pater noster* and the prayer "O God, etc.," (p. 311,) performing the same number of acts of charity. In these acts of charity may be included the least kindness done to another for the love of God—such as a kind word, or a kind act, or even a fervent prayer.

Litany of the Faithful Departed.

Lord, have mercy on us.
Christ, have mercy on us.
Lord, have mercy on us.
Christ, hear us.
Christ, graciously hear us.
God, the Father of heaven, *Have mercy on them.*
God, the Son, Redeemer of the world, *Have mercy on them.*
God, the Holy Ghost, *Have mercy on them.*
Holy Trinity, one God, *Have mercy on them.*
Holy Mary,
Holy Mother of God,
Holy Virgin of Virgins,
All ye holy Angels and Archangels,
All ye holy orders of blessed spirits,
All ye holy Patriarchs and Prophets,
All ye holy Apostles and Evangelists,
All ye holy Disciples of our Lord,
All ye holy Innocents,
All ye holy Martyrs,
All ye holy Bishops and Confessors,
All ye holy Doctors,
All ye holy Priests and Levites,
All ye holy Monks and Hermits,
All ye holy Virgins and Widows, } *Pray for them.*

310 Litany of the Faithful Departed.

All ye men and women, saints of God,
                              Make intercession for them.
Be merciful unto us.   *Spare us. O Lord.*
Be merciful unto us.   *Graciously hear us, O Lord.*

From all evil,
From Thy wrath,
From the rigor of Thy justice,
From the power of the devil,
From the gnawing worm of conscience,
From long-enduring sorrow,
From cruel flames,
From horrible darkness,
Through the mystery of Thy holy Incarnation,
Through Thy coming,
Through Thy nativity,
Through Thy baptism and holy fasting,
Through Thy cross and passion,
Through Thy death and burial,
Through Thy resurrection,
Through Thy admirable ascension,
Through the coming of the Holy Ghost, the Comforter,

                                        O Lord, Deliver them.

We sinners, *We beseech Thee to hear us.*
That Thou spare them,
That Thou pardon them,
That Thou deliver the souls of our parents, kinsfolks, and benefactors, from all their sufferings,
That Thou vouchsafe to give eternal rest to all the faithful departed,
That Thou vouchsafe to confirm and preserve us in Thy holy service,
That Thou lift up our minds to heavenly desires,
That Thou vouchsafe to bring us to true penance,
That Thou vouchsafe graciously to hear us,
Son of God,

                                        We beseech Thee to hear us.

Lamb of God, Who takest away the sins of the world,
                                        Spare us, O Lord.
Lamb of God, Who takest away the sins of the world,
                                        Graciously hear us, O Lord.
Lamb of God, Who takest away the sins of the world,
                                        Have mercy on us.

Christ, hear us.   *Christ, graciously hear us.*
Lord, have mercy on us.   *Christ, have mercy on us.*

LET US PRAY.

O God, Whose property is always to have mercy and to spare, receive our petition that the souls of all Thy servants, who are still detained in the flames of Purgatory, may, by the compassion of Thy goodness, be mercifully absolved.

Grant, O Lord, we beseech Thee, that while we lament the departure of Thy servant, we may always remember that we are most certainly to follow *him*. Give us grace to prepare for that last hour by a good and holy life, that we may not be taken unprepared by sudden death, but may be ever on the watch, that, when Thou shalt call, we may go forth to meet the bridegroom, and enter with him into glory everlasting. Through the same Jesus Christ our Lord. Amen.

O most wise and merciful Lord, Who hast ordained this life as a passage to the future, confining our repentance to the time of our pilgrimage here, and reserving for hereafter the state of punishment and reward; vouchsafe to us who are yet alive, and have still the opportunity of reconciliation with Thee, the grace so to watch over all our actions, and to correct every slightest wandering from the true way to heaven, that we may not be surprised with our sins uncancelled, or our duties unfulfilled; but when our bodies shall go down into the grave, our souls may ascend to Thee, and dwell with Thee for ever in the mansions of eternal bliss. Through Jesus Christ our Lord and only Saviour. Amen.

AN INVOCATION OF THE MOST HOLY TRINITY FOR THE SOULS IN PURGATORY.

O God of all goodness, Father of mercies, Who, at the prayers and fastings of Thy faithful people, didst vouchsafe to send Thy angels to break assunder the fetters of Thy holy apostle Peter, and to open the doors of his prison; hear even also on this day the prayers and supplications of Thy Church, and send Thy angel to the souls for whom we pray, that, the doors of their prison being opened wide, they may be happily received into the bosom of Thy mercy.

Pater.   Ave.   Gloria.

O Son of God, Saviour of souls, Who didst refresh the three children in the burning fiery furnace, pour down upon the souls that cry to Thee from the flames Thy heavenly dew. Thy precious blood alone can quench the flames of purgatory; oh, let it now flow down upon these suffering souls, and do Thou, O Lord, have mercy upon them.

Pater. Ave. Gloria.

O Spirit of love, have compassion on the cruel torment which these souls endure, that are filled with the purest charity, and aspiring without ceasing towards their God, cry aloud in their distress, "I thirst: I thirst after my God!" and yet cannot attain unto the object of their love, nor receive the least drop of that torrent of pure delights. O Holy Spirit, grant that, having felt the fiercest pangs of love, they may taste its heavenly delights in a blessed eternity. Amen.

Pater. Ave. Gloria.

O God, Who by sin art offended, and by penance pacified, mercifully regard the prayers of Thy people making supplication to Thee for the souls in Purgatory, and turn away from them the scourges of Thy anger which they deserve for their sins.

O God, the Creator and Redeemer of all the faithful, give to the souls of Thy servants departed, the remission of all their sins, that through pious supplications they may obtain the pardon which they have always desired.

O almighty and eternal God, Who hast dominion over the living and the dead, and art merciful to all whom Thou foreknowest shall be Thine by faith and good works, we humbly beseech Thee that all those souls for which we have determined to offer up our prayers, may, by the clemency of Thy goodness and by the intercession of all Thy saints, obtain pardon and full remission of all their sins, through our Lord Jesus Christ Thy Son, Who liveth and reigneth, one God with Thee and the Holy Ghost, world without end. Amen.

V. O Lord, hear my prayer.

R. And let my cry come unto Thee.

V. May the almighty and most merciful Lord graciously hear us.

R. Amen.

V. And may the souls of the faithful departed, through the mercy of God, rest in peace.

R. Amen.

Rule of Life.

I. IN THE MORNING.

Before you get up, make the sign of the cross, and say, Jesus, Mary and Joseph, I give you my heart and my soul. (Each time you say this prayer you get an indulgence of one hundred days, which you can give to the souls in Purgatory.) Get up directly at a fixed time, and while you are dressing yourself do not think of your dreams or other foolish things, but remember that God is looking at you.

II. MORNING PRAYERS.

When you are dressed kneel down and say the Our Father, Hail Mary and Creed. Then make a meditation:

1. *Morning Offering.* Say to yourself, "what shall I have to do from now till evening"—think for a moment what ?—and how you will do each action well, prayers and school duties, work, meals, conversation, &c., then say, My God I offer to Thee the thoughts, words, actions and sufferings of this day, with those of Jesus Christ.

2. *Examination about the sins of the day.* Say to yourself, "what is the greatest sin I commit, or what sin do I commit oftenest"—what is

it?—think how you will avoid it. Then say, My God, keep me to-day from all sin. Amen.

It is good to say also, "Dear Mary, Mother of Jesus, pray for me. St. Joseph and my holy patrons, pray for me. My dear angel guardian, I love you, take care of me this day. Sweet Jesus, have pity on the poor sinners and save them from hell; have mercy on the souls suffering in Purgatory."

It is better to say short prayers, Our Father and Hail Mary, or to say your prayers going to or at your work, than to say no prayers at all.

About the meditation, remember, 1. To say the prayers slowly, and to stop on them as long as you can, like a bee stops in a flower, till it has got all the honey out of it. 2. A boy was walking along a road where there was a great stone. When he came to the stone, he tumbled over it and fell down, because he was not looking before him. Temptations to sin are the devil's stones, and if you do not try to foresee them, and get ready for them in your morning meditation, very likely when you come to them, you will fall into sin. 3. You never forget to take your breakfast. Meditation is the breakfast of the soul, so make your meditation every morning.

III. MEAL PRAYERS.

Before and after your meals bless yourself.— You may also say grace. *Before meals*: "Bless us, O Lord, and these Thy gifts, which of Thy bounty we are going to receive, through Christ our Lord. Amen." *After meals*: "We give Thee thanks, Almighty God, for all Thy benefits, Who livest and reignest for ever. Amen. May the souls of the faithful departed, through the mercy of God, rest in peace. Amen." At your meals it is good not to eat some very little bit, at least a crumb, for the love of the infant Jesus.

IV. NIGHT PRAYERS.

Before you go to bed, kneel down and say your night prayers. 1. The Our Father, Hail Mary and Apostles' Creed. 2. Examine your conscience. Say: "Did I miss my prayers or commit any sin to-day?" Think for a moment what sin—then say, "O God, be merciful to me a sinner."

V. WHEN IN BED

Bless yourself, and put your arms in the form of a cross for the love of Jesus, Who died on the cross for the love of you. Then say, Jesus, Mary and Joseph, I give you my heart and my soul.

VI. DAILY VIRTUES.

1. Be meek and humble of heart like Jesus.—
2. Give everything you do to Jesus. If you pray eat, drink, sleep, dress yourself, talk, sing, walk, sit down, go on an errand, light a candle, sweep the house, go to school, read, write, mend a pen, sew, work—in every action, great or little, at the beginning or middle or end of it—say, my Jesus, I do this for the love of Thee, or all for Thee, my Jesus, or if you like say only "Jesus and Mary," or the Hail Mary. 3. If anything happens to you which you do not like, say, my God, may Thy holy will be done. 4. Be kind to everybody, and give a bit of bread or anything to the poor if you can. 5. Forgive those who offend you, and speak kindly to them. 6. Love, respect and obey your parents, masters and superiors. Jesus the great God was obedient to Mary and Joseph. Obey quickly, cheerfully, and in every thing, and because it is the will of God.

VII. GOOD PRACTICES.

Every day make a meditation (page 219)—hear mass—visit the blessed sacrament, (prayer pages 90–99,) visit some picture or image of the blessed virgin, and say the hail Mary — say the angelus, morning, noon and night—say the rosary, at least one decade for the love of Mary your dear mother. If you have no beads, count the Hail Marys on your fingers.

It is good for every family to meet together in the evenings, and say the rosary, and this with the examination of conscience (page 18,) would do for night prayers Be in some pious confraternity. Read this rule of life every Sunday.

VIII. TEMPTATION.

1. If a temptation comes to you, turn away from it and say, "Jesus and Mary, help me," or say the Hail Mary till it goes away. 2. Put a bad thought out of your heart as quickly as you would shake a burning spark off your hand.— 3. Keep your eyes, ears and tongue from what is bad. 4. Keep away from bad company, public-houses, whiskey-shops, dram-shops, bad dancing and singing-houses, gambling-houses, theatres, bad wakes, bad books, novels and romances. Against temptations of impurity, it is good to say every day three Hail Marys in honor of the purity of the Immaculate Mary.

IX. SINS COMMITTED.

1. *Mortal Sin.*—If you commit a mortal sin, make an act of Contrition directly, and go to Confession as soon as you can. 2. *Venial Sin.*

—Live in the firm purpose of never committing a venial sin. If you fall into venial sin even many times, do not be vexed at yourself, or discouraged, but always strike your breast, or at least be sorry for a moment, and resolve not to commit it again.

X. THE SACRAMENTS.

Go to Confession and the Holy Communion at Easter, and at least once a month. Do not wilfully conceal a sin in Confession.

XI. DAYS OF THE WEEK.

Give Sunday to the Blessed Trinity: Monday to the souls in Purgatory; Tuesday to your Angel Guardian; Wednesday to St. Joseph; Thursday to the Blessed Sacrament; Friday to Jesus crucified; Saturday to your Mother, Mary.

XII. DEATH.

Live every day as if you were to die that day. When death comes, be sure to make an act of Contrition—say, O my God, I am very sorry that I have sinned against Thee, because Thou art so good, and I will not sin again. This act of Contrition from your heart will save your soul if there is no priest to hear your Confession when dying. If you are near any poor creature who is dying, whisper the act of Contrition into his ear, and perhaps you will save a soul from hell.

For the love of Jesus and Mary, do the twelve things which are in this Rule of Life.

Explanation of the Commandments.

FROM THE WORKS OF ST. ALPHONSUS.

FIRST COMMANDMENT.

I. *Faith.* You must be very careful to know the four great truths, because no one can go to heaven without knowing them. 1. One God. 2. Which are the three Persons in God. 3. Who was made man, and died on the Cross for our sins. 4. Heaven and hell. You must know also the Sacraments, especially Baptism, the Holy Eucharist, and Penance: the Our Father, Hail Mary and Apostles' Creed: the commandments of God and of the Church. It is a mortal sin wilfully to doubt or disbelieve or deny the Catholic faith. It is bad to go to prayers or sermons in Protestant places of worship, and much worse to go where it is strictly forbidden, as in many parts of Ireland, or where you give scandal by it, or your faith is likely to be weakened, or if you join with them in worship. You must not read Protestant books or tracts. Say your morning and night prayers. A distraction in prayer against your will, or when you do not remember that you are distracted, is not a sin. It is not a sin to give over saying scapular or confraternity prayers, but it is commonly a sign of spiritual sloth.

II. *Hope, Despair* and *Presumption.*

III. *Charity.* 1. Not helping the poor when you can especially if they are in great need : it would be a mortal sin for any one to save up all his money to get rich, and give nothing to the poor. You must also do good to the souls of others, especially when they are not able to help themselves; for example, if a child was dying without baptism, or if a sinner was dying who did not know how to make an act of contrition and you could help him. 2. *Scandal,* or what is likely to make others sin, such a bad example, or teaching them what is bad, or any way leading them into sin.

IV. *Religion.* 1. *Superstition.* It is very bad to ask fortune-tellers to tell your fortune, or dumb persons, or those who use charms or signs, or toss cups, and the like. It is bad to do any of these things yourself, especially if you believe in them. Do not give attention to dreams, lucky days, and such things. You must not read or keep superstitious books. 2. *Sacrilege and irreverence.* To behave ill in church, or to priests and religious, or to sacred things, for example, crucifixes and religious ceremonies, the holy scriptures, the relics of the saints, sacred images, beads, &c. It would be still worse to use any sacred thing for the purpose of committing sin. When you go to confession tell your sins sincerely. If you knowingly and wilfully conceal a mortal sin in confession through fear or shame, it is a bad confession, your sins are not forgiven and you will have to make the confession over again. If you forget a great sin in confession, it is pardoned along with the other sins, but you must confess it the next time you go to confession. It is commonly a venial sin not to say at all, through your own fault, a penance given in confession for venial sins, and it is a mortal sin not to say a great penance given for a mortal sin. It is a mortal sin wilfully to receive the blessed sacrament not fasting. If you have received with bad dispositions a sacrament which you can receive only once, for example, confirmation, you must repent and confess it, and then God will give you the grace you would have got in the sacrament. 3. *Simony.* It is a mortal sin to buy or sell anything sacred, for example, the relic of a saint, but it is not a sin to sell the case containing the relic for its just value, or to sell blessed beads for what they are worth without the blessing.

SECOND COMMANDMENT.

I. *To take the name of God in vain.* To say, for example, good God, or, O Lord, habitually and without respect, is a venial sin.

II. *Blasphemy* is to speak ill of God or the saints, or what is sacred; to say that God is cruel or unjust, or takes no care of us; to wish there was no God; to say the sacraments are of no use; the holy scriptures contain lies; to damn anything sacred. It is a mortal sin to say these and the like blasphemies, if you know the harm of what you are saying, and that it is an injury to God.

III. *Curses.* It is very bad to use God's name in a curse, for example, that God may damn any one, or that the curse of God may be on them, etc. Other curses without God's name —that people may die, never stir, or about the devil, or hell, or bad luck, etc., if not said from the heart, are venial sins; but if they are said from the heart, and you really wish some grievous harm to a person, then it is a mortal sin.— N. B.—If you repent of the habit of saying a bad word and it slips out of your mouth against your will, it is not a sin; but you must do your best to correct yourself by striking your breast or blessing yourself when this happens.

IV. *An oath* is to call God or something sacred to witness that what you say is the truth; for example to swear on the Book, or by the name of God or the holy name—by heaven— on my soul—so help me God. Mat. v. "Let your speech be yea, yea, and no, no, and that which is over and above these is of evil." Do not then in conversation say faith—troth—on my life—on my conscience—true as I stand here —true as gospel. Do not in talking say, I swear—God's truth—God knows—I declare to God. To say such words is commonly a venial sin, but not an oath unless God is called to witness the truth. 1. It is a mortal sin to take an oath in a lie, and worse in a court of justice, or that you will do something which is a sin, and such oaths must never be kept. 2. It is a venial sin to take an oath not false or bad, but without any necessity for taking it. 3. It is a sin not to keep a good oath, especially in a great thing. 4. It is very bad to have a custom of taking oaths when you talk. 5. It is no sin to take a good oath on a proper occasion; for example, in a court of justice.

V. *Vows.* It is a mortal sin to break a vow or a promise made to God, in a great thing—a venial sin to break a vow in a little thing; for example, a vow about saying the Hail Mary. You should ask the advice of your Confessor before you make a vow.

THIRD COMMANDMENT.

I. *Servile work.* 1. It is a sin to work on Sundays. 2. It is a mortal sin to work for about two hours, or two hours and a half. 3. It is not a sin to work if there be necessity for it.

For example, if a person has not food enough for the day—in case of certain works which cannot be interrupted without grievous inconvenience, such as the carriage of letters, and certain manufactories—if it be necessary for a funeral and the like—poor people, who have no other time, are allowed to wash and mend their clothes—servants may do household work, cooking, etc.—to avoid any great loss, for example, if a farmer's hay, or corn, or fruit is in danger of being destroyed or much injured by the weather—in buying or selling, if there is any custom permitted by the Bishop—it is allowed to sell things which are necessary on Sunday, as medicines and food—poor people who come out of the country, are allowed to buy, if they cannot buy on any other day. It is not servile work to write, or teach, or draw, or sing, or play music, or travel. If a person does on Sunday what is not servile work, it is not a sin to be paid for it.

II. *Hearing Mass.* 1. It is a sin wilfully to lose any part of a mass of obligation. 2. If through your own fault you lose much of the mass on Sundays or days of obligation, you commit a mortal sin, unless you know that you can hear another mass. 3. It is a mortal sin to play or talk, etc., during a great part of a mass of obligation, so that you cannot attend to it. 4. During mass you may read the prayers in your book, or say the beads, or your penance, or any other prayer, or meditate, or examine your conscience, or attend devoutly to what the Priest does. 5. It is not a sin to be absent from mass for a just reason.

Those are excused from hearing Mass who are sick, or so weak that it is dangerous for them to go, also those who have to take care of the sick, servants who cannot leave the house without grievous inconvenience to the master or themselves, those who have to cook, or mind a baby, take care of cattle, etc.; such persons are excused, if by going they would be in danger of losing their places and could not easily find another, but they should try to take turns in going to Mass, or rise a little earlier; and if they can seldom or never get to Mass and the Sacraments, they should seek another place. Children are excused if hindered by their parents; or wives by their husbands, soldiers, people in prisons and workhouses, if they can not get to Mass, those who are on a journey if it would be a grievous inconvenience to stop, those who cannot go to Mass without exposing themselves to the danger of some great temporal or spiritual evil, those who live far from a chapel, especially if they are weak or the weather bad, the death of a near relation excuses where such is the custom, he who is asleep does not hear Mass, but he who is troubled with sleepiness hears Mass if he can give some attention to it, to help at Mass, by serving, singing, playing the organ, is no hindrance to hearing Mass.

FOURTH COMMANDMENT.

I. *Children.* 1. *Love.* Children must love their parents, and it is very wrong to cause them great sorrow, or not to help them when they are sick, or old, or poor. 2. *Respect.* It is a mortal sin to strike your parents, or in their presence to put out your tongue at them, or mock them, or the like, through spite or contempt, or in their hearing to curse them or call them very bad names, such as fools, beasts, drunkards. It is also very bad to threaten or scold them, cast up their faults to them—not to speak to them through pride. These things are a less sin if they do not see or hear you, also to look sullen or give disrespectful answers. 3. *Obedience.* It is very bad to disobey your parents in any great thing, such as going out at night, or into bad company, or to dancing-houses and the like, or playing about the streets with any one you meet, or leaving your parents. It is wrong to stop away from school, or not to learn your lessons. If you know that your brothers or sisters go into bad company or do other bad things, you should tell your parents. Do not by your own fault provoke your parents to curse, and do not follow their bad example. It is generally a mortal sin to make a runaway marriage You must ask the consent of your parents before you marry. Children must not go to Protestant or soupers' schools, or schools forbidden by bishops or parish priests.

II. *Servants.* 1. *Respect* to master and mistress. It is foolish for servants to give notice in a passion that they will leave. 2. *Obedience.* 3. *Justice.* Not doing the work they agreed to

—wasting things—stealing—to eat out of meals against the will of the master, things commonly given to servants is often a venial sin. It is sinful to give away their master's things against his will; to let strangers steal, or let their fellow-servants steal the things given to their charge. If servants do not hinder their fellow-servants from stealing or injuring their master's things, when they can easily, they sin, and if these things were given to their charge, and they allow them to be stolen by their fellow-servants, they must make restitution. When servants cannot make restitution to their master, they must try to make amends by more diligence, and laboring harder in his service. Female servants or girls in service must take care lest men living in the same house, especially if they are alone, should lead them into sin. If they are tempted to great sin, they must leave their place. If they are in a place where they can seldom or never go to Mass and the Sacraments, they should seek another place, they must avoid as much as possible being in service in whiskey-shops and public-houses, dram-shops, and such like places.

FIFTH COMMANDMENT.

I. *Suicide* or killing one's self is a grievous mortal sin, also to risk one's life without some just reason.

28*

II. *Murder* or unjustly taking away another's life, is a grievous mortal sin.*

III. It is very wrong to do any great *bodily injury* to ourselves or others, by fighting or any other way. The sin of fighting is commonly greater in older people than in children.

IV. It is bad to *desire our own death* impatiently, but it is lawful to desire our own death to go to heaven, or be free from sin, or from some temporal evil which may lead to despair or other sin.

V. *Anger, hatred, enemies.* If any one has injured you, it is a sin, 1. Not to forgive him, or keep spite. 2. To wish some harm to him — 3. Not to answer him when he speaks to you. 4. If you were accustomed to speak to him before, you should not pass him by, without saying a word, or in some way showing him that you forgive him, unless you are afraid it will make him worse, or have some other just reason, for example, to avoid bad company. 5. To take revenge. Take notice. If you feel a dislike to

---

* It is a mortal sin to do anything for the purpose of destroying or grievously injuring a child before or after its birth.

It is not a sin to defend your own life or another's life, chastity or property of great value when unjustly attacked, even though it cannot be defended without taking away the life of him who attacks it. It is not a sin to desire some temporal misfortune to another in order that it may make him cease to give scandal or be converted, or not persecute the good.

a person and try to put away the dislike and are kind to him, it is no sin if you cannot get rid of the dislike.

VI. *Drunkenness.* It is a mortal sin to get drunk so as to lose your senses. You must not go to places, houses, fairs or markets, where you know, from experience, that you are likely to get drunk. A person is answerable for all the sins he could foresee he was likely to commit in drunkenness. "Avoid all occasions of drunkenness. Drunkards shall not obtain the kingdom of heaven."' Gal. v.

SIXTH COMMANDMENT.

I. *Sins with others, or by one's self.* To go into bad company—liberties—to do what is bad, or immodest, with any person or thing—or to one's self, alone. It sometimes happens that people do some of these things when they are children, and do not think of telling them afterwards in confession.

II. *Thoughts and desires.* Not putting away bad thoughts and desires, but taking pleasure in them; also curiosity to know bad things. Take notice: a bad or impure thought in the mind for some moments before you can be sufficiently on your guard against it, is not a mortal sin. A bad thought which is not wilful, is no sin; but not to try to put away the bad thought, to take pleasure in it, to consent to it—that is a sin.

III. *Senses.* To look with pleasure at bad things — to say or listen with pleasure to very bad words, especially if you take pleasure not only in the words, but in the bad thought itself —also to encourage others to say such words— to sin with any of the senses.

IV. *Bad things.* Bad songs, books, pictures and the like. These things must be destroyed.

Take notice, 1. *Scandalous things.* It is a great sin for women or girls to go wilfully and unnecessarily into company where they know that liberties will be taken with them, although these liberties are against their will. Immodesty of dress is sinful. It is a great sin to do anything to raise bad thoughts in the minds of others.— It is a sin for men to make women think they are going to marry them when they have no such intention. Girls should take care if men or boys come to them when *alone*, especially if they say anything which may have a bad meaning, or ask them to come alone with them and offer them something. So let girls when they fear anything evil, fly away. Also girls in the country, who have to take care of cattle or beasts, or work in the fields, or in harvesting, must be on their guard against men or boys if they work with them, or come to them when *alone*. It is very bad for girls to go and drink with men or boys.

2. *Dangerous places and things.* Bad dancing-houses, bad wakes, gambling-houses, fights, theatres, races, whiskey-shops, gin-shops, dram-shops, public-houses, sometimes lodging-houses, and the streets at night, shows, if there is anything bad in them. People must be much on their guard at fairs, markets and the like occasions. The reading of novels and romances is often very dangerous. It is better for girls not to go to schools taught by men, unless the priest approves of these schools; it is proper for boys to play with boys, and for girls to play with girls; it is very dangerous for men and women to keep company, especially if alone; in some cases it is very dangerous for girls or women to receive presents or letters from men; on many occasions when women or girls have to make visits, it is very proper for some one else to be with them; the same may be said of many occasions when they have to receive visits. On Sunday there is sometimes more sin, because people have more time and liberty. The time before marriage is very dangerous; women must not allow the man they are going to be married to, to take the least liberty with them, and it is strongly advisable that they should not be in company *alone* with him, but along with their

parents, and other well-behaved persons. They will learn his character much better by inquiring, than by being alone with him, for, before marriage, people seldom show themselves such as they really are.

SEVENTH COMMANDMENT.

I. *Stealing.*—1. *Different ways of stealing.* 1. To steal all at once. 2. To take and keep things by little and little. 3. To help others to steal. 4. To let others steal when you have charge of a thing — for example, a servant. — 5. To receive stolen goods, or things from servants, or those who have no right to give them away. 6. To keep a thing found without trying to find the owner. 7. To destroy or injure wilfully what belongs to another. 8. To make a person lose anything by lies, detraction or other unjust means—for example, so to make a servant lose her place, or a shop-keeper his customer. It is worse if you steal by force, or from a church, or anything sacred.

2. *Sin of Stealing.* 1. It is a sin to steal except in some cases of most grievous distress : for example, if a person was almost dying of hunger and he took only what was necessary to save him. 2. It is a venial sin to steal a little. 3. It is a mortal sin to steal much: for example,

to steal from a workman a day's wages, or to steal less from a poorer man, or more from a richer man, or from parents. If you steal from a rich person you commit a sin, because it is always a sin to steal. But if you steal the same from a poor man, you commit a greater sin, because the poor man suffers more from the loss. If you steal often a little it is a sin each time and when the little sums come to make altogether a large sum, then it becomes a mortal sin. It is also a mortal sin to steal a little, if at the same time you have the will and intention to steal much if you could.

II. *Bargains or contracts.* 1. Ignorance of your employment, and thus injuring others, as in a doctor or druggist. 2. To make a bargain or contract to do what is sinful, or do something which you are unable to do, to cheat in fulfilling a contract: for example, by using unsound materials, or doing the work ill, or doing only part, and taking the whole price, to break an agreement without just reason. 3. To cheat in buying or selling, to sell for more than a reasonable price, to lend or sell what is hurtful to the buyer: for example, bad books, to sell what is in itself bad and useless to the buyer, to sell what is imperfect for the same price as if it were perfect, except in some cases where there is a common understanding that a thing is to be sold for what it will fetch. He who sells must be content with a reasonable profit, and when custom has fixed the price, then no more should be charged; about not paying wages to servants or others, St. James says, that the wages due to the laborer and not paid, cry to God for vengeance against him who withholds them. "Behold the hire of the laborers which by fraud has been kept back by you, crieth, and the cry of them has entered into the ears of the Lord."—James v. 4. It is a sin to sell to those who have no right to buy: for example, to children who buy in the name and without the leave of their parents. 4. To take too much interest for lending money, or to sell provisions, meal, etc., to the poor on credit, and charge them an excessive price.— 5. Also to imitate any writing for some bad purpose, to pass false money, to beg pretending to be poor, or under a false pretext. 6. Unjust lawsuits. 7. It is commonly a mortal sin to break a promise of marriage without just reason. 8. To break a simple promise to give something to another is commonly not more than a venial sin, and many promises are no more than the expressions of one's intention. A promise to give does not oblige at all, if it is about anything hurtful, unlawful or useless, or when things change so much afterwards that if you had foreseen it you would not have made the promise.

9. To get into debt, not meaning to pay, or to pay at proper time, when you are able, or not to lessen your expenses in order to pay.

III. *Restitution.* 1. If you have stolen anything you must give it back; if you have injured any one in his person, character, honor or goods, you must make amends. You are not obliged to restore, if the injury you did was by accident and you did not mean to do it. You may delay restitution, if you cannot do it at present without very great difficulty; for example, if a workman would have to sell his tools, or if a person would lose his character, but you must have the will and intention to do it as soon as possible; at least, by little and little. If you do not know how to restore, ask the priest.

2. *To whom.* You must make amends to the person injured, or his heirs, and if you cannot, then to the poor.

EIGHTH COMMANDMENT.

I. A *Lie* is a sin—a lie which does a grievous injury to another is a mortal sin, it is of such lies that the holy scripture speaks when it says, "the mouth that lieth killeth the soul." Wisdom, i, 11.

II. *Calumny.* To injure much or take away any one's character by a lie is a mortal sin, and you must recall the lie. You might say you were mistaken, or the like.

III. *Detraction.* 1. To injure much or take away any one's character by making known to others something very bad about him, which is true, but which was not known before you made it known. It is a mortal sin, unless, you have some good reason for it, such as to ask advice, or tell his superiors that he may amend. 2. It is sinful to encourage others who detract; for example, by asking them questions—it is wrong to be pleased with hearing the detraction through curiosity, but worse if you are pleased at the injury done to a person's character. 3. Superiors must not let their inferiors detract—parents must hinder their children from detracting, and masters their servants. 4. If you commit the sin of detraction, you must repair it as well as you can.

IV. *Rash judgment* is a sin, and it would be very bad, if, for little or no reason, you firmly believe or say something very bad about a person.

V. *Unjust suspicions* are wrong, but they are seldom great sins, except they are quite wilful, and about some very bad thing indeed, such as murder. If there is some foundation for a suspicion, it is not a sin.

VI. *Telling a secret* is wrong, and is very bad if it is a great secret, and telling it does great harm or gives great sorrow. It would not be wrong to tell it to some one for a good reason, such as to ask advice.

VII. *To read letters or private papers* is wrong, and would be very bad if you think perhaps there is something in them the owner would be very sorry for you to know.

VIII. *To dishonor or insult* any one by striking him or calling him bad names, or the like, or to scoff and laugh at people because they are pious and good, is sinful.

IX. *Talebearing and whispering* is bad, especially if you do some great harm by it, such as making friends into enemies.

NINTH AND TENTH COMMANDMENTS.

Thou shalt not covet thy neighbor's wife, thou shalt not covet thy neighbor's goods— these commandments are examined in the sixth and seventh.

COMMANDMENTS OF THE CHURCH.

When you are seven years old, you must go to Confession every year, receive the Blessed Sacrament at least every Easter after your first Communion; you must not eat flesh-meat on days of abstinence unless you are ill, or can get nothing else, when you are twenty-one years old, and until you are sixty years of age, you must fast on fasting days, except you are weak, or have hard labor, or cannot get a full meal in the day. To break these Commandments of the Church is a mortal sin, unless you do it by mistake or forgetfulness, or have some lawful reason.*

Holidays of Obligation. New Year's Day, the Epiphany, the Annunciation of the blessed Virgin, the Ascension, Corpus Christi, SS. Peter and Paul, the Assumption, All Saints, Christmas Day.†

Fasting Days. Lent. All Fridays in *Advent.* Ember Days, that is, Wednesdays, Fridays and Saturdays in the first week of Lent, in Whitsun week, in the third week of September, and the third week of Advent. The *eves* of Whit-Sunday, of the Assumption, of All Saints, and of Christmas.

Days of abstinence from flesh-meat. Fridays and fasting days.

---

* It is a venial sin to break the fast by eating two ounces of food, or the abstinence by eating one-eighth of an ounce of flesh-meat.

† 1. In the dioceses of *New Orleans, St. Louis, Mobile, Dubuque, Little Rock,* and *Chicago,* the Circumcision, Epiphany, Annunciation, and Corpus Christi are not festivals of obligation.

2. In *Lower Canada,* all the above-mentioned festivals, together with the Feasts of SS. Peter and Paul, and the Immaculate Conception of the B. V. Mary, are holidays of obligation.

3. In *Upper Canada,* the Annunciation, Corpus Christi, and Assumption, are excepted. In the diocese of *Halifax,* the Feast of St. Peter and St. Paul is of obligation.

Duties of Particular States.

I. FATHERS AND MOTHERS.

1. *Love to Children.* Hatred, cruelty, beating them too much, or without cause, or in a passion, cursing them, too much love and fondness for any of them, letting them have their own way. 2. *Education in temporal things.* Care before and after their birth. It is a great sin to put brothers and sisters in the same bed; parents must send their children to good schools, and it is a great sin to send children to schools forbidden by bishops or parish priests, such as soupers' schools and Protestant schools. It is wrong to send children to beg instead of bringing them up to some trade or employment, it is a great sin to go away and leave children. Parents must not unjustly deprive some of their children of what they leave at their death. — 3. *Education in religion.* Care about their baptism in the Catholic church, and not delaying it, teaching them when very little, and making them say their prayers, when they are seven years old making them go to Confession, to Mass and Catechisms, or questions or class on Sundays and Holidays, not letting them say bad

words, or go into bad company, or keeping dangerous company with persons of the other sex, or play about the streets, correcting them for their faults, and not keeping in the house bad or irreligious books. It is a mortal sin for parents to hinder their children from following the call which God gives them to become nuns, etc., or without just reason to hinder their marriage, or force them to marry.

II. HUSBANDS AND WIVES.

People must take great care not to receive the sacrament of marriage with bad dispositions, for this is often the reason why many things happen afterwards to make them unhappy. *Invalid marriages.* Married persons cannot marry again unless they are quite sure their former wife or husband is dead. There can be no marriage betwixt blood relations as far as third cousins included, nor betwixt a man and the relations of his wife, as far as third cousins included, and the wife the same, the child baptized, and its parents cannot marry either the person who gave the baptism or the godfather and godmother. There can be no true marriage in Ireland and some other places, except the marriage is before the parish priest and two witnesses.— There can be no marriage betwixt a Catholic and a person not baptized. In all these and some other cases, there can be no true marriage without a dispensation. The church disapproves of marriages betwixt Catholics and those who are not Catholics. But if such a marriage takes place, it is necessary that the children should be baptized in the Catholic church, and brought up in the Catholic religion. It is a mortal sin to agree or consent that children shall be brought up in a false religion. *Love.* Hatred, cruelty, beating, giving their affections to another person. *Living together.* Leaving one another without just cause, the husband spending his evenings and his time in idle or bad company. *Family duties.* The husband must work for the support of his family, and not spend his wages in drinking, gambling and the like, or spend unjustly what belongs to the wife or children. The wife must take care of the household, and not spend too much money, and she must obey her husband. *Particular duties of marriage.* 1. A wrong or improper use of marriage. 2. The wife must obey her husband in the lawful duties of marriage. 3. Anything done before children which may scandalize them. Observe, it is a mortal sin to do anything for the purpose of destroying an infant unborn, even to save the mother's life.

III. MASTERS.

1. *In temporal things.* Ill treatment of servants, over working them, not giving them food enough, or paying their wages, breaking the agreement. 2. *In morals.* Keeping wicked sevants, especially if they have the care of children, allowing servants to use bad words, or go into bad company, asking servants to do anything forbidden by the law of God. 3. *Religion.* Masters must make their servants attend to their religious duties, and give them time for it.— When it is necessary that some one should stop at home during Mass, it would be wrong not to let the servants take turns to go to Mass. It is a sin to make servants do servile work on Sundays, without just reason.

ACT OF CONTRITION.

O'Reilly's Catechism.

O my God, I am heartily sorry for having offended Thee, because Thou art the chief good and worthy of all love; and everything that is sinful is displeasing to Thee. I am resolved, by the assistance of Thy divine grace to amend my life.

The Arch-Confraternity

FOR

THE RELIEF OF THE SOULS IN PURGATORY.

IN order to give a satisfactory idea of the object of this Arch-Confraternity, and to induce as many of the clergy and laity as possible, to become active promoters and members of the same, it will suffice to explain in simple language those truths of our holy Religion, upon which the Arch-Confraternity is based, and the practical exercise of which it professes to promote, together with a short statement of the spiritual advantages and privileges which it enjoys.

As to the truths of our holy Religion upon which the Arch-Confraternity is based, the Catholic Church teaches, that, after this life there is a middle state of suffering, to which the souls of those are doomed for a time, who, though in the state of grace and in friendship with God, yet have not fully satisfied the divine justice for the debt of temporal punishment due for their smaller sins, or for their more grievous sins, whose guilt has been pardoned in the sacrament of penance, or who die under the guilt of smaller sins or imperfections.

The Church further teaches that the living, by the offering of the Holy Sacrifice of the Mass, through prayers, alms-deeds, indulgences and other good works offered for the departed, can shorten their sufferings, ameliorate their condition and deliver their souls from their place of torment, and finally, that to assist these suffering souls is an act of charity most holy, most salutary and most pleasing to Almighty God.

THE BELIEF IN THIS DOCTRINE

Is much more ancient than Christianity itself. We have a most decisive proof of it from Scripture, among the people of God under the Old Law, in the time of Judas Machabeus, about two hundred years before Christ. For, upon the occasion of a great victory gained by that valiant general over the enemies of their religion, after the battle, in which many of his people had been slain. "Judas making a gathering, he sent twelve thousand drachms of silver to Jerusalem for a Sacrifice to be offered for the sins of the dead, thinking well and religiously concerning the resurrection, and because he considered that they who had fallen asleep in godliness, had great grace laid up for them. It is, therefore, a holy and wholesome thought to pray for the dead, that they may be loosed from sins."—(2 *Macca.* 12, 43.)

In this passage of Holy Writ, we have the following particulars established: 1. That the whole people of God, long before Christ, did hold it holy and laudable to pray for the dead. 2. That they believed this to be a means of benefitting the souls of the departed, by freeing them from their sins. 3. That the word of God declares this to be holy and wholesome. If, therefore, the souls of the faithful departed are benefitted by the prayers of those on earth, this establishes a Purgatory beyond all contradiction, since those in heaven are in need of no help, and those in hell can receive none.

Now, were this not sound doctrine our Saviour would certainly have reprehended the Jews for this practice, as upon all occasions He censured the Pharisees for the corruptions they had introduced, some of which were even of much less consequence than this. Nothing is more reasonable than this doctrine. The word of God assures us that none "but the clean of heart shall see God." (*Matt.* 5, 8.) When, therefore, a soul leaves this world in perfect charity with God, undefiled by the smallest stain of sin, doubtless that soul will immediately be admitted into the presence and enjoyment of God. If, on the contrary, a soul leaves this world in disgrace with God and dead to Him by the guilt of mortal sin, that soul will undoubtedly be condemned to the eternal torments of hell. But when a soul leaves this world in the friendship of God, yet sullied with the stains of venial sins and imperfections, it is plain that such a soul cannot in that state go to heaven where "nothing defiled can enter" (*Apoc.* 21, 27;) neither can it be condemned to hell, because it is in friendship with God and a living member of Jesus Christ. Therefore, there must be some middle state, where such a soul is confined for a time, till, by suffering, it is cleansed and purged from all these defilements of venial sins and rendered fit to be admitted to the presence and enjoyment of God. In this view our blessed Saviour says: "He that shall speak against the Holy Ghost it shall not be forgiven him, neither in this world nor in the world to come," (*Matt.* 12, 32,) in which words He plainly insinuates that some sins shall be forgiven in the world to come, otherwise it would be superfluous and trifling to say of the sin against the Holy Ghost, in particular, that it shall never be forgiven, either in this would or in the next. Now this truth necessarily establishes a middle state where some sins shall be forgiven. This place cannot be heaven, for no sin can enter there to be forgiven; it cannot be hell, for in hell there is no forgiveness; therefore, it must be in a middle place distinct from both. Neither can these sins which are forgiven in the next life be mortal sins, for a soul that dies in mortal sin is immediately condemned to hell, like the rich glutton in the gospel. Therefore, it is only venial sins from which the soul is purged in Purgatory. The true reason for this doctrine is found in God's infinite sanctity, justice and love.

His sanctity requires such an expiatory punishment, because every thing that is not good and perfect, is essentially opposed to His divine nature; hence He cannot admit into heaven to the contemplation of His divine essence, a soul that is still defiled with the least stain of sin.

His justice requires no less severity than His sanctity, because every sin is an offence and outrage to His divine majesty; for this reason He cannot help defending His divine right and absolute dominion over all creatures, by requiring full satisfaction from every soul that offends against His divine majesty.

Neither can His infinite love be less severe, because He wishes to see His elect quite pure, quite beautiful, quite perfect; for this reason He purifies them from every stain, as gold is refined in a furnace, until they are His true image and likeness, according to which He created the first man in sanctity and righteousness. He takes no pleasure in seeing these souls suffer, but wishes to render them capable and worthy of being united to Him as to their supreme happiness.

We may then, fairly conclude with St. Thomas Aquinas, that those who speak against this doctrine, "speak against God's justice," (*in* IV *Sent. dist.* LXV *qu.* 1,) Sanctity and love.

The holy fathers and doctors of the Church in speaking to the faithful upon

THE PAINS OF PURGATORY,

Could not find comparisons strong enough to describe the same.

The greatest of all is

THE PAIN OF LOSS,

Or the pain of the privation of the beatific vision of God. Love, says St. Thomas, is not satisfied with the mere feelings thereof; it longs for the possession of and union with the object beloved. Even in this world the greater part of men are not satisfied with the mere sentiments of their mutual charity and benevolence, but wish to see and converse with one another. Jacob, the aged Patriarch, would have died of grief, had his well beloved son Benjamin never returned from Egypt and so deprived him of his presence for ever.—When Joseph, to try his brothers, pretended to retain the youngest with him, Judas said: "Therefore, if I shall go to thy servant, our father, and the boy be wanting (whereas his life dependeth upon the life of him,) and he shall see that he is not with us, he will die, and thy servants shall bring down his grey hairs with sorrow into hell." (*Gen.* 44, 30)

If such be the grief of men, how great must be the longing of the souls departed to see and possess God, their supreme good and happiness. How great soever our natural or supernatural love for a human creature may be, it will never be free from imperfection, or able to satisfy the heart; nay, should it withdraw us from God, it will turn into a source of many troubles, so much so as even to lead us to hell. But God being the source of everything good, holy, sweet, and amiable, souls, by possessing Him, enjoy an everlasting happiness to the extent they are capable of. "Our heart," says St. Augustine, "is not at rest, O Lord, until it rests in Thee for Whom it was created." How much, then, must the souls in Purgatory yearn for this eternal rest in God, especially since they can no longer have the least desire for anything terrestrial! When in this life, they knew, to a certain degree, by the light of reason and of faith, how great God was in His divine attributes. How perfect soever this knowledge may have been, at all events, it was defective like everything else in this world.

But no sooner had they departed this life and appeared before Jesus Christ their eternal judge, than they knew Him in an incomparably more perfect manner, and this knowledge of God was at once so deeply and vividly impressed upon them, that from that very moment they were incapable of being occupied with anything else, their will being so violently impelled and drawn by this knowledge, as to find it utterly impossible to wish, to seek, and to love anything but God, the supreme Lord of all things visible and invisible. Being, however, at the same time, excluded from the enjoyment of their supreme good for the period of their expiation, they were at once enkindled with the consuming fire of an insatiable longing, which torments them more than the flames of Purgatory and which will not be quenched until they will have obtained the object of their longing. With the royal prophet they are unceasingly exclaiming: "As the heart panteth after the fountains of waters, so my soul panteth after Thee, O God. My soul hath thirsted after the strong living God; when shall I come and appear before the face of God? My tears have been my bread day and night, whilst it is said to me daily: Where is thy God." (*Ps.* 41, 1.)

After Anthony Corso, a Capuchin brother, a man of great piety and perfection, had departed this life, he appeared to one of his brethren in religion, asking him to recommend him to the charitable prayers of the community in order that he might receive relief in his pains, "for I do not know," said he, "how I can stand any longer the pain of being deprived of the sight of my God. I shall be the most unhappy of creatures as long as I must live in this state. Would to God all men would understand well what it is to be without God, in order that they might firmly resolve to suffer everything during their life on earth, rather than to expose themselves to the danger of being damned forever." (*Annal. P. P. Capuc. ad* 1548.)

Besides this pain of the privation of the sight of the divine essence, the souls in Purgatory have also to endure

THE PAINS OF THE SENSES,

The greatest of which is that of fire. According to the apostle St. Paul, "the fire shall try every man's work, of what sort it is. If any man's work burn, he shall suffer loss, but he himself shall be saved, yet so as by fire." (I. *Cor.* 3, 15.) "Stains of sin being taken away by fire," says St. Gregory of Nyssa, commenting on this passage, "a soul defiled by them, must of necessity enter into this fire and stay therein until it is cleansed from everything unjust, unclean and unholy." In what manner this is done we know not; but this matters little. "We know," says St. Gregory the Great, "that the rebellious angels are tormented in hell by a corporeal fire; in the same manner such a fire can torment the souls of the damned as well as those in Purgatory. It is just as easy for the justice of God to punish a spirit by means of corporeal substances, as it is for His omnipotence to vivify a body by means of a spirit." We may, then, easily imagine what these pains of the senses are, if we but think of the pains caused by our fire on earth whenever we come in contact with it. This, however, will give us but a faint idea of it, because the burning quality of the fire in Purgatory is far more intense and penetrating; for our terrestrial fire, as theologians say, was not created by God to torment men, but rather to benefit them, whilst the fire in Purgatory was created by God for no other purpose than to be an instrument of His justice.

St. Severinus, Archbishop of Cologne, was a prelate of great sanctity, so much so that God wrought through him many remarkable miracles. One day after his death, he was seen by a canon of the Cathedral, deeply plunged into the waters of the Rhine. Upon being asked why he was standing there so deep in the water, he who, on account of his sanctity ought to be reigning gloriously in heaven: "If you wish to know," he replied, "give me your hand that you may have an experimental proof of the pains which I have to suffer in Purgatory." Whereupon he took the canon by his hand and dipped it gently into the water, but so intense was its heat, that the flesh of the hand was immediately scalded as far as it had been dipped in. After this the saint went on to say: "This pain I suffer merely for having recited the canonical hours hurriedly and with wilful distraction." Then begging the canon to join with him in prayer for the cure of the hand and also for his own liberation from so great pains, he disappeared suddenly, leaving his friend miraculously cured and full of the fear of God's judgment. (*St. Pet. Dam. Epist.* 14, ed. *Desid. c.* VII.)

One day, when a certain man declared in the presence of St. Augustine, that he was not in the least afraid of Purgatory, provided he would escape hell, he was at once reprimanded by the saint for his inconsiderate language. "The fire of Purgatory," said the saint, "is but too often made light of, because, according to St. Paul, we are saved by fire, but this fire is more frightful than anything we can endure in this life."— St. Gregory the Great, St. Anselm, St. Bernard, and St. Thomas, teach the same, saying that no pain of this life can be compared to that of this fire. "Although this fire is not everlasting," says St. Augustine, (*Ps.* 37.) "yet it is of the most intense heat, and the agony from it surpasses in degree all that any one on this earth has ever suffered. Such pains have never been endured by the flesh of man although the holy martyrs suffered extraordinary tortures." St. Cyril, patriarch of Alexandria, (*cit. ab Horn conc.* 27,) says: "Every living soul should prefer to be tormented with all possible tortures even to the end of the world, rather than endure the pains of Purgatory for a single day." "The smallest spark of the Purgatorial fire," says St. Thomas Aquinas, "produces a suffering more intense than the most severe pains endured in this life." St. Bernard, (*tom.* 2. *serm.* 15,) comparing the fire of Purgatory to the fire of this world says: "The difference is as great as between natural and painted fire." "Nay, a soul in Purgatory," says St. Mary Magdalene de Pazzi, "if the transition were possible, would consider the hottest earthly fire, compared with that of Purgatory, a pleasure garden."

A religious of the Order of St. Dominic, when about to depart this life, most earnestly begged a priest to say Mass for the repose of his soul immediately after his death. The good religious had scarcely expired when the priest went to say mass for him with great fervor and devotion. He had hardly taken off the sacred vestments after mass, when the soul of his deceased friend appeared, rebuking him severely for the hardness of his heart in leaving him in the torments of Purgatory for thirty years. Quite astonished, the good priest exclaimed: "What! thirty years! an hour ago you were still alive!" "Learn then from this," said the deceased, "how excruciating are the pains of Purgatory, since one hour's stay therein appears as long as thirty years; and learn also how to sympathize with us and to obtain relief for us by your charitable prayers and other good works." (*Da Fusign. Tom.* IV.)

The souls in Purgatory, however, do not all experience the intensity of this fire in the same degree. Its expiating and purifying flames are proportioned to God's justice. The souls in Purgatory suffer in proportion to their indebtedness, and those powers of the soul which rendered themselves most guilty, suffer most the intensity of this fire; for "the Lord," says St. Paul, "renders to every man according to his works," (*Rom.* 2, 6,) and before this the Prophet had already declared: "O most Mighty, Great and Powerful, the Lord of Hosts is Thy name, great in counsel and incomprehensible in thought; Whose eyes are upon all the ways of the children of Abraham, to render unto every one according to his ways, and according to the fruit of his devices." (*Jerem.* 32, 18.) For this reason St. Bonaventure said: "They are tormented in proportion to the stains with which they departed this life, and which are to be cancelled by the flames of this fire." O how much grieved are these souls for the unlawful, miserable and transitory pleasures of this world, for the neglect of the mortification of their senses, and for the little fear they had of the judgments of God! Now they know what it is: "One fault more or less;" now they know that this is as much as one pain more or less in Purgatory.

In the life of Blessed Margaret Mary Alacoque, it is related that the soul of one of her departed sisters appeared to her and said: "There you are, lying comfortably in your bed; but think of the bed on which I am lying and suffering the most excruciating pains." "I saw this bed," says the saint, "and I still tremble in all my limbs at the mere thought of it. The upper and lower part of it was full of red-hot sharp iron points, penetrating into the flesh. She told me that she had to endure this pain for her carelessness in the observance of her rules. 'My heart is lacerated,' she added, 'and this is the hardest of my pains. I suffer it for those fault-finding and murmuring thoughts which I entertained in my heart against my superiors. My tongue is eaten up by moths, and tormented, on account of uncharitable words, and for having unnecessarily spoken in the time of silence. Would to God, that all souls consecrated to the service of the Lord, could see me in these frightful pains! Would to God I could show them what punishments are inflicted upon those who live negligently in their vocation! They would indeed, change their manner of living, observing most punctually the smallest point of their rules, and guarding against those faults for which I am now so much tormented.'"

"No defiled thing shall enter the heavenly city of Jerusalem," says St. John in the Apocalypse. How could it be possible that a soul spotted with the least stain of sin, could be united with God, Who is sanctity itself! Now, even the least venial sin, not duly expiated by penance, every little disorderly affection, every attachment to creatures, is such a spot or stain; hence, the soul cannot be admitted into heaven before it is cleansed from these faults by passing through the ordeal of the purgatorial fire. But it is indescribable how severe God is in purifying them from these stains. It is beyond all human conception, because we are never able to to comprehend the attributes of God, especially His sanctity and His justice. The judgments of God are very different from those of men. "My thoughts are not your thoughts," says the Lord through the Prophet Isaias, (55, 8,) "nor your ways My ways. For as the heavens are exalted above the earth, so are My ways exalted above your ways, and My thoughts above your thoughts."

We know that souls of great perfection were deprived of the beatific vision of God, for having committed little faults. We know this from many apparitions of the souls of the faithful departed, who have been saved and who praised the mercy of God, declaring, at the same time, that the judgments of the Lord were strict and terrible beyond description, and that mortals could never reflect upon and penetrate themselves enough with this truth. Although the judgments of God are so very strict, yet they are, at the same time, very just. "Unto whomsoever much is given, of him much shall be required." (*Luke* 12, 48.) The Lord requires a greater faithfulness in His service from such souls as have received His gifts in a larger measure. If they are careless in corresponding to them, the least unfaithfulness of theirs will be so much the more severely punished. Besides they must be purified in proportion to the degree of glory to be occupied by them in heaven.

It is related in the life of St. Mary Magdalene de Pazzi, that one day she saw the soul of one of her deceased sisters kneeling in adoration before the Blessed Sacrament in the Church, all wrapped up in a mantle of fire, in expiation of her neglecting to go to Holy Communion on one day, when she had her confessor's permission to communicate.

In a Convent of the Dominicans at Cologne, two brothers died on the same day. One of them was a priest and a professed member of the Order; the other was still a novice. On the third day after their death, the latter appeared to a brother of the Convent, telling him that he was already in heaven on account of the sincerity of his conversion and the zeal with which he had commenced the spiritual life. A few months after, the soul of the priest, also all radiant with heavenly glory, appeared to the same brother. On being asked by the brother why he had not been delivered from Purgatory with his brother, and what was the meaning of the insignia which he wore, he answered: "My too great familiarity with seculars, and my useless conversations with them, were the cause of my long stay in Purgatory. My glory in heaven however, is greater than that of my brother.—The sun on my breast signifies the purity of my intentions and of my zeal in working for the glory of God; the precious gems on my habit represent the souls which I have saved from eternal destruction, and the crown of gold on my head signifies the reward for my labor in the vineyard of the Lord." (*Vitæ P. P. Ord. Præd. P. V. c.* 5.)

It is a great relief for us in the sufferings of this life to know for certain that after a certain lapse of time they will be over. A sick person is easily resigned to his pains and readily takes bitter medicines, when he is told by the physician that in a few weeks his sickness will have left him. A prisoner will find the state of his captivity so much the more supportable, the more he is assured of his speedy deliverance. It is a consolation for him to count the days to the time of his delivery. But the uncertainty of the duration of our sufferings adds to their weight. In this state of uncertainty are the souls in Purgatory, at least, many of them. They are, it is true, sure of their salvation; but they are ignorant of the duration of their sufferings, unless it be revealed to them by God. Many, therefore, besides their other tortures are greatly tormented by the thought that the time of their deliverance may be still far off.

After St. Vincent Ferrer had learned the death of his sister Frances, he at once commenced to offer up many fervent prayers and works of penance for the repose of her soul. He also said thirty Masses for her, at the last of which it was revealed to him, that, had it not been for his prayers and good works, the soul of his sister would have suffered in Purgatory to the end of the world. (*Marches. Diar. Dom.* 5. *Apr.*)

The venerable Bede relates that it was revealed to Drithelm, a great servant of God, that the souls of those who spend their whole lives in the state of mortal sin and are converted only on their death-bed, are doomed to suffer the pains of Purgatory to the day of the last judgment. (*Hist. Anglic. L.* V. *c.* 13.)

In the life and revelations of St. Gertrude we read, that those who have committed many grievous sins and die without having done due penance, are not assisted by the ordinary suffrages of the Church until they are partly purified by divine justice. (*Chap.* XIV.)

Could the souls in Purgatory derive any spiritual advantage from their sufferings they would find them less difficult to bear. How great soever our pains and sufferings may be in this world, yet there is always in them a great consolation for us, knowing, as we do, that by bearing them patiently we gain new graces, accumulate greater merits, and advance in the love of God. For this reason many saints, instead of shrinking from sufferings, embraced them joyfully, and ardently wished for more. But what pains soever the souls in Purgatory may endure, they can no longer increase either in grace or in merit, for the time of merit has passed away with that of their trial. They can only suffer in expiation of their faults to satisfy the divine justice. Upon these souls is come that night of which Jesus Christ said: "The night cometh when no man can work," (*John* 9, 4;) that is to say when no one can merit any longer, every one remaining in that state of merit in which he left this world.

Moreover, in the sufferings of this life, we may derive consolation, relief, strength and courage, from fervent prayer to our Lord and to the Blessed Virgin Mary and other saints of heaven, as well as from the meditation of the passion of our Lord Jesus Christ and the reception of the sacraments. How often does not the Lord favor pious souls, in reward for their patience, faith, and confidence, with so abundant interior consolations, as make them forget all their sufferings. The souls in Purgatory, however, are altogether unable to do anything that might give them any relief in their sufferings. It might seem that they do not feel their pains so sharply on account of their resignation to God's holy will. But however great this resignation may be, it lessons not the pain of loss, or of their privation of the beatific vision of God. They know, it is true, that they are unfit to be admitted into heaven, not being sufficiently cleansed and purified; but, at the same time, they are aware that it is through their own fault they are condemned to this state of suffering; they see clearly how many admonitions, exhortations, inspirations and divine lights they have rejected, how many prayers, opportunities to receive the sacraments, and to profit by the other means of grace they have neglected through mere caprice, carelessness and indolence; they see their ingratitude towards God, and the deep wounds which they made in the Sacred Heart of Jesus Christ, and their grief and sorrow for this is a worm, never ceasing to gnaw them. The more they are penetrated with a sense of their unworthiness, the more painful for them is the thought of being themselves the cause of it. Now, these suffering souls are utterly unable to help themselves in their torments, and from many of the faithful in this world they have but little relief to expect, for the greater part of Christians will think of every thing else rather than of relieving the souls of their departed brethren by their prayers and charitable works. Hence, they exclaim day and night with the Prophet: "Woe is me that my sojourning is prolonged." (*Ps.* 119, 5.) "Woe to us that our stay in this country of exile, of sorrow and of torments is prolonged, and that we cannot see the end of our pains and sufferings. Lamenting, sobbing and sighing, shedding torrents of tears and crying aloud, we stretch out our hands for one to help and console us, and there is none to be found." A sick man weeps on his bed, and his friend consoles him. A baby cries in his cradle, and his mother at once caresses him; a beggar knocks at the door for an alms and receives it; a malefactor laments in his prison, and comfort is given him; a dog whines at the door, and is taken in; but we poor suffering souls cry day and night from the depths of the fire in Purgatory: "Have pity on me, have pity on me, at least you my friends, because the hand of the Lord hath touched me," (*Job* 19, 21,) and there is none to listen! O what great cruelty, my brethren!

But it seems to me that I hear these poor souls exclaim: "Priest of the Lord, speak no longer upon our sufferings and pitiable state. Let your description be ever so touching, it will not afford us the least relief. When a man has fallen into a fire you do not long consider his pains, but try to draw him out or quench the fire with water. This is a true compassion. Tell the people to do the same for us. Explain to them the second truth mentioned in the beginning of your discourse. Show them how

BY THE OFFERING OF THE HOLY SACRIFICE OF MASS, THROUGH PRAYERS, ALMS-DEEDS, INDULGENCES AND OTHER GOOD WORKS OFFERED UP FOR US TO THE ALMIGHTY, THEY WILL DIMINISH OUR SUFFERINGS, SHORTEN THEIR DURATION AND ACCELERATE OUR DELIVERANCE FROM OUR PLACE OF TORMENT."

Indeed, dear reader, it seems to be a kind of folly to reflect long upon the pains of the souls in Purgatory, in order to be induced to assist them. To know that they are tormented by fire, should be enough for us to come to their relief at once, especially as we can do it so easliy without much inconvenience to ourselves.

In the Catholic Church, or in the spiritual body of Christ, there exists a most intimate spiritual union of all the members of the militant, suffering and triumphant Church. The Lord has disposed all things in a manner most wise and most admirable. The severity of His judgments He has reserved to Himself, whilst He has left a portion of His mercy to His creatures, in order that thus the severity of His justice might yield again to the commiserations of His infinite charity. The members of the triumphant Church, or the blessed in heaven pray both for us and for the souls in Purgatory, no longer with sobs and tears, but with most fervent affections, proceeding from love most pure and most perfect

We on earth, as members of the militant Church, implore the saints in heaven to intercede for us, we pray for one another to be enabled to fight valiantly for the recovery of the heavenly Kingdom, and we can and we should also pray most fervently for the members of the suffering Church, that is to say, for the souls in Purgatory, especially for those to whom we are under greater obligations.— Although these souls cannot do anything for their own relief, yet they can pray to God for their benefactors, that He may reward them for their charity; and the Lord is pleased with their prayers, because He loves these souls, being, as they are, forever confirmed in His grace and love.

All this charity exercised by the members of this threefold church towards one another is a fruit of the Redemption, and is exercised in the name of Jesus Christ, their common head; and all the mercy which the Lord bestows on account of this charity, is bestowed in the name and by virtue of the infinite merits of His well-beloved Son. "For there is no other name under heaven given to men whereby we must be saved than the name of Jesus Christ," says St. Peter, the Apostle. (*Acts* 4, 12.)

Our holy mother, the Church, unceasingly implores the divine mercy for the suffering souls in Purgatory. She is a good, faithful and tender mother; she does not forget her children, though they have already departed this life; she desires nothing more earnestly than that they may soon be admitted into the presence of God. It is, above all, the holy sacrifice of Mass which she offers up for them, and which affords them great assistance, because in holy Mass, our Saviour Jesus Christ offers Himself to His heavenly Father in atonement for the sins of the world. This great and most holy sacrifice has of itself an infinite value, and, considered in itself, a single Mass would be sufficient to free all the poor souls from Purgatory; yet the distribution of its fruits is limited because this depends on the acceptance of God, and on the dispositions and the condition in which the souls in Purgatory are found. It is for this very reason that the holy sacrifice of Mass may be repeatedly offered for the poor souls in general, as well as for particular individuals. In those Masses which are offered for the living, the Church, in the canon of the Mass, likewise commemorates the souls of the faithful departed, and also in the divine office which each priest is obliged to recite daily, she closes the different portions of it with the words: "*Fidelium animæ per misericordiam Dei requiescant in pace.*" "May the souls of the faithful departed, through the mercy of God, rest in peace."

The Church has, furthermore, a particular office for the dead, which is recited in choir every month. She has also set aside one day of the year for the commemoration of all the faithful departed. Finally, she has granted numerous indulgences which may be applied to the poor souls, and she exhorts all the faithful to make use of these treasures of grace for the benefit of the suffering souls.

We read in the Acts of the Apostles that the faithful prayed unceasingly when St. Peter was imprisoned, and that an angel appeared, who broke his chains and released him. In like manner, the angels at the prayers of the Church, descend into Purgatory in order to liberate the poor souls from their captivity. O how good, how beautiful, how consoling it is to be a child of our holy Church.

However, the most efficacious of all means which the Church has in her power to obtain relief for the souls in Purgatory, is undoubtedly the holy sacrifice of Mass. This is the common doctrine of the Fathers. St. Jerome says, that by every Mass, not one only, but several souls, are delivered from Purgatory, and (*Apud Bern. de Busto, Serm. 3 de missa,*) he is of opinion that the soul for which the priest says Mass, suffers no pain at all while the holy sacrifice lasts. The Fathers of the Council of Trent declare, that by the sacrifice of the Mass the souls in Purgatory are most efficaciously relieved.— This was clearly the belief of St. Monica, the mother of St. Augustine, when she replied, on her death-bed, to her son's enquiries concerning her place of burial. "Bury me," said she, "wherever you please; all that I ask of you, is to remember me at the altar of the Lord."

In the time of St. Bernard, a monk of Clairvaux appeared after his death to his brethren in religion, to thank them for having delivered him from Purgatory. On being asked what had most contributed to free him from his torments, he led the enquirer to the Church, where a priest was saying Mass. "Look," said he, "this is the means by which my deliverance has been effected; this is the power of God's mercy; this is the salutary sacrifice which takes away the sins of the world." Indeed, so great is the efficacy of this sacrifice to obtain relief for the souls in Purgatory, that the application of all the good works which have been performed from the beginning of the world, would not afford so much assistance to one of these souls, as would be imparted by a single Mass. I will illustrate this by an example drawn from the life of St. Dominic. The blessed Henry Suso made an agreement with one of his brethren in religion, that as soon as either of them died, the survivor should say two Masses every week for one year, for the repose of his soul. It came to pass that the religious with whom Henry had made this contract, died first. Henry prayed every day for his deliverance from Purgatory, but forgot to say the Masses which he had promised. Whereupon the deceased religious appeared to him with a sad countenance, and sharply rebuked him for his unfaithfulness to his engagement. Henry excused himself by saying that he had often prayed for him with great fervor and had even offered up for him many penitential works. "O brother," exclaimed the soul, "blood, blood is necessary to give me some relief and refreshment in my excruciating torments. Your penitential works, severe as they are, cannot deliver me. Nothing can do this but the blood of Jesus Christ, which is offered up in the sacrifice of the Mass. Masses, Masses, these are what I need!"

We read of St. Gregory, the Great, that he had Mass said for thirty days in succession for a deceased monk named Justin, who, according to a revelation, was detained in Purgatory for having kept some money without permission. On the last day Justin appeared to his brother telling him that he now was released from Purgatory, after enduring intense torments.—(*Life of St. Gertrude, chap.* XVI.)

"My children," said the Curé of d'Ars one day, "you remember the story I have told you of that holy priest who was praying for his friend; God had, it appears, made known to him, that he was in Purgatory; it came into his mind that he could do nothing better than to offer the holy sacrifice of Mass for his soul. When he came to the moment of consecration, he took the sacred host in his hands and said: 'O holy and eternal Father, let us make an exchange. Thou hast the soul of my friend who is in Purgatory, and I have the body of Thy Son, Who is in my hands; well, do Thou deliver my friend, and I offer Thee Thy Son, with all the merits of His death and passion.' In fact, at the moment of the elevation, he saw the soul of his friend rising to heaven, all radiant with glory. Well, my children, when we want to obtain anything from the good God, let us do the same, after consecration, let us offer Him

His well beloved Son, with all the merits of His death and His passion He will not be able to refuse us anything."—(*Spirit of Curé d'Ars.*)

A remarkable example of the efficacy of the public prayers of the Church for the relief of the souls in Purgatory is also related by Genandius. (*Def. Conc. Flor. L.* III.)

The Greek Emperor Theophilus, was, after his death condemned to the pains of Purgatory, because he had been unable to perform the penances which towards the end of his life he had wished to perform. His wife, the pious Empress Theodora, was not satisfied with pouring forth fervent prayers and sighs for the repose of his soul, but she also had prayers and Masses said in all the convents of the city of Constantinople. Besides this she besought the Patriarch, St. Methodius, that, for this end he would order prayers to be said by both the clergy and the people of the city. Divine mercy could not resist so many fervent prayers. On a certain day when public prayers were again offered up in the church of St. Sophia, an angel appeared to St. Methodius and said to him: "Thy prayers, O Bishop, have been heard, and Theophilus has obtained pardon." Theodora, the Empress, had at the same time, a vision in which our Lord Himself announced to her that her husband had been delivered from Purgatory. "For your sake," He said, "and on account of the prayers of the priests, I pardon your husband."

But not only the holy sacrifice of Mass and other public prayers of the Church, but also the prayers and pious exercises performed by the faithful in private are of great benefit to the suffering souls, because they are performed by the faithful as living members of the Church according to her doctrines and exhortations and in her spirit. It is, however, to be observed that this efficacy of private prayers and devotions is proportioned to the zeal, fervor and charity with which they are performed. This was one day expressly declared by our Lord to St. Gertrude when asking Him: "How many souls were delivered from Purgatory by her and her sisters' prayers." "The number," replied our Lord, "is proportioned to the zeal and fervor of those who pray for them." He added: "My love urges me to release a great number of souls for the prayers of each religious and at each verse of the psalms which they recite, I release many."—(*Chap.* XVI.) Praying one day for a lay brother lately deceased, St. Gertrude saw his soul under a hideous form as if consuming by a devouring fire, full of excessive anguish and bent down by an overpowering weight in punishment for having failed in holy obedience, in elevating his soul to heavenly things and in acquiring temporal goods without the permission of his superiors and even concealing what he thus acquired. When reading the psalms and keeping vigil, she asked our Lord what remedy could be applied to this soul. He replied: "Although the souls of the departed are much benefitted by these vigils and other prayers, nevertheless a few words, said with affection and devotion, are of far more value to them." And this may be easily explained by a familiar comparison; for it is much easier to wash away the stains of mud or dirt from the hands by rubbing them quickly in a little warm water, than by pouring a quantity of cold water on them without using any friction; thus, a single word, said with fervor and devotion, for the souls of the departed, is of far more efficacy than many vigils and prayers offered coldly and performed negligently.

After St. Gertrude had prayed for a long time for a certain deceased person who had led a sinful life for a considerable time, he appeared to her under a horrible form, as if blackened by fire and contorted with pain, each member suffering for the sins to which it had been accessory. St. Gertrude was given to understand that a soul like this cannot avail itself of the prayers of the faithful until it has been partly purified by divine justice. She then inquired of our Lord what work or prayers would most easily obtain mercy from Him for those sinners who have died in a state of grace, so that they might be delivered from this terrible impediment which prevents them from obtaining the benefit of the Church's prayers. Our Lord replied: "The only way to obtain such a favor is divine love; neither prayers nor any other labors will avail without this, and it must be such a love as you now have for me; and as no one can have this grace unless I bestow it, so also no one can obtain these advantages after death unless I have prepared him for it by some special grace during life.— Know, however, that the prayers and labors of the faithful relieve these souls gradually from this heavy burden and that they are delivered sooner or later according to the fervor and pure intentions of those who thus serve them, and according to the merit which they have acquired for themselves when in this life." *Life, chap.* XIV.

When Mass was offered for the deceased Brother Hermann, his soul appeared to Saint Gertrude, all radiant with light and transported with joy. Then Gertrude said to our Lord: "Is this soul now entirely freed from its sufferings?" Our Lord answered: "He is already free from much suffering, and no human being can form an idea of his glory; but he is not yet so perfectly purified as to be worthy to enjoy My presence, though he is approaching nearer and nearer to this purity by the prayers which are offered for him and is more and more consoled and relieved:" *Life, chap.* X.

The merits of our Lord and Saviour Jesus Christ are an infinite treasure, by which the contrite sinner obtains not only the remission of his sins, but also of the temporal punishment which he has deserved for them. To this treasure we must add all the merits of the most pure and most holy Virgin, the mother of our Saviour, which, though not infinite as those of her divine Son, still surpass the reach of the human understanding. Besides these, there are the merits of the holy apostles and martyrs, and of so many other saints, who, during their lives, have done more penance and performed more meritorious works, than was necessary for the atonement of their own transgressions. Now all this treasure has by our Lord been confided to His holy Church, and the Church, under certain conditions, opens this treasure to all the faithful, that thereby they may obtain the remission of the temporal punishment, both for themselves and for the souls of the faithful departed.

Still there is an essential difference between indulgences for the living and indulgences for the dead. The former are granted by the Church in virtue of the power and jurisdiction which she holds over all faithful living on this earth. These, therefore, surely have their effect in the manner expressed by the Church, if the faithful punctually fulfil the prescribed conditions. The latter, on the contrary, rest on intercession, because the Church has no jurisdiction over the dead. She can, therefore, only beg Almighty God that He would deign to accept these indulgences and apply them to the poor souls for whom they have been offered. But we cannot know to what extent they are received by Almighty God. This depends not only on the dispositions of the souls, but also on secret circumstances and causes, known to God alone; for His decrees are inscrutable, and human reason will never discover the manner in which God's mercy and justice are reconciled. This should, however, not deter us from gaining indulgences for the poor souls, for it is certain that no indulgence will be lost if it is duly applied, and that by them they obtain, if not entire deliverance, at least consolation and relief, or an abbreviation of their suffering.

A very pious nun had just died in the Convent in which St. Mary Magdalene de Pazzi lived. Whilst her corpse was exposed in the Church, the saint lovingly looked upon it and prayed fervently that the soul of her sister might soon enter eternal rest. Whilst she was thus rapt in prayer, her sister appeared to her, surrounded with great splendor and radiance, in the act of ascending into heaven. The saint, on seeing this, could not refrain from calling out to her: "Farewell, dear sister! When you meet your heavenly Spouse, remember us who are still sighing for Him in this vale of tears!" At these words our Lord Himself appeared and revealed to her that this sister had entered heaven so soon, on account of the indulgences gained for her. *Vita S. Magd. de Pazzi, L I, c. 39.*

The blessed Mary Lataste delivered from Purgatory the soul of a pious woman, named Jane, who had died a short time previous, merely by saying for her, after holy Communion, the prayer, "Look down upon me, good and gentle Jesus," (p. 32;) together with the prayers for the wants of the Holy Church. She offered up for her also the plenary indulgence attached to these prayers; whereupon the soul of the deceased appeared to her and thanked her for her charity.—(*Cf. La vie et les œuvres de Marie Lataste.*)

Among the many good works, which, besides prayer and other acts of devotion, we can offer up for the poor souls, we may especially reckon alms-deeds; for, since this is a work of mercy, it is more especially apt to obtain mercy for the poor souls. But not the rich alone can give alms, but the poor also, since it does not so much depend on the greatness of the gift. Of the poor widow who gave but one penny, our Lord said, that she had given more than all the rich who had offered gold and silver, because these offered only of their abundance, whilst the poor widow who gave what she saved from her daily sustenance. The poor are in general more charitable than the rich. It is true, there are many wealthy persons who distribute, with a generous heart, many and great alms; yet the poor are in general more inclined to mercy, because from their own experience they know what it is to be in want, and also because they need less and are not so much attached to temporal goods. Even if one is so poor as to be obliged to live on alms, still he will always find an opportunity to perform charitable services to his neighbor; and we know from the Gospel, that even a drink of cold water given for God's sake, will not remain unrewarded.

We, too, shall one day belong to the number of those souls who are justly called *poor*, because no one is poorer than they. In this life, the poorest beggar can, at least, expose his wants to others, and beg them for an alms; but in general, the poor souls cannot even do this, and those cases in which they were permitted to come and ask assistance from the living, are but exceptions. What great consolation will it not afford us, if the poor, whom in this world we have supported by our alms, and the poor souls for whom we have offered up these works of mercy, will assist us by their prayers. It is for this reason that the book of Ecclesiasticus says: "Do good to thy friend before thou die: and according to thy ability, stretching out thy hand give to the poor."—(*Eccl.* 14, 13.)

A pious priest, attending the Church of St. Cecilia, in Rome, had the following vision. He saw the Queen of heaven sitting on a splendid throne surrounded by the holy virgins, St. Cecilia, St. Agnes and St. Agatha, together with a great number of angels. He was quite enraptured by the charms and the majesty of the most holy virgin and the splendor of the vision; when suddenly, he beheld a poor woman wearing a very rich fur, approaching the throne of the blessed Virgin and asking mercy for a certain deceased patrician, whose name was John, and whose soul was suffering great torments in Purgatory. Thrice did she thus repeat her petition without receiving a reply. Finally, she added: "Remember, O glorious Virgin and mother of my Lord, that I was standing at the door of a Church dedicated to thy name, shivering with cold; and when I asked this John for an alms for the love of thee, he took off this fur with which he was clothed, and presented it to me out of devotion and love for thee." The mother of mercy, moved by these words, and seeing the saints also join their prayers to those of the poor woman, ordered John to come forth. He came, laden with heavy chains; but Mary, with a kind and tender look, ordered the chains to be removed. The priest then saw how his soul, freed from all sufferings ascended into heaven with the other saints. He understood from this vision, that the grateful and persevering prayers of the poor woman, had obtained the deliverance of the patrician from Purgatory.

The venerable servant of God, Father Clement Hoffbauer, of the Congregation of the Most Holy Redeemer, who died in Vienna in the year 1820, and whose cause of beatification has already been introduced, once assisted a man of distinction for death. A short time afterwards, the same man appeared to his wife in a dream, in a very pitable condition, his clothes in rags, and quite haggard and shivering with cold. He begged her to have pity on him, because he could scarcely endure the extreme hunger and cold which he suffered. His wife went without delay to Father Hoffbauer, related her dream and asked his advice on this point. The confessor, enlightened by God, immediately understood what this dream meant, and what kind of assistance was especially needed and asked for by this poor soul. He accordingly advised her to clothe a poor beggar. The woman followed the advice, and, soon after, her husband again appeared to her, dressed in a white garment and his countenance beaming with joy, thanking her for the help which she had afforded him.

We can assist the poor souls not only by prayers, devotions, exterior works of penance, alms-deeds, and other works of charity, but we can also aid them by interior mortifications.— Everything which appears to us difficult and which costs us a sacrifice, the pains of sickness, and all the sufferings and troubles of this life, may be offered up for these poor souls. We may, indeed, pray to God that He would deign to receive these mortifications and sufferings, first and above all as a penance and in atonement for our own sins; but this in no way prevents us from uniting with this, the intention of applying all the merit which we may gain, to the poor souls. The only coin which is of value before God, and which is received in payment for our own debts and for the debts of others, is charity and good intention. How brilliant soever some works may appear in the eyes of the world, if this stamp of charity and good intention is wanting to them, they are before God nothing more than a valueless counterfeit. But, on the contrary, wheresoever this stamp is found the smallest action becomes precious and meritorious in the eyes of God. Consequently, all without exception, learned and unlearned, rich and poor, sick and healthy, can aid the poor souls with this coin. And how many opportunities do we not find in the course of each day! If, in order to aid the poor souls we were obliged to make a pilgrimage to the Holy Land, to fast on bread and water, to perform severe and extraordinary penances, the greater part of the faithful would have reason for excuse. They might justly object that these things surpasses their strength, and that they are unable to perform them. But since it is so very easy to afford help to the poor souls, who will be able to find an excuse? Nothing more is required than a lively faith and an ardent charity, a frequent remembrance of the four last things, and of the unspeakable sufferings of the poor souls, together with a heartfelt compassion for them. With these sentiments in our hearts, we shall soon discover many means and ways of assisting them. Those, of course, who want one or the other of these sentiments, will never find out any means, because they do not find time even for seriously providing for the salvation of their own soul, much less for those of others.

As St. Gertrude prayed for the repose of the soul of brother Hermann, a lay brother lately deceased, he appeared to her in a state of great suffering. "This soul," said our Lord to the saint, "has been prevented from being relieved by your prayers as speedily as he would otherwise have been, on account of his obstinacy in following his own will, and his disinclination to submit to the will of others."

When St. Gertrude asked this soul for what fault he had to suffer most, he replied: "For self-will and self-opiniatedness; for when I did any kindness for others, I would not do as they wished, but as I wished myself; and so much do I suffer for this, that if the mental agonies of all mankind were united in one person, he would not endure more than I do at present." And when St. Gertrude recited the Our Father for this soul, she observed, to her extreme surprise, that his sufferings appeared greatly increased when she repeated the words: "Forgive us our trespasses, as we forgive those who trespass against us." As she inquired the reason of this suffering, he replied: "When I was in the world, I offended God frequently by my unwillingness to forgive those who injured me in any way; and even when I had forgiven them, I showed my resentment by a grave manner when I met them, and I suffer for this whenever these words are repeated for me." "And what remedy," asked St. Gertrude, "will be most efficacious for you?" He answered: "To perform acts of the contrary virtue, and to avoid committing the same fault."—(*Life, chap.* X.)

The only son of a rich widow of Bologna had been murdered by a stranger. The culprit fell into her hands, but the pious widow was far from taking revenge by delivering him up to the hands of justice. She thought of the infinite love of our Saviour when He died for us upon the cross, and how He prayed for His executioners when dying. She, therefore, thought that she could in no way honor the memory of her dear son better, and that she could do nothing more efficient for the repose of his soul, than by granting pardon to the culprit, by protecting him and by even adopting him as her son and heir to all her riches. This heroic self-denial, and the sacrifice which she thereby offered to our Lord in memory of His bitter passion, was so pleasing to God, that in reward thereof, He remitted to her son all the pains of Purgatory. The happy son then appeared to his mother in a glorified state, at the very moment when he was entering heaven. He thanked her for having thus delivered him from the sufferings of Purgatory much sooner than any other good work could have effected it.

The relief which we afford the poor souls of Purgatory, is reckoned among the works of mercy. Now, it can easily be proved that in many respects it is far superior to other similar works. To feed the hungry, clothe the indigent, visit and attend the sick, are all very good, praiseworthy and meritorious acts, still they are but corporal works of mercy, and consequently, mercy shown to the dead is superior to them, because it is shown to the soul and not to the body. Besides this, our natural feelings are always moved to compassion at the sight of human misery; but the sufferings of the poor souls we cannot see with the eyes of the body, but we must look at them with the eyes of faith, and consequently, our compassion is purer, more spiritual and more meritorious. Finally, well-ordered charity looks upon those sufferers in preference to others, who endure most and who are most in want of assistance: now, who suffers more and is in greater need of assistance, than the poor souls in Purgatory? There are many spiritual works of mercy, such as converting sinners, instructing the ignorant, removing an occasion of sin, &c., which are undoubtedly very good, and the best of the kind; still, we may say, that in many cases the spiritual want of the living is entirely voluntary, because they have sufficient means to free themselves from this want. But the poor souls are, on the contrary, thrown entirely upon the mercy of others, because their condition is purely passive, excluding all action. We should then relieve the wants both of the living and the dead. Whenever we have an opportunity, we should perform both spiritual and corporal acts of mercy for the living; but we should also at all times practise charity towards the dead, and in case we wish to unite both, we need only make the intention of applying the merit of our good works to the suffering souls in Purgatory. The holy apostle St. James says: "My brethren, if any one of you shall err from the truth, and any one convert him: he must know that he who causeth a sinner to convert from the error of his way, shall save his soul from death, and shall cover a multitude of sins." (*St. James*, 5, 19, 20.) Whosoever, therefore, converts a sinner and offers up the merit of his exertions for the poor souls, at the same time saves a soul from eternal death and procures, or at least hastens the admission of one or more poor souls into eternal life.

Two brothers of the Order of Friars-Preachers were one day conversing on the question—which act of charity was the greater, to labor for the conversion of sinners, or to aid the poor souls in Purgatory. The one whose name was Bertrand, obstinately maintained the former opinion, and that in a manner which proved that he cared little for charity towards the poor souls. The other brother, whose name was Benedict, endeavored by all possible reasons to overcome this obstinacy by urging that the poor souls loved God and were loved by Him; whilst, on the contrary, sinners hate God and are hated by Him; that they remain voluntarily in this unhappy state, whilst the poor souls are powerless to free themselves; that, further, our endeavors to help them never remain fruitless, and that this act of charity could be performed at all times and in all circumstances, &c., &c. Still, in spite of all his endeavors to change the mind of the brother, he did not succeed, because Bertrand's heart lacked all compassion for the poor souls. A short time afterwards a soul from Purgatory appeared to this brother during the night, covered with an enormous weight, which it placed for an instant upon his shoulders, in order that he might learn from experience what sufferings the poor souls endure in Purgatory and how much they deserve our compassion.— The good brother now saw his error, and from that moment that zealous laborer for the salvation of souls became also a fervent intercessor for the poor souls in Purgatory, thus gaining a two-fold measure of graces and merits.

There are, perhaps, few barbarous nations in such a savage state as not to honor their dead. The pagans of old erected to their dead splendid mausoleums, statutes and pyramids, at an enormous expense; nay, they even went so far in their folly as sometimes to place them among their gods. We Christians, enlightened by the light of faith, know better in what manner we should honor the memory of the dead, and show them our love. We may, and even should, besides the celebration of their obsequies according to their rank in life, raise to them Christian monuments and tombstones: still the main point always is the alleviation of their sufferings and their deliverance from Purgatory.— For, of what use to a soul are all the marks of honor shown it on earth, while it is meanwhile languishing in the consuming flames of Purgatory?

How painful will it not be to many a soul honored and distinguished on earth, to see its surviving friends concerned about the exterior display alone, and not even thinking of reciting one Our Father for its repose!

Friends may, besides the customary suffrages, render a departed soul a great act of charity by fulfilling obligations which it neglected to fulfil in life and failed to discharge at the hour of death, either for want of time or opportunity: viz., by cancelling an act of injustice which the deceased person had committed, by making restitution for damages caused by him, by removing a scandal to which he had given rise, and by instantly paying the debts left unpaid. Although by this supplementary satisfaction the indebtedness as well as the well-deserved punishment of such a soul, cannot be removed, as the Venerable Cardinal Bellarmine teaches, the pains which its friends undergo, or the sacrifices which they offer are accepted by the Divine Justice in expiation of its faults.

Pope Benedict XIII. relates in one of his works the following occurrence, which he had heard from a lay-brother of the Dominican Order. The father of this brother had been accustomed to have his horses shod by a certain blacksmith for several years; he failed, however, from culpable neglect to remunerate him for his services. After his death, he appeared to a faithful servant, charging him to go to his wife and beg her to discharge this debt, on account of which he was suffering great pains in Purgatory. His wife immediately hastened to discharge not only this, but all other debts of her husband; after which he appeared to her surrounded with flames and bound from head to foot with strong cords: "For God's sake," he exclaimed, "loosen these ropes."— Having done so instantly, her husband thanked her for having complied with his request, and told her that he had been obliged to suffer this torment until the debts were paid.

If it be an obligation for us to assist the poor souls, especially those who were closely connected with us by the ties of blood, or for other reasons, this duty is doubly binding upon those to whom the departed bequeathed their earthly possessions. They ought then, from a sense of gratitude, to assist their deceased benefactors. But, if the deceased in their last will have left legacies for Holy Masses, or other pious works to be offered for the repose of their souls, then it is not only a duty of charity, but an obligation of the strictest justice for their heirs and executors to execute their last will most punctually and without delay. Whoever neglects this duty is guilty of a sacrilegious injustice, and incurs excommunication, according to the decrees of the Church; and although he may afterwards comply with his duty, yet he will be severely punished by God for his neglect. Every practical and conscientious Christian, bearing love towards the poor souls in Purgatory, will not only abhor and detest such a crime, but even, if the deceased have left no pious legacies, will at least, have Masses said for the repose of their souls, because by merely mourning for them, from which they draw no profit, he will not fulfil the duty of gratitude.

Those who give themselves up to immoderate grief at the loss of beloved friends, should bear this in mind also. Instead of injuring their health by a grief which is of no avail to the deceased, they should endeavor to deliver their souls from Purgatory by Masses, prayers and good works; nay, the very thought that they thus render to the souls of their beloved friends the greatest possible act of charity, will console them and mitigate their sorrow. For this reason St. Paul exhorts the Thessalonians not to be afflicted on account of the departed after the manner of heathens who have no hope.— (*Thess* 4, 12.)

Thomas Cantipratensis relates that a celebrated warrior of the army of Charlemagne, left, on his death-bed, his charger, together with saddle and harness, to a nephew, charging him to sell it and apply the proceeds for Masses and pious works, to be offered up for the repose of his soul. His nephew, however, kept the horse for his own use for a long time. But how great was his fright when, one night, the voice of his deceased uncle aroused him from sleep, reproaching him most bitterly for his impiety. "Why," said he, "did you not execute my order? Why did you break your word? You are the cause of my having had to suffer great and severe pains in Purgatory, and which I should still be suffering, had not the mercy of God remitted part of my temporal punishments. I am now going to enjoy the delights of Paradise. But you must know that in punishment for your faithlessness, a premature death is awaiting you, and after death, a peculiar chastisement, for you will have to discharge in Purgatory both your own indebtedness to the Divine Justice, and that part of mine which it was pleased to remit." The youth was horror-struck at these words. He repented of his sin, confessed it, and hastily made all possible amends for it; by this means he escaped the eternal, but not the temporal punishment, for he was soon after carried off by a sudden death. (*L.* II. *Apum* 53, 25.)

The same Thomas Cantipratensis relates also of a certain mother, that she wept day and night over the death of her darling son, so much so that she forgot to assist his soul in Purgatory. To convince her of her folly, God one day permitted her to be rapt in spirit and see a long procession of youths hastening towards a city of indescribable beauty. Having looked for her son in vain for some time, she at last discovered him walking slowly along at the end of the procession. At once her son turned towards her and said: "Ah, mother, put an end to your useless tears, and if you truly love me, offer up for my soul, Masses, prayers, almsdeeds, and such like good works." Then he disappeared, and his mother, instead of any longer wasting her strength by foolish grief, began henceforth to give her son proofs of a true Christian and motherly love, by complying with his request. (*L. II. Appar.* 5, 17.)

Having thus far shown how we should aid the souls in Purgatory, I will now proceed to the explanation of the third truth, namely,

THAT TO COME TO THE ASSISTANCE OF THE SUFFERING SOULS IN PURGATORY IS A WORK MOST HOLY, MOST PLEASING TO THE ALMIGHTY AND HIS SAINTS, AND MOST SALUTARY TO OURSELVES.

First, it is a most holy work, for it is the fruit of great faith, firm hope, and ardent charity. Although each prayer and good work of ours may be considered a fruit of these three theological virtues, if practised with a good intention and in the spirit of the Church, yet they are so in a more special manner if performed for the relief of the souls in Purgatory. Above all, they are the fruit of faith, because by these good works offered up for the faithful departed, we profess, in a more than common manner, our faith in God's sanctity, justice, and mercy, showing as we do by deed, our heartfelt sympathy for these souls, though we do not see their sufferings. Moreover, these good works are the fruit of a firm hope, because we would not perform them were it not for the great confidence which we place in the infinite merits of our Saviour Jesus Christ and in His promises that we trust our prayers and good works will be accepted by God in behalf of the souls in purgatory.— Finally, our prayers and good works for these souls are also the fruit of charity towards God and our neighbor, because we accelerate their deliverance out of Purgatory and their admission to the beatific vision of God, in order that thus they may be enabled to love, bless and glorify Him in a most perfect manner.

Besides these three theological virtues, we also practise many other moral virtues by assisting the souls in Purgatory. Hence, should we not be moved by natural compassion to aid them, the great spiritual profit derived from such charitable assistance, should be a strong inducement for us to give it. Indeed, experience teaches that those who are in the habit of practising great charity towards the souls in Purgatory, always live in the holy fear and love of God, are addicted to prayer to the frequent reception of the sacraments, and to all kinds of good works. A tree is known by its fruit, says our Lord in the gospel. Charity shown to the souls in Purgatory must then be something very holy, since it produces such good and holy fruits.

It is related in the life of the Venerable Mary of Antigua that a deceased sister of her convent appeared to her and said: "Why do you not make the Stations of the Way of the Cross for me?" Whilst the servant of the Lord felt surprised and astonished at these words, Jesus Christ Himself spoke to her thus: "The exercise of the Stations is of the greatest advantage to the souls in Purgatory, so much so that this soul has been permitted by Me to ask of you its performance in behalf of them all. Your frequent performance of this exercise to procure relief for these souls, has induced them to hold intercourse with you, and you shall have them for so many intercessors and protectors before My justice. Tell your sisters to rejoice at these treasures and the splendid capital which they have in them, that they may grow rich upon it."

The holy fruits growing on the tree of charity towards the souls in Purgatory, will appear still more precious by the consideration of the great pleasure which they cause to our Lord, to the Blessed Virgin, His glorious mother, and to all the saints of heaven.

It must be a thought no less sublime than consoling for us, that by our prayers for these suffering souls we imitate, nay in some manner complete the work of redemption. By His death on the cross, Jesus Christ delivered us from eternal damnation and restored to us our right to life everlasting; but by offering up our prayers and good works for the souls in Purgatory we free them from the temporal punishment still due for their indebtedness to the divine justice, thus enabling them to enter into the posession of their heavenly inheritance. Jesus Christ stands not in need of our co-operation, it is true to complete the redemption of His elect; but He wishes us to co-operate towards it for our own spiritual good and that of these suffering souls; He wishes that by our charity and holy fervor, His justice may be sooner appeased, and that He may be enabled to display greater mercy towards His captive spouses, and that we may have an opportunity to increase in grace and merits. In His farewell discourse to His disciples He said: "Greater love than this no man hath, that a man lay down his life for his friends." (*John* 15, 13.) What He taught in these words, He soon afterwards accomplished by dying for us on the cross in order to deliver us from eternal death. He desires that His followers should imitate Him, in some degree; if not by the sacrifice of their lives, at least, by liberating the souls of their deceased brethern from the pains of Purgatory, through pious aspirations, fervent prayers, and other good works.

After the Venerable Sister Catherine Paluzzi, had for a long time, and with the utmost fervor offered up prayers and pious works for the soul of her father, she, at last, gave herself up to the firm hope that he was already enjoying Paradise. But how great was her consternation and grief, when our Lord, in company with St. Catherine, her patroness, led her one day in spirit to Purgatory, where she beheld her father in an abyss of torments imploring her assistance. Melting into tears, she cast herself at the feet of her heavenly spouse, begging Him, through His precious blood, to free her father from His excruciating sufferings, and having begged St. Catherine to intercede for Him too, she continued: "Lord, charge me with my father's indebtedness to Thy justice. In expiation of it, I am ready to take upon myself all the afflictions Thou art pleased to impose upon me." Our Lord graciously accepted this act of heroic charity, releasing at once her father's soul from Purgatory. But how heavy the crosses were which she henceforth had to suffer, may more easily be imagined than described.

The souls in Purgatory are holy souls. They are confirmed in grace and no longer in a condition to offend God or to forfeit heaven. They love God above everything; all their disorderly affections and passions have died away, and as they love God, so are they loved by Him in an unutterable manner. For this reason, our Lord wishes that they should be united to Him as soon as possible, but as he is a God most holy and most just, His holiness and justice forbid Him to admit them into the city of the heavenly Jerusalem before their indebtedness to His divine justice has been fully discharged, either by their own sufferings or by the prayers and good works of their brethren on earth. To remove then, by our charity this bar to the divine goodness, and to assist these souls in being sooner united to the angelic choirs and the number of the blessed in heaven, there to love, praise and glorify God in a most perfect manner, cannot but be a work most pleasing and most acceptable to the Almighty. "I was hungry," He will say to the elect on the day of judgment, "and you gave me to eat; I was thirsty, and you gave me to drink; I was a stranger, and you took me in; naked, and you clothed me; sick, and you visited me; I was in prison, and you came to me." And when the just will ask the Lord upon what occasion they acted thus toward Him, He will answer: "Amen, I say to you: so long as you did it to one of these, my least brethren, you did it to Me," (*Matt.* 25, 34-40.) Truly, if our Lord so highly values the least act of charity, what value will He not set on that charity which freed from their expiatory place such souls as were already espoused to Him for all eternity.

We read in the life and revelations of St. Gertrude, that she one day inquired of our Lord why the recital of the Psalter for the soul of the departed was so agreeable to Him, and why it obtained such great relief for them, since the immense number of psalms and the long prayers after each, caused more weariness than devotion. Our Lord replied: "The desire which I have for the deliverance of the souls of the departed, makes it acceptable to me; even as a prince who had been obliged to imprison one of his nobles, to whom he was much attached, and was compelled by his justice to refuse him pardon, would most thankfully avail himself of the intercession and satisfaction of others to release his friend. Thus do I act towards those whom I have redeemed by My death and precious blood, rejoicing in the opportunity of releasing them from their pains and bringing them to eternal joy." "But," continued the Saint, "is the labor of those who recite this Psalter acceptable to Thee?" He replied: "My love makes it most agreeable to Me; and if a soul is released thereby, I accept it as if I had been Myself delivered from captivity and I will assuredly reward it at a fitting time, according to the adundance of My mercy." (*Chap.* XVI.)

When we reflect on the superabundant merits of the blessed Virgin and consider for a moment the unspeakable love which the Most August Trinity bears her, we cannot doubt that she is able to free the suffering souls,—nay, to empty at once that abode of torments, Purgatory, provided such were the will of God. But God has other designs in His ineffable wisdom, justice and mercy, as was placed before us in the previous consideration. If even the precious blood and the copious merits of Jesus Christ do not effect the immediate deliverance of the poor souls, how much less can the prayers and tears of the blessed Virgin, together with her inconceivably great merits, bring it about. Mary does not pray God to free all the suffering souls at once, she rather asks that the will of God be done. For, although she is occupied incessantly in interceding for them, above all for such as honored her especially during life, and though she assuages their torments in a great degree and extends her hand to them the moment their term of punishment has expired, yet she does not overstep certain limits in affording them assistance. It remains for the faithful of the Church Militant to offer good works in behalf of the poor souls, which works can, according to the plan of God, satisfy his rigorous justice. The blessed Virgin Mary is, on the other hand, greatly delighted when the faithful extend aid to the suffering souls—indeed she looks upon such acts of charity as done to herself. She is our common mother. Our dear Lord, before expiring on the cross, addressed the disciple thus: "Son, behold thy mother." Hence she loves us all as children, and if her love for us whilst we are yet in this vale of tears is so intense, who shall attempt to describe it when we have run our earthly career and are confirmed in the favor of her Son forever?

It is the pious belief of Catholics, a belief resting on the evidence of numerous unobjectionable revelations, and founded on the authority of many holy authors, that Mary liberates each year a host of poor souls on the Feast of her glorious Assumption into heaven. The reason is simple. If kings are wont to dispense special favors on the day of their accession to the throne, if they throw open dungeons, remit the punishment of criminals—how much more becoming is it in the blessed Virgin to remember the poor souls in Purgatory and let them experience the mercy and compassion of her mother's heart on the day of her coronation in heaven. The "Privilege of Saturday," attached to the scapular of our Lady of Mount Carmel, is equally celebrated. Of the almost innumerable instances of the signal intercession of the blessed Virgin in favor of the poor souls, we cannot refrain from mentioning the following example.

It is related in the biography of the venerable Sister Catherine of St. Augustine, that there once lived a woman, Mary by name, in a grotto in the neighborhood of a city in Italy. This woman had been banished from the city for misdemeanor. She was attacked by a fatal disease and hurried to an untimely death without receiving the sacraments. When dead, she was denied Christian burial because of her public scandal. Sister Catherine, hearing of her sudden and wretched death, thought it useless to pray for this unhappy soul, though she had made it a rule to pray for all the departed.— After the lapse of four years, a poor suffering soul appeared to her saying: "O, sister Catherine, how wretched am I! You pray for all the poor souls, but for me you have no prayers." "Who are you?" enquired the servant of God. "I am Mary who died four years ago in the lonely grotto." "Are you then saved?" "I am, thanks to the mother of God." "But how?" "As I lay in my agony and reflected on the multitude and the heinousness of my sins, I recollected that Mary is the refuge of sinners, the mother of mercy. Then arose within me the firm conviction that no one need despair who invokes her succor. I at once had recourse to her merciful intercession with these words: 'O, Queen of heaven, here I am abandoned by God and man by reason of my enormous sins. Thou art my sole refuge! Have mercy on me!' The mother of mercy listened to my repentant sigh and obtained for me perfect contrition for my sins. But not satisfied at seeing me rescued from eternal torments, she obtained, in addition, the abridgment of my temporary punishment in Purgatory, and now only a few prayers and several Masses are required to effect my entire deliverance. Pray, do not refuse me this slight ransom." Catherine consented — did as she was requested, and after a few days the soul of Mary reappeared to her, beaming with loveliness and spoke as follows: "I thank you, sister, for your kind service. I am now on my way to heaven, there to praise the mercies of God and Mary, there to pray for you;"—whereupon she disappeared.

The angels of God are our constant companions. We learn from Holy Writ that they offer our prayers before the throne of God. The arch-angel Raphael said to Tobias: "When thou didst pray with tears, and didst bury the dead, and didst leave thy dinner and hide the dead by day in thy house and bury them by night, I offered thy prayers to the Lord."—(*Tob.* 12, 12.) Moreover, in the revelations of St. John, it is said that "an angel with a golden censer stood before the throne of God and offered the incense, which is the prayers of the saints, on the golden altar which is before the Most High; and the fragrance thereof ascended before the Almighty" (*Apocal.* 8, 3.) We know likewise that God has accorded each one of us at the moment of our birth an angel whose duty it is to accompany us through life, to succor us in bodily and spiritual necessities and dangers, to spur us on to good, to advise and counsel us, that we may gain our final destiny. Even after his client has come off victorious and ended his earthly career happily, the guardian angel considers his task but half done and rests not till he beholds him safe in heaven in the never-ending enjoyment of bliss. Supposing the soul to be detained in the flames of Purgatory, even here the angel guardian is solicitous about its welfare, exerts his utmost to afford relief, and intercedes for the abridgment of the term of suffering, because he cherishes this soul as a trust confided to his care by God. Hence, the holy angel guardians are very grateful toward those who extend aid to their respective clients and never cease praying for the benefactors of their poor and suffering souls. It has certainly happened more than once to one or the other of us that he has felt himself suddenly impelled to pray for a certain departed soul, and it is very probable that its guardian angel excited and urged him to offer up a prayer for his client. Not a few theologians maintain that it is the office of the angel guardians to bring to the poor souls the tidings of all the good works done in their behalf by the faithful on earth. These theologians appeal to the words of the apostle speaking of the angels: "Are they not all ministering spirits sent to minister for them who shall receive the inheritance of salvation." (*Heb.* 1, 14.)

The following incident took place at Dole, in France. One day, in the year 1629, long after her death, Leonarda Colin, niece to Hugueta Roy, appeared to her and spoke as follows: "I am saved by the mercy of God. It is now seventeen years since I was struck down by a sudden death. My poor soul was in mortal sin, but thanks to Mary whose devoted servant I had ever striven to be, I obtained grace in the last extremity to make an act of perfect contrition, and thus I was rescued from hell-fire, but by no means from Purgatory. My sufferings in those purifying flames are beyond description. At last, Almighty God has permitted my guardian angel to conduct me to you in order that you may make three pilgrimages to three churches of our Blessed Lady in Burgundy. Upon the fulfilment of said condition my deliverance from Purgatory is promised." Hugueta did as she was requested, whereupon the same soul appeared in a glorified state, and thanking her benefactress, and promising to pray for her, and admonishing her always to remember the four last things.

The saints of the Church Triumphant imitate their glorious queen, Mary. Although they are safely lodged in the heavenly mansions, they cannot look down from their exalted thrones upon our combats with indifference. Nay, they are filled with compassion at the sight of us tempest-tossed voyagers. Their most intense desire is to see us one day safely anchored in the unruffled harbor of eternal bliss; and to this end they leave no means untried to fly to our assistance at the moment they hear our cry of misery, and support us vigorously in every necessity of body and of soul. Innumerable examples go to prove this most clearly. The saints are by no means satisfied with aiding us whilst yet in the flesh; their solicitude reaches its perfection when we have departed this life. Then the saints, especially our patron saints, endeavor as far as the will of God allows, to abridge the term of our banishment, or, at least, to assuage our torments. They, too, are grateful for the services rendered their poor clients by the faithful, and never fail to repay such acts of charity both here and hereafter, by their most effectual intercession with God. Almighty God warns us, by the parable of the unjust steward, to gain advocates by means of our wealth, gifts, and the faculties which we enjoy from Him. Devotion to the poor souls in Purgatory is the means best calculated to gain for ourselves the friendship of the saints in heaven, because, by being devout to the souls of the departed and by offering up good works for them, we move the saints to intercede with God for our own salvation. Happy we, if we are so fortunate as to secure the patronage of one saint. The words of the son of Sirach will be fulfilled in our regard. "A faithful friend is a strong defence, and he that hath found him has found a treasure. Nothing can be compared to a faithful friend, and no weight of gold and silver is able to countervail the goodness of his fidelity. A faithful friend is the medicine of life and immortality, and they that fear the Lord shall find him." (*Eccl.* 6, 14.)

Cardinal Baronius relates in his annals of the year 647, that King Dagobert I. cherished a tender devotion to the glorious saints and martyrs Maurice and Dionysius, and made it his special study to propagate devotion to them. He died a holy death, but not being found spotless in the sight of God, he was necessarily detained in Purgatory. It so happened, that as a certain person was praying for the soul of Dagobert, it was shown to him in a vision, that the king had gone to rest, his two patrons, having obtained for him, the abridgment of his banishment from God, had themselves gone to Purgatory to escort him thence with great rejoicings.

We have had the consolation to see in the foregoing reflections, how, by good works done in behalf of the suffering souls in Purgatory, we can secure for ourselves the protection of the queen of heaven, of the angels and of the saints of God In addition to all this, the poor souls themselves pray for their benefactors; although they are unable to merit anything for themselves, says St. Alphonsus, yet their prayers in favor of others find mercy before God. The reason is simple. They are friends of God, and gratitude is as agreeable to Him as the contrary vice is hateful in His eyes; how then could God turn a deaf ear to the prayers of gratitude sent up by the suffering souls? God hears such intercessions willingly, nay, He not unfrequently allows the poor souls to assist their benefactors in a most striking manner, not merely in trifling matters but in great necessities of body and soul. St. Gregory the Great relates in his dialogues several miracles wrought at the intercession of the poor souls.

Whenever St. Catherine of Bologna, wished to obtain a certain favor, she had recourse to the souls in Purgatory, and her prayers were immediately heard. She declared that by praying to these holy souls she obtained many favors, which she had sought through the intercession of the saints, but had not obtained.

It is a well-known fact that, to awaken at a fixed hour of the night, it is only necessary to say a prayer to the poor souls. Experience has shown this in numerous cases, although persons were buried in the deepest sleep. Above all, the devotion to the poor souls is a sure means of obtaining help in spiritual wants and dangers, it being their earnest desire to see their benefactors saved forever. The holy ties by which the Church Suffering and the Church Militant are united, consist in their mutual endeavors to help each other on to the destiny of both—God and the enjoyment of everlasting bliss. The Triumphant Church alone needs no assistance, whilst she is continually occupied in affording aid.— More effectual however are the intercessory prayers of the poor souls after they have entered the kingdom of heaven. In this world favors are soon forgotten, and even the most grateful are, in the lapse of time, brought to disregard their former benefactors. The angels and saints, on the other hand, exercise the virtue of gratitude in its entire perfection.

A certain knight, not less pious than valiant, was in the habit of stopping for awhile to pray for the souls of the departed whenever he passed a graveyard. One day, as he went out without his usual weapons of defence, he was suddenly attacked by his enemies. The knight tried to save his life by running off as fast as he could, and in his flight arrived at a graveyard. Here he knelt down to recommend himself to the Lord and to the souls in Purgatory for protection. Wonderful to relate, when his enemies were quite near, they saw the knight surrounded by a host of armed men to defend him. Being frightened at this sight, they took to flight themselves in the greatest confusion. We may most piously believe that these armed men were the souls of those faithful departed, for whom the good knight had prayed, and whom our Lord had permitted to assume those forms to protect their benefactor in his danger. (*Segola triumph. anim. c.* 22, *Rossignoli Marav.*)

A certain servant of the Lord was, on his death-bed, most violently assailed by the evil spirits. Such was the fury of the demons who assailed him, that the dying man was well-nigh beside himself, not knowing what means to adopt against the attacks of his enemies. But having been in the habit of praying for the souls in Purgatory, he beheld at the moment his distress was greatest, a multitude of celestial spirits who put the infernal spirits to flight, and told the dying man that they were those souls whose deliverance from Purgatory had been accelerated by his prayers and good works, and that they had come to reward him for his charity by assisting him in his passage to a happy eternity. At these words the dying man felt unspeakably consoled; all his fear had disappeared and in great peace he breathed forth his last. (*Binet de Statu. Anim. c.* 1.)

From what has been said, it follows that our charity towards the souls in Purgatory

IS MOST SALUTARY TO OURSELVES.

It will, however, not be amiss to add a few reflections to make this truth still more evident. The better we understand the spiritual fruits which grow on this tree of charity the more carefully shall we cultivate it, that it may bear still greater fruits.

Heaven allures us, it is true, with eternal and precious rewards and admonishes us to avoid neither labors, conflicts, nor sacrifices to merit an imperishable crown, and hell threatens us with everlasting and unendurable punishments, and reminds us of "what does it profit a man to gain the whole world and lose his own soul;" but Purgatory, between these two eternities of the blessed and the miserable, with its temporary yet terrific sufferings is equally salutary, to make us flee from sin in order to escape being consigned to its punishments. The thought of Purgatory is a powerful motive to induce us to do penance for the sins of our past life, that we may not have to undergo sufferings in the next world, far surpassing those of which we read in the lives of the most severe penitents.

Purgatory reminds us how in this world we should long and seek for nothing but God, Who alone is able to satisfy the cravings of the heart, and earnestly endeavor to become more and more united to our Lord, to the supreme and only source of all happiness here below and in the world to come. In Purgatory, this ardent longing for God is a source of unspeakable pain, but here below it proves to be a source of unspeakable graces and blessings in all the troubles and struggles of this life.

Purgatory tells us to be patient and resigned to God's holy will in all our crosses and sufferings in this vale of tears, since the least degree of the pains of Purgatory far surpasses the most excruciating torments of this world.

Purgatory tells us to profit well by our time, to apply to the frequent reception of the sacraments, to assiduous prayer and other good works, as death may overtake us and deprive us of every opportunity to do good to ourselves, and that it is great folly to depend on the charity of our friends, since they too easily forget the departed, for whom the proverb "out of sight, out of mind," proves to be but too true.

Purgatory tells us to be careful always to keep ourselves in the grace of God, as otherwise all our good works would be neither of any merit to ourselves, nor of any profit to the souls in Purgatory if offered for them.

A certain father begged his son to pray much for him after his death. The son did so most earnestly. Thirty years after, his father appeared to him, all surrounded with fire, and suffering most intensely. "Cruel son," said he, "why have you not procured any comfort for me in the space of thirty years." "How is that," said the son quite surprised and amazed, "have I not offered up for you so many prayers, alms, fasts and the like? Did so many pious works not avail you anything?" "Know, my son," replied the father, "that all the good which you have done and are still doing, as it has availed you nothing, so it has not profited me anything either, because you have done it in the state of mortal sin, all your confessions being bad for want of true sorrow. God, in his mercy, has permitted me to tell you this both for my and your advantage." After this, the father suddenly disappeared leaving his son salutarily touched and frightened, so much so that he went to make a good general confession, and commenced to lead a truly Christian life, and by the practice of many good works he soon freed the soul of his father from Purgatory, and his own from eternal perdition. (*Campadelli, disc. sacr.* 191.)

What can be more wholesome for us than all these reflections? Are they not a most powerful incentive to make us embrace a holy life? Is not charity toward the souls in Purgatory an admonitor that makes us remember these truths? Is it not a kind of an alarm-clock, awakening in us so many wholesome thoughts? How salutary, then, to ourselves, is not this charity towards the souls in Purgatory? Would to God we were faithful in its daily, nay hourly practice! How pure and how holy would our lives soon be!

But where shall we find this faithful admonitor, this alarm-clock, reminding us regularly of our charity toward the faithful departed? This admonitor has been provided in

THE ESTABLISHMENT OF THE ARCH-CONFRATERNITY FOR THE RELIEF OF THE SOULS IN PURGATORY.

To become an active member of it, is to have at once several faithful admonitors to call to our mind our duty toward the departed in connection with so many salutary reflections.

Believe me, dear, dear reader, I tell you a great truth. Give it a fair trial by being regularly enrolled in this Arch-Confraternity, and the poor souls will daily put you in mind of your duty both toward them and toward yourself.

As our mother, the Holy Catholic Church, harbors within her bosom various religious Orders to supply her different wants, temporal as well as spiritual, so in like manner has she established different confraternities to preserve among the faithful a lively faith in certain mysterious truths of her holy religion, such as the Confraternity of the Blessed Sacrament and of the Precious Blood, for the preservation of faith in the mystery of love, the blessed Eucharist and in the mystery of our holy Redemption.

The Arch-Confraternity for the relief of the souls in Purgatory, has been established for a similar purpose, viz: to keep up among the faithful, a lively faith in those three truths which have just been explained and which proceed from the ninth article of the Creed, namely: "I believe in the communion of saints." The promotion of practical faith in these truths, is the particular object of the Arch-Confraternity. A simple statement of its history and special spiritual advantages and privileges together with those already mentioned, will not fail, it is confidently hoped, to induce pastors to establish it in their respective churches, and the faithful to become active members of it. After it had been established in the year 1840, by the Redemptorist Fathers in Rome, in their Church of S. Maria Monterone, as a pious society, for the object just mentioned, the Holy Father Gregory XVI, not only approved the design, but extended to it his special patronage, and in a Papal Brief, dated August 8, 1841, raised the society to the rank of an Arch-Confraternity with all the rights and privileges belonging thereto. Moreover, in order to show how highly they valued and esteemed this Arch-Confraternity, and in order to stimulate the zeal and piety of its members, and to induce the faithful in general to become members of it, the sovereign Pontiffs Gregory XVI, and Pius IX, have most generously and most munificently enriched them

WITH THE TREASURES OF THE CHURCH

Granting them no less than thirty-five plenary and over two-hundred partial indulgences to be gained in the course of the year, on the following occasions:

INDULGENCES.

By virtue of Briefs and Rescripts of the Sovereign Pontiffs, Gregory XVI, and Pius IX, dated Jan. 19, 1841; Sept. 30, 1859; Jan. 22, 1861; Feb. 18, 1861; and March 27, 1863, the members of the Arch-Confraternity, who after Confession and Communion, shall visit any church or oratory they choose, and pray for the exaltation of our holy mother, the Church, for unity and peace among Christian princes, and for the extirpation of heresies, may gain the following Indulgences. The sick, as well as those unable to visit a church, may gain these Indulgences, provided they make a good confession and perform some other pious work prescribed by their confessor; and be it ever remembered that every member is left free to go to confession and communion and make his visit in *any Catholic Church whatsoever.*

A PLENARY INDULGENCE.

1. On the day of admission into the Arch-Confraternity.
2.* On Christmas Day.
3. On the Epiphany.
4. On Corpus Christi.
5. On the Fest. of the Immaculate Conception, B.V. M., Dec. 8.
6. On the Fest. of the Nativity, B. V. M., Sept. 8.
7. On the Fest. of the Annunciation, March 25.
8. On the Fest. of the Purification, B. V. M., Feb. 2.
9. On the Fest. of the Assumption, B. V. M., Aug. 15.
10. On the Fest. of St. Michael, the Archangel, Sept. 29.
11. On the Fest. of the Apparition of St. Michael, May 8.
12. On the Fest. of St. Joseph, March 19.
13. On the Patronage of St. Joseph, third Sunday after Easter.
14. On the Fest. of St. Peter and St. Paul, June 29.
15. On All-Souls' Day, Nov. 2.
16. Once a month, on a day at option.
17. At the hour of death, if, confession and communion being impossible, they invoke the holy name of Jesus interiorly, if not with the lips.

PARTIAL INDULGENCES.

1. Of seven years and seven times forty days on the following Festivals of our Lord.

On the Fest. of the Circumcision, Jan. 1.
On the Fest. of the Holy Name of Jesus, *i. e.* second Sunday after the Epiphany.
On Easter Sunday.
On the Fest. of the Ascension of our Lord.
On the Fest. of the Finding of the Holy Cross, May 3.
On the Fest. of the Sacred Heart of Jesus.
On the Fest. of the Most Precious Blood.
On the Fest. of the Transfiguration, Aug. 6.
On the Fest. of the Exaltation of the Holy Cross, Sept. 14.

---

* To gain the indulgences attached to Feast-Days, the conditions may be performed on the day, or any day during the octave.

2. Of seven years and seven times forty days on the following Festivals B. V. M.

On the Friday before Palm Sunday, the Fest. of the Compassion B. V. M,

On the Fest. of the Visitation, B. V. M., July 2.

On the Fest. of the B. V. M. of Mt. Carmel, July 16.

On the Fest. of the Dedication of St. Mary ad Nives, Aug. 5.

On the Fest. of the Holy Name of Mary, the Sunday within the octave of the Nativity of the B. V. M.

On the Sunday following the Festival of the seven dolors, B. V. M.

On the Fest. of the B. V. M., Lady of Mercy.

On the first Sunday of October, the Fest. of the Holy Rosary.

On the Fest. of the Presentation of the B. V. M., Nov. 21.

3. An indulgence of seven years and seven times forty days on the Feasts of the Holy Apostles.

On the Fest. of St. Matthias, Feb. 24 or 25.

On the Fest. of St. Philip and St. James.

On the Fest. of St. Barnabas.

On the Fest. of St. Paul.

On the Fest. of St. James, the Greater.

On the Fest. of St. Matthew.

On the Fest. of St. Simon and St. Jude.

On the Fest. of St. Andrew.

On the Fest. of St. Thomas.

On the Fest. of St. John, the Evangelist.

4. An indulgence of seven years and seven times forty days on the seven days following All-Souls' Day.

To gain the above Indulgences it is necessary to visit a church or oratory, and pray for the intention of our holy mother, the Catholic Church. The sick, as well as those unable to visit a church, may gain these Indulgences by performing some other good work.

5. An Indulgence of seven years and seven times forty days on Saturday before Septuagesima Sunday and on each of the ten days following.

6.* An Indulgence of seven years and seven times forty days on the first Monday of every month.

---

*It is a pious custom with many Christians to observe every Monday in the year as a day of commemoration and prayer for the faithful departed.

The above Indulgences may be gained by the members of the Arch-Confraternity, if they visit a church or oratory and pray for the exortation of the Church, etc.

The sick and those unable to make this visit, may perform, in its stead, some other good work suitable to their condition.

7. An Indulgence of three hundred days as often as a member of the Confraternity visits a church or oratory.

8. An Indulgence of one hundred days as often as a member of the Confraternity performs some work of piety or fraternal charity: for example, assists at the holy sacrifice of the mass or sermon; prays for the living or dead, gives alms, instructs the ignorant, reconciles enemies, restrains any one from sin, either by advice or example.

9. The Indulgences attached to the devout visits to the Churches of the Stations in Rome.

The practice of visiting the Churches of the Stations, where are preserved the most striking religious memorials of the saints, and of the Martyrs especially, dates its institution from the first ages of Christianity, and on certain days in the year, the people, clergy and even Popes, used to go there in procession, to pray. To maintain this pious and time-honored devotion, Pope Gregory the Great, granted several Indulgences to those who, on certain days, would visit the assigned churches. To these Indulgences others were added in the course of time by the Roman Pontiffs. According to a Brief of Pope Pius IX., dated Jan. 22, 1861, all the members of the Arch-Confraternity, living out of Rome, may gain all the Indulgences of the Stations in Rome, if they visit, on the appointed days, a church or oratory, and pray for the intention of the Holy Father.

The following Indulgences were granted by a Decree of Pope Pius VI., July 6, 1777.

PLENARY INDULGENCES.

1. On the Feast of the Nativity of our Lord.
2. On Thursday in Holy Week.
3. On Easter Day.
4. On Ascension Day.

PARTIAL INDULGENCES.

1. An Indulgence of thirty years and thirty quarantines.
On the Feast of St. Stephen, the first Martyr, Dec. 26.
On the Feast of St. John, the Evangelist.
On the Feast of Holy Innocents.
On the Feast of the Circumcision, and on the Epiphany of our Lord.
On Septuagesima Sunday.
On Sexagesima Sunday.
On Quinquagesima Sunday.
On Good Friday.
On Holy Saturday.
On every day in Easter Week, Low Sunday included.
On the Feast of St. Mark.
On the Rogation Days.
On Whit-Sunday.
On every day of the octave of Whitsun-week, Ember days included.

2. An Indulgence of twenty-five years and twenty-five quarantines.
On Palm Sunday.

3. An Indulgence of fifteen years and fifteen quarantines.
On the third Sunday in Advent.
On the vigil of the Nativity of our Lord.
At the first Mass of this Feast, celebrated at midnight.
At the second Mass, celebrated toward day-break.
On Ash-Wednesday.
On the fourth Sunday in Lent.

4. An Indulgence of ten years and ten quarantines on all Sundays and Week-days in Lent, not yet mentioned, Ember-days included.
On the Vigil of Pentecost.
On the Ember-days in September and December.

To these Indulgences Pope Leo XII., in a Decree dated Feb. 28, 1827, added others for the devout visits to the Churches of the Stations in the course of Lent. These Indulgences, too, may be gained by the members of the Arch-Confraternity, living out of Rome, if they visit a church or an oratory, and pray there according to their devotion, say the third part of the Rosary, and the Litany of the blessed Virgin, and finish by reciting the psalm: "*Out of the depths*," or one Our Father, Hail Mary, and the versicle, "*Eternal rest, etc.*," for the repose of the souls departed. By complying with the above conditions, the members of the Arch-Confraternity may gain an Indulgence of forty years and forty quarantines on every day of Lent, and by complying with the same on three different days, they may gain a Plenary Indulgence on any day at option, after having confessed, received holy communion, visited a church or oratory, and prayed for the intention of the Holy Father. Sick people or prisoners may gain these Indulgences by performing such good works as may be prescribed for them by their confessor.

10. The Indulgence attached to the Devotions in the month of November.

According to the Brief of Pius IX., dated Jan. 22, 1861, the members of the Arch-Confraternity, as well as the rest of the faithful, may gain an Indulgence of seven years and seven quarantines every time they assist at a public devotion performed in the month of November for the relief of the souls in Purgatory, in a church in which the Arch-Confraternity has been established, and pray, with contrite hearts, for the exaltation of the Church. Those who have assisted at these devotions twelve times, may gain a Plenary Indulgence on the usual conditions. The sick may gain these Indulgences, if they recite three times the 129th Psalm: "*Out of the depths*," instead of each devotion.

According to a Brief of the same Pontiff, dated March 27, 1862, the members of the Arch-Confraternity may gain the above Indulgence of seven years and seven quarantines for each visit to a grave-yard, praying there for the repose of the departed, and a Plenary Indulgence, on the usual conditions, for four such visits made within a month.

Great though these favors and treasures of the Church are in themselves, yet experience teaches that they are sought for only in proportion as they are appreciated, and they are appreciated by the generality of the faithful in proportion to the knowledge which they have of the nature and conditions of these treasures — This knowledge being in many too superficial, too deficient and too incorrect, it will not be amiss to explain, in a few words, the

TRUE NATURE AND CONDITIONS OF INDULGENCES.

Sin produces in the soul two bitter fruits: First, *guilt*, which deprives us of the grace and friendship of God; and secondly, *its penalty*, which forbids us the enjoyment of God in paradise. The penalty of sin is twofold, being partly eternal, partly temporal. Guilt, together with the eternal penalty of sin, is entirely remitted to us by means of the infinite merits of Jesus Christ in the sacrament of penance, provided we approach that sacrament with fitting disposition. The temporal penalty of sin is, however, not always remitted to us by this sacrament. This is removed by penance, or by works of satisfaction, that is to say, prayers, alms, fasting, etc; or by the patient endurance of troubles and adversities sent us by God; or by the satisfaction of our Lord Jesus Christ and the saints, applied to us by the Church, under certain conditions, which application we call an *Indulgence*. Those who do not pay the debt of temporal punishment in this world, in any of the above ways, will have to discharge it in Purgatory, as we have seen above, in that prison from which they shall not go out, "till they have paid the last farthing." (*Matt.* V. 25, 26.)

An *indulgence*, then, is not a pardon for sin, because sin must be remitted before an indulgence can be gained. Much less is it a permission to commit sin, as so many malicious or ignorant persons assert it to be; for even God Himself could not give such a permission. It is simply an act by which the Church applies to us the superabundant satisfactions of Jesus Christ and His saints, to satisfy for the *temporal punishment* due to those sins which we trust God has already pardoned, as to the *guilt and eternal punishment*.

Indulgences are distinguished into two classes. Some are called *plenary*, or, as it is sometimes technically said, "in form of Jubilee." Plenary indulgences, or indulgences in form of Jubilee, are one and the same thing in their effect, the only difference being, that where the indulgences are granted in form of Jubilee, confessors have power of jurisdiction conferred on them to absolve in reserved cases, to dispense from or commute all simple vows, etc. By *all* such indulgences that temporal punishment is remitted, which we owe to God for all those sins for which, though pardoned, we were still debtors, so that were we to die immediately after gaining a *plenary indulgence*, we would go straight to heaven. The same may be said of the holy souls in Purgatory, whenever in suffrage for them, we gain a plenary indulgence, provided the divine justice deign to accept it in their behalf.

Other indulgences are called *partial*, because they remit part only of the punishment. These are given for days, or periods of forty days, called "quarantines," or for a year, or some years. An indulgence of three hundred days, however, does not mean that it remits a pain of three hundred days to be otherwise endured in Purgatory, but remits only as much of the punishment due to sin as God would have remitted for the sake of a canonical penance faithfully performed for the same length of time.

In order to gain an indulgence, several conditions are requisite:

First, it is necessary that we should be in the state of grace. For whosoever, before God, is living in his guilt of unremitted sin, and liable to its eternal penalty, is not and cannot be, whilst continuing in that state, in a capacity to receive the remission of the temporal punishment. No better advice can then, be given, than, before performing the works enjoined for gaining an indulgence, if we cannot go to confession, to make, at least, an act of true contrition, accompanying it with a firm resolution to go to confession, in order that by so doing we may regain the grace of God, should it happen to have been lost.

Secondly, *all* the works enjoined by the church, both as to time, manner and object, according to the precise letter of the grant, by which the indulgence has been conceded, must be fulfilled: as for instance, if it be there said that the work ought to be done kneeling, or standing, or at the sound of the bell, or at such an hour, such a day, or contrite, or having confessed and communicated, etc; so that, should any of the works enjoined be omitted, either wholly or in some notable portion of them, be it through ignorance, or negligence, or inability; or should any one of the conditions of time, place, etc., prescribed, fail to have been observed for any reason whatsoever, then the indulgence in question is not gained.

For a Plenary Indulgence, the *ordinary* conditions are to go to confession and communion, and to pray for the intention of the Pope. No particular prayer is prescribed. It would suffice to say for the intention of the Holy Father, six Our Fathers and six Hail Marys, or the Litany of the Blessed Virgin. The communion may be made on the eve of the Feast to which the Indulgence is attached. Those who are accustomed to confess every week, can gain all the indulgences that occur in the course of the week, without again confessing, provided they remain in a state of grace. Indulgences, however, granted in the form of a Jubilee, are excepted from this rule, inasmuch as in order to gain such indulgences, besides the works enjoined, the confession ought to be made within the time appointed in the grant of such indulgences.

Thirdly, in order to gain a Plenary Indulgence, it is required that we detest even all venial sins, and, moreover, lay aside every affection to all such sins, in general, as well as to each in particular.

Fourthly, in order to gain an indulgence, we must also have the intention to gain it, so that, if we perform an act to which an indulgence is attached, without having had the intention, we do not gain it. If we make an intention in the morning to gain all the indulgences that we can possibly gain that day, the intention is supposed to continue, even if inadvertently lost sight of. It would be well to add to this intention another, *i. e.* that of applying these indulgences to the souls in Purgatory, as far as they are applicable to them.

It is well to determine which of the suffering souls we wish to assist; for example, we may propose to ourselves the deliverance of that soul for which we are most bound to pray, by an obligation of justice, charity or gratitude.

Partial Indulgences may be gained as often as we repeat the act to which they are annexed, unless the contrary is specified in the grant.

The Arch-Confraternity based upon the authority of the Holy See being now firmly established, has chosen

THE EVER BLESSED VIRGIN MARY UNDER THE TITLE OF THE ASSUMPTION, AS ITS ESPECIAL PATRONESS,

Partly because the Church of S. Maria Monterone, the central point of the association, was consecrated under this title, and partly from a pious belief supported by many revelations, not to be lightly rejected, that the glorious queen of all the saints, on the Feast of her Assumption, comes in an especial manner to the relief of the suffering souls who were her devout clients on earth

The Heads of several Religious Orders have also concurred in favoring the Arch-Confraternity by granting to the Directors thereof, power to *bless and indulgence the Rosary of Saint*

Dominic, the Chaplets of the Most Holy Trinity, of *Our Lord,* of *the Immaculate Conception of the Blessed Virgin Mary, the Cord and Chaplet of St. Augustine and St. Monica,* as well as to *bless the Scapulars of the Most Holy Trinity,* of *the Passion of our Lord Jesus Christ,* of *our Lady of Mount Carmel,* and of *our Lady of Mercy,* and to invest therewith the faithful, together with all the privileges and rights annexed thereto.

Moreover, the *Superiors Generals* of *the Carmelites,* of *the Augustinians,* of *the Trinitarians,* of *the Franciscans,* and of *the Capuchins* have affiliated *all the members* of the *Arch-Confraternity,* as *Oblates of their respective Orders,* and they grant them the privilege of *sharing in all the good works* which are performed in these Orders.

The Arch-Confraternity being under the direction of *the Redemptorist Fathers* in Rome, all the members of it share also, in a particular manner, in *all the good works* which are performed in the congregation of the Most Holy Redeemer.

The Arch-Confraternity being thus favored in a most extraordinary manner, a quarter of a century had not elapsed since its foundation, when four hundred confraternities were already incorporated with the mother association at

Rome; and the number of its members scattered throughout Europe, Asia, and America, exceeded *one million*.

According to a Brief of his Holiness, Pope Pius IX., dated August 23, 1861,

THE ARCH-CONFRATERNITY MAY BE ESTABLISHED

With the consent of the Bishop, in any church or station whatsoever of the diocese. *Branches of the Arch-Confraternity* may also be established in *the chapel of Conventual Houses of Religious Ladies* living cloistered, *for themselves, their out-sisters* and *pupils*.

Moreover, by virtue of the aforesaid Brief of Gregory XVI., and a Decree of Pius IX., dated August 23, 1861, *plenary power* is imparted not only to *all other societies* having the same title, but also to *associations of different names*, established for the same purpose, to *aggregate* or *embody* themselves with this Arch-Confraternity, and to *partake* of *all the indulgences, graces,* and *privileges* set forth in this book, if they will add to or incorporate in their original title the words: "*And for the relief of suffering souls.*"

If the pastor or members of any congregation desire to establish a branch of the confraternity in the parish, or if any similar association, already organized, wishes to affiliate with the Arch-Confraternity for the relief of suffering souls, they can address for this purpose *the Procurator-General of the Congregation of the Most Holy Redeemer at Rome*, or *the Very Rev. Provincial of the same Congregation at St. Alphonsus' church, Baltimore, Md.*

The *names* of those who wish to be enrolled in the Arch-Confraternity should be recorded in a book made for the purpose, either by the director of the Arch-Confraternity himself, or by a sub-delegated priest, which sub-delegation may be obtained from the *Very Rev. Father Provincial* of the Redemptorists, to whom the number of those thus enrolled should be forwarded every five years. *No pecuniary dues* are required of the members either on admission or afterwards.

The following is

A SUITABLE FORM FOR A CERTIFICATE OF MEMBERSHIP.

I, (N. N.) associate myself to this pious Confraternity out of pure love for the suffering souls, and in union with the Brotherhood thereof, earnestly resolve to help the same, and form the intention to apply all the good works as well as all the indulgences granted by the Holy See to this Arch-Confraternity in satisfaction for my own sins and for the relief and deliverance of the suffering souls in Purgatory.

O, good and merciful Jesus, graciously regard the suffering souls, soothe their pains, assuage their sufferings, and grant to all the faithful, and particularly to the members of this Arch-Confraternity, a compassionate desire and an ardent zeal to assist them, that so helped, they may sooner enjoy Thy presence, and attain to their everlasting happiness! Amen.

Done in this Confraternity, this day   of   in the year 186 .
Signed.   N. N.

The *Director* of each affiliated Confraternity *is required*, if possible, to have *Mass said* on an altar of the association on all Mondays, or, at least, on the first Monday of every month, for all suffering souls, especially for those who have been members of the Arch-Confraternity, for the neglected, and for those most in need of help.

Let it be remembered here, that *each altar* of the *association* is *privileged* for *each Mass* and for *every priest, regular* or *secular*, no matter whether he be a member or not of the Arch-Confraternity. This favor has been granted by the Holy See in behalf of the faithful departed, and its meaning is, that for each holy Mass said on such an altar, a plenary indulgence is granted by the Holy See for any specified departed soul that may be detained in Purgatory, that by its application the same may be delivered from its sufferings.

On the second of November all the Masses enjoy this privilege, no matter at what altar they are said. On this day, that is to say on *All Souls' day*, which is the *chief solemnity* of the Brotherhood, and during the octave, if practicable, some devotions shall be performed both morning and evening, with tapers lighted. The several confraternities are also advised to observe and use during the whole month of November, such prayers as they will find composed for this purpose in this book, and as are used in the Church of S. Maria Monterone. Beyond this the rules of each association need not necessarily be the same; but they must be approved by the Bishop of the diocese.

Each member should induce others to be enrolled in the association, and to form new societies, which should be aggregated to the Arch-Confraternity of S. Maria Monterone. *Each member* of the Confraternity *should* also sometime during the year *perform some acts of devotion for* the relief of the suffering souls; if a layman, he might have a Mass said for them, or make the Stations of the Cross, or say the Rosary, or assist at Mass with this intention, or offer up a Communion; if he is a priest, he should offer the Holy Sacrifice. This is not obligatory upon the members under the pain of sin, but it is requisite to gain the indulgences. All further suffrages, works, &c., are left to the discretion of the members, but all should consider it a pious duty to assist the suffering souls as much as possible, by prayers, devotions, or other good works. The most fervent might even make the following

HEROIC ACT OF CHARITY;

OR,

Offering of all works of satisfaction and suffrages in behalf of the souls in Purgatory.

This heroic act of charity in behalf of the souls in Purgatory consists in a voluntary offering made to them by any one of the faithful of all works of satisfaction done by him in this life, as well as of all suffrages which shall be offered for him after his death; he thereby depositing them into the hands of the Blessed Virgin, that she may distribute them in behalf of those holy souls whom it is her good pleasure to deliver from the pains of Purgatory, declaring at the same time that by this offering he only foregoes in their behalf that special fruit of the Mass which belongs to himself; so that if, being a priest, he make this offering, he is not hindered from applying the Holy Sacrifice of the Mass according to the intention of those who give him alms to that end.

This heroic act of charity, called also a vow or oblation, was instituted by F. Gaspar Oliden, a Theatine; for although it was not unknown in former ages, it was he who propagated it, and it was at his prayer that it was enriched with many indulgences: first by Pope Benedict

XIII., in a decree of August 23, 1728; and then by **Pope Pius VI.,** in a decree of Dec. 12, 1788; and lastly, these indulgences were specified by the Sovereign Pontiff **Pius IX.,** in a decree of the S. Congr. of indulgences of Sept. 30, 1852. They are as follows:

I. The Indult of a privileged altar, personally, **every day in the year,** to all priests who have made this offering.

II. The Plenary Indulgence, applicable only to the departed, to all the faithful who have made this offering, whenever they go to holy communion, provided they visit a church or public oratory, and pray there for a time according to the mind of his Holiness.

III. The Plenary Indulgence, every Monday, to all who hear Mass in suffrage for the souls in Purgatory, provided they visit, &c., and pray as above.

IV. All Indulgences granted or to be granted, even though not applicable to the dead, which are gained by the faithful who have made this offering, may be applied to the holy souls in Purgatory.

V. Lastly, our Holy Father and Lord, Pope Pius IX., having regard to the young who are not yet communicants, as well as to the poor sick, to those who are afflicted with chronic disorders, to the aged, to farm-laborers, prisoners, and others who are debarred from communicating and unable to hear Mass on Mondays, vouchsafed by another decree of the S. Congr. of Indulgences, of November 20, 1854, to declare, that for all the faithful who cannot hear Mass on Monday, the Mass heard on Sundays should be available for gaining the Indulgence, No. III.; and that in favor of those who are not yet communicants, or who are hindered from communicating, he has also left it to the will of their respective ordinaries to authorize confessors to commute the works there enjoined.

And note, 1. That although this act of charity is denominated a vow in some printed tracts, in which also is given a formula for making the offering, no inference is to be drawn therefrom that this offering binds under sin.

2. That to make this vow, it is not necessary to pronounce the words: it suffices to wish it, and to make it with the heart;

nor is it any frequent repetition of it prescribed, although such a practice might be very useful to excite the fervor of charity, and to cause more diligence in gaining spiritual assistance for the relief of the blessed souls in Purgatory.

3. That this vow is not at all opposed to the rule of charity, which obliges us to pray first for deceased relations, for our brethren in the congregation of which we may be members, &c. For it is to be borne in mind, that the prayer to which the fruit of impetration corresponds (with which this vow has nothing to do,) is quite different from the suffrages to which corresponds the fruit of satisfaction; and although in this duty of offering suffrages, charity obliges us first towards our relatives, still the most blessed Virgin knows better than we, what are our wants, and therefore she will take care that our good works may be useful, first, to our relatives and brethren, and afterwards, to others, as in the sight of God they may deserve them.

Thus we may practise without doubt all our accustomed devotions for obtaining any grace of God, of the blessed Virgin, or the saints, since this is not opposed to the vow by which the satisfactory part alone of our good works is applied to those holy souls; the meritorious, propitiatory, and impetratory parts, which, being personal, cannot be communicated, being reserved for ourselves.

FORMULA OF THE PIOUS AND CHARITABLE VOW, TO CO-OPERATE IN THE LIBERATION OF THE SOULS IN PURGATORY FROM THEIR TORMENTS.

For Thy greater glory, O my God, one in essence and three in person! and in order to imitate more closely my dear Redeemer, Jesus Christ, as also to show my sincere love for the most holy Virgin Mary, mother of mercy, and of the poor souls in Purgatory, I, N. N., resolve to co-operate in the redemption and deliverance of those imprisoned souls, still debtors to the divine justice, on account of the punishment due to their sins; and in the manner I lawfully can, without obliging myself under pain of any sin, I sincerely promise and I here offer to Thee my own free vow, to wish the liberation from Purgatory of all those souls whose deliverance the blessed Virgin may wish; and to that effect I place in the hands of this most pious mother all my satisfactory works, and those of others applied to me, in life or death, and after my passage to eternity.

I pray Thee, O my God! deign to accept and confirm this my offering, as I here renew and confirm it, to Thy honor and the good of my soul.

And if perhaps my works of satisfaction be not sufficient to pay the debts both of those souls which the blessed Virgin wishes to liberate and also my own for my sins, which I heartily detest and abhor, I offer myself, O Lord, if it please Thee, to make up by my sufferings in Purgatory, what is wanting for their release, committing myself into the arms of Thy mercy, and those of my most sweet mother. This my oblation and protest I call the blessed in heaven to witness, and the whole Church Militant, on earth and suffering in Purgatory. Amen.

On   day of   the year 18

This act is called heroic because it is very contrary to our selfishness. The greater part of Christians little understand the words of St. Paul, "charity seeketh not her own." (I. *Cor.* 13, 5.) Were they do practise better this great truth, they would say with St. Sidonius, Bishop of Clermont: "In my opinion, that man sees best to his own interest who lives for the interest of others, showing his sympathy for his fellow-men by the performance of charitable works."— (*Rohrbacher's Hist. Univ.*) But it is not given to all to understand this truth; for this reason, very many hesitate to make the above act of charity for the benefit of the souls in Purgatory. However, to make this act, is not to lose, but gain. By it, you enhance considerably the merit of all your actions, which are, in the sight of God, so much the more meritorious, the greater the charity is with which they are performed; nay, to make this act, is to increase all your good works and their merit a hundred-fold. What man would hesitate to loan one hundred dollars to his neighbor to free a poor man from his painful captivity, if he knew for certain that a hundred times more money would be returned? "This is indeed a rich bargain," he would say, "by which I become wealthy at once." Now, has not Jesus Christ promised a hundred-fold for the least act of charity? Would it not, then, be blasphemy for you to believe for a moment, that, after making the above act of charity, Jesus Christ would not make good His promise and return to you a hundred-fold whatever you may have given in charity to His captive spouses for His sake?

And has not our holy mother, the Catholic Church, guided as she is by the Holy Ghost, sufficiently intimated this great gain by attaching to this act, such unusual privileges and spiritual advantages, to induce her children to make it? Would she grant and hold out such favors to her children in order to throw them into a state of spiritual poverty? Must you not then firmly believe, that by making this act at the intimation of your mother, you will be a great gainer? The saints understood this but too well. Hence they found no difficulty in practising great charity towards the souls in Purgatory. In his famous work "Christliche Mystik," 3 B., J. Gœrres says:

"Among so many saints who excelled in charity towards the souls in Purgatory, the discalced nun, Frances of the Blessed Sacrament, is very remarkable. She had inherited from her father a tender love and affection for these poor suffering souls. Her feelings of compassion were considerably increased by repeated apparitions of her deceased mother and sister, whose pitiable state had impressed itself on her soul in indelible characters. From that time, she sympathized most extraordinarily with all those souls that were in the same condition.— Many of them seemed to know her great compassion for them; for, daily, nay even, hourly, by day and by night, these souls would come to her cell in crowds, asking her charitable prayers. Departed souls of every condition of life, those of popes, archbishops, priests, monks, nuns, nobles and beggars, would surround her and tell her of their excruciating pains and of the faults for which they had to endure them, asking her to offer up fervent prayers to the Almighty for their deliverance. Sometimes they appeared to her all surrounded with fire; at other times, in forms as black as coal, from which sparks of fire were issuing, or in forms too hideous to behold, resembling more a wild beast than a human being; at other times, she would see only one of their limbs black."

"As Frances, in such cases, often fainted away from fright, these souls would not again appear to her in their true shape, but would assume the form of a shadow, until she became more used to behold them in different forms. The different states of life in which they had lived on earth, were represented to her by the respective signs of these conditions; for instance, the soul of a notary-public would appear to her with writing materials; that of a lock-smith, with a red-hot hammer; that of a vain lady, in old ragged clothes."

"Whilst Frances was assisting at the divine office in the choir, these souls would wait for her at the entrance near the holy water font, to accompany her, to her cell, where they would speak to her about their great distress and affliction. When she was in company with any of her sisters or in a place of recreation, they would give her a sign to draw nearer to them. By the different looks of their eyes and the expression of their countenances, she could easily tell in what condition they were. It was especially in the night of All Soul's day that they would surround her in great number, particularly such as were to be delivered on that day. These would converse with her quite familiarly and communicate to her many secret things."

"Whilst she was asleep, they would stay around her bed until she awoke by herself, that she might not be frightened. She could however, never conquer her fear; for this reason, she always felt sad toward night. Many of these souls begged her to tell certain things to their friends, which she did for some time; but as several annoyances to the convent arose from it, her superiors forbade her to continue doing so. At this, these souls felt much grieved; but they praised her for her obedience. Many souls came to bring her tidings from such as were not allowed to approach her."

"Thus her sympathy for them was very great. She did all in her power to give them comfort. For this purpose she prayed for them almost unceasingly, had Masses said, fasted on bread and water almost throughout the whole year, took the discipline for hours, offered up her communions, pains, privation of sleep, her fears, labors, troubles, anxieties, and all her steps, not reserving for herself as much as one breath."

"Johanna of Jesu Maria, Gertrude of St. Domenica, Bernardine of the Cross, and Benedicta of Brescia, are also known to have been such Sisters of Charity to the souls in Purgatory."

It is beyond human conception what the wonderful virgin Christina, who lived at St. Trond, in Belgium, did for the relief of the souls in Purgatory. No human strength could have endured what she underwent for their sakes; no one can read her life without shuddering at the sufferings through which she passed in order to obtain comfort for these souls. She was induced to go through so many tortures by the vision God had once given her of the frightful torments of Purgatory. Being left by Him at liberty to choose either immediate admittance into heaven or a longer stay on earth for the sake of procuring relief for the departed souls, she preferred the latter, and upon being asked why she performed so many extraordinary penances and treated her body so cruelly, she answered: "You speak in this way, because you know not what they suffer in Purgatory. Did you but know this as well as I do, you would do for the relief of the blessed souls what you see me do." (*Benedict XII., Sacr Triges, I. Serm. 25.*)

We read in the life of St. Gertrude, that, after having offered all her merits for the dead, she said to our Lord: "I hope, O Lord, that Thou wilt frequently cast the eyes of Thy mercy on my indigence." He replied: "What can I do more for one who has thus deprived herself of all things through charity, than to cover her immediately with charity?" She answered: "Whatever Thou mayest do, I shall always appear before Thee destitute of all merit, for I have renounced all I have gained or may gain." Our Lord replied: "Do you not know that a mother would allow a child who was well clothed to sit at her feet, whilst she would take one barely clad into her arms and cover her with her own garment?" He added: "And now what advantage have you, who are seated on the shore of an ocean, over those who sit by a little rivulet?" That is to say, those who keep their good works for themselves, have the rivulet; but those who renounce them in charity, possess God, Who is an inexhaustible ocean of beatitude. On another occasion, when she reflected upon what she had done, she commenced to be frightened at the thought that she would have to appear with empty hands before the tribunal of God. But Jesus Christ, her Spouse, appeared to her and said: "My daughter, why do you feel so much alarmed?" "My Lord," she replied, "it is because I have given every thing in suffrage for the souls in Purgatory, reserving nothing for myself, as a necessary satisfaction for my sins." "My daughter," replied our Lord, "your charity towards the souls in Purgatory has pleased Me so much, that, in reward for it, I have forgiven all the temporal punishment due to your sins.— Moreover, I, Who have promised a hundredfold for every good action, intend to reward you more liberally than you can conceive, by increasing your glory and happiness in heaven.— Finally, I will order all those souls whom you have delivered from Purgatory to come and be present at your death, and to accompany your soul with hymns of praise and thanksgiving to paradise." Were you favored with such a revelation, would you still hesitate for a moment to imitate St. Gertrude and other saints? Would you not feel too glad to make this heroic act, and thus exchange, as it were, your beggar's dress, *i. e.* your poverty of soul, for the nuptial robe of charity, in which you must appear at the gate of heaven to obtain admittance. Alas! shall a revelation have with you more weight and persuasive power than the pious wish and intimation of the Church and especially the infallible promise of Jesus Christ, to reward a hundredfold the least good action? Why should you then hesitate any longer to make this act, both to aid the poor souls more effectually, and to benefit yourself more abundantly? One hesitates when a great loss is to be apprehended, but not when a hundredfold gain is certain.

Having considered **Purgatory**, its pains, the manner of relieving its sufferers, the merit of this relief and charitable aid, the privileges of the members of the Arch-Confraternity, I will conclude with a brief enumeration of the principal advantages which you, as a member of the Arch-Confraternity, derive from your charity toward the souls in Purgatory.

1. As an active member of this Confraternity, you are, as it were, in the ark of Noah, in which you will find refuge from the deluge of temptations and sins.—"We see in the course of our missions," says St. Alphonsus, in his "Glories of Mary," "the utility of Confraternities. Generally speaking, one person who does not belong to any is under the guilt of more sins, than twenty persons are, who are members of one or more confraternities."

2. You will feel anxious to avoid venial sin and subdue your passions.

3. You will carefully practise works of penance to cancel the punishments due to your sins.

4. You will experience a great desire to sanctify yourself.

5. You will always be filled with a holy fear of God's judgments.

6. You will feel solicitous to profit by your time and make up for time lost.

7. You will be watchful to preserve yourself in the grace of God.

8. You will be induced to do more good to the poor and indigent, in order to apply the merit of your works to the souls in Purgatory, thus earning a double reward for this twofold charity.

9. You will feel more and more confirmed and strengthened in faith, hope and charity.

10. You will practise more perfectly holy patience and resignation to the will of God, in all your troubles and sufferings.

11. You will be more assiduous in praying, in hearing Mass with devotion, in gaining indulgences, and in preparing for confession and communion, so as to secure these indulgences,

12. You will be more punctual in complying with all your obligations towards your neighbor.

13. You assist, as it were, Jesus Christ to complete the work of Redemption in those souls of His elect, who are detained in Purgatory, and you are instrumental to His justice giving way to His mercy.

14. You give particular pleasure to Jesus Christ, to the Blessed Virgin Mary, and to the whole heavenly court.

15. You put the souls delivered from Purgatory by your prayers, under perpetual obligations to yourself.

16. The Blessed Virgin and all the saints of heaven, especially the patron saints of those souls, as well as their guardian angels, will become intercessors for you before the throne of God in a most special manner.

17. Those souls themselves will, from a sense of gratitude, take a particular interest in your welfare, both temporal and spiritual, and promote the same by their prayers to the best of their power, even whilst detained in Purgatory; and we read of St. Catherine of Bologna, that she had recourse to these souls whenever she wished to obtain a grace and her prayers were heard immediately.

18. You shall not have to pass through Purgatory, or, at least, you will not stay there very long.

19. Can there be a greater or a purer joy for you than to deliver a captive soul from its prison of fire and open the gates of heaven for it?

20. You are aggregated to the Oblates of five, and partake in all the good works of six Religious Orders. Who can count all their good works in which you share in so special a manner?

21. Count, if you can, how many thousands of Masses are offered up for the deceased members of the Arch-Confraternity. How many millions of prayers, of good works, of indulgences, especially those attached to the privileged altars and to the heroic act of charity above mentioned, which is certainly made by hundreds of the members of the Confraternity. O, what great consolation and comfort for you in the hour of death, and, far more, in Purgatory, to have been a member of this Arch-Confraternity! How soon must the souls of its deceased members be delivered from their place

of torment! Ah! when millions of tongues cry every day to our Lord, "Have mercy, O Lord, have mercy on the souls of our departed brethren." His justice will be put to the blush, as it were, and give way to His mercy, either by releasing them at once from their prison of fire, or by shortening the duration and diminishing the intensity of their sufferings.

22. Not to mention the special privilege granted to the Directors of the Arch-Confraternity, you will, as active member of the same, be also a good member of the Church Militant, always remaining in the communion of the Saints, and, as such, be one day admitted to the Church Triumphant, there to receive your inexpressible and everlasting reward.

23. To secure all these blessings, so little is required, and no obligation contracted under pain of sin.

Truly, he who is not as yet a member of the Arch-Confraternity, and knows all this, must be blind to his own spiritual welfare, if he feels not anxious to be admitted to membership and to assist the suffering souls in Purgatory, to the best of his ability. Their sufferings he would not willingly make his own, yet there is good reason for him to believe that they will be some day his portion ; for he who disregards charity for the poor souls, and remains as hard as stone to their pitiable condition, will one day—even supposing him to have saved his soul—cry in vain for the help he so sorely needs, but which he once refused. The words of the Gospel will ring in his ears when he begins to complain of his dereliction : "With what measure you shall mete, it shall be measured to you again." (*Matt.* 7: 12.) The aid and relief which he shall experience in Purgatory, shall be in proportion to the assistance which he will have extended to the poor souls. It will be in vain for him to deplore his unhappy lot, if, whilst yet alive, he was sparing in his charity to the poor souls. "He who soweth sparingly shall also reap sparingly." (II *Cor.* 9: 6.) To avoid this, we should fly with all our might to the relief of these suffering souls; we should ponder over the inspired words: "Stretch out thy hand to the poor, that thy expiation and thy blessing may be perfected. A gift hath grace in the sight of all the living, and restrain not grace from the dead. Be not wanting in comforting them that weep, and walk with them that mourn Be not slow to visit the sick, for by these things thou shalt be confirmed in love." (*Eccles.* vii, 36.) To whom do these words refer better than to the souls in Purgatory who are here called the poor, the sick, the weeping, and the mourning

" Blessed the man who fails not to succor the poor souls by his prayers." These words were heard by St. Bridget, when in an ecstacy in which she saw how the poor souls were purified like gold in a furnace. A little while after, she heard another voice, saying: " O, Jesus, our Lord, inspire religious souls on earth, Thy priests, Thy religious, all the pious laity, to cool our devouring flames by Masses, prayers, penances, and indulgences." At another time, she heard voices, saying: " Reward, O, just Judge, those who afford us the relief we ourselves cannot obtain!" Scarcely had these words died away, than she saw the dread pit lighted up with a brilliancy, like unto that of the aurora announcing the rising sun, and another deep and solemn strain, like the mingling notes of many singers, burst from the mouth of the pit: "O, God of mercies, award a hundred fold to all those by whose charity we are now ascending imperishable glory." (*St. Bridg Revel.* 4, 7.)

With St. Bernard, then, every one should say: " I will forthwith come to the relief of the suffering souls in Purgatory; with sobs and sighs, I will conjure the Lord; with tears, I will entreat him, I will be their advocate by my prayers, I will especially offer up for them the holy sacrifice of Mass, that the Lord, with the eyes of His unspeakable mercy, may look down upon them, changing their desolation into peace, their misery into joy, and their pains into everlasting glory and bliss " All this I will do, and that I may never forget to be faithful to this my solemn resolution, I will be a member of the Arch-Confraternity for the relief of the souls in Purgatory, that the words of St. Paul may be verified in me: "He who soweth in blessings, shall reap in blessings." (II *Cor.* 9: 6.)

LIST OF PLENARY INDULGENCES
To be Gained in the Course of the Year.
(See Explanation at the End.)

MONTHS.	DAYS.	Plenary Indulgences, TO BE Gained on the Following Festivals. By the Members of the	Purgat. Arch-confraternity.	Scapular of the Immac. Concep.	Scapular of Mt. Carmel.	Scapular of the Blessed Trinity.	Scapular of the Seven Dolors.
JANUARY.		Once a month on a day at option	D*	—	—	—	—
	1	Circumcision of our Lord,	—	D	D*	—	—
	5	Epiphany of our Lord,	D*	—	—	—	—
		Sunday within Octave of Epip'y,	—	—	—	—	—
	18	Chair of St. Peter at Rome,	—	—	—	—	—
	23	Espousal of the Blessed Virgin,	—	—	—	—	—
	25	Conversion of St. Paul,	—	—	—	—	—
	27	St. John Chrysostom,	—	—	—	—	—
	28	St. Agnes,	—	—	—	D*	—
FEBRUARY.		Once a month on a day at option	D*	—	—	—	—
		Sunday preceding Septuagesima	—	—	—	—	—
	2	Purification of the Blessed V.	D*	D	D*	D*	—
		First and last Sunday,	—	—	—	—	—
	4	St. Andrew Corsini,	—	—	D*	—	—
	8	St. John of Martha,	—	—	—	D*	—
	22	Chair of St. Peter and St. Marg't	—	—	—	—	—
	24	St. Matthias, Apostle,	—	—	—	—	—
		Ash Wednesday,	—	—	—	D*	—
		First Sunday in Lent,	—	—	—	—	—
MARCH.		Once a month on a day at option	D*	—	—	—	—
	5 6	St. Joseph of the Cross,	—	—	—	—	—
	9	St. Catharine of Bologna,	—	—	—	—	—
	12	St. Gregory, the Great,	—	—	D*	—	—
	19	St. Joseph,	D*	D	D*	—	—
	25	Annunciation of Blessed Virgin,	D*	D	D*	—	—
		Third Sunday in Lent,	—	—	—	—	—
		Passion Sunday,	—	D	—	—	D*
		Every Saturday in Lent,	—	D	—	—	—
APRIL.		Once a month on a day at option	D*	—	—	—	—
		Wednesday in Holy Week	—	D	—	—	—
	26	Thursday do. do.	D*	D	D*	D*	D*
		Friday do. do.	—	D	D*	—	—
		Every day do. do.	—	—	—	—	—
		Every Friday in the Year,	—	—	—	—	—
		Easter Sunday,	D*	D	D*	D*	D*
		Third Sunday after Easter,	D*	—	D*	—	—
MAY.		Once a month on a day at option	D*	—	—	—	—
		First Sunday,	—	—	—	—	—
	1	St. Philip and James, Apostles,	—	—	—	—	—
	2	St. Athanasius,	—	—	—	—	—
	3	Finding of the Holy Cross,	—	D	D*	—	—
	4	St. Monica,	—	—	D*	—	—
	7	Crowning our Lord with Thorns	—	—	—	—	—
	8	Apparition of St. Michael,	D*	D	—	—	—

Copyright secured.

LIST OF PLENARY INDULGENCES.

(Continued.)

Scapular of the Passion.	† Third Order of St. Francis.	Absolut'n in Third Order.	† Sacred Heart of Jesus.	† Sacred Heart of Mary.	† Confraternity of the Rosary.	Living Rosary.	Confraternity of Precious Blood.	† Confraternity of Bona Mors.	Society of Holy Childhood.	Society of the Blessed Trinity.	† Sodality of Mary.	Society of the Propag'n of the Faith.	Arch-confr. of the Holy Family.
—	D*	—	—	D	—	D*	D*	—	—	—	—	—	—
—	—	A	D*	D	—	D*	D*	D*	—	—	—	—	D*
—	—	—	—	—	D*	—	—	—	—	—	—	—	—
—	—	—	—	D	—	—	—	—	—	—	—	—	—
—	D*	—	—	—	—	D*	—	—	—	—	—	—	—
—	—	—	—	D	—	—	—	—	—	—	—	—	—
—	—	—	—	—	—	—	—	—	—	D*	—	—	—
—	—	—	—	D	—	—	—	—	—	—	—	—	—
—	D*	A	D*	D	D*	D*	D*	D*	—	D*	—	—	D*
—	—	—	—	D	—	—	—	—	—	—	—	—	—
—	—	—	—	—	—	—	—	—	—	—	—	—	—
—	D*	—	—	—	—	—	—	—	—	—	—	—	—
—	—	—	—	—	—	—	—	D*	—	D*	—	—	—
—	—	—	—	—	—	—	—	—	—	—	—	—	—
—	D*	—	—	—	—	—	—	—	—	—	—	—	—
—	D*	—	—	—	—	—	—	—	—	—	—	—	—
—	—	—	D*	—	—	—	—	—	—	—	—	—	—
—	—	—	D*	D	—	—	—	D*	V	—	D*	D*	D*
—	D*	A	D*	D	D*	D*	D*	D*	—	—	D*	D*	—
—	—	—	—	—	D*	—	D*	—	—	—	—	—	—
—	D*	—	D*	—	D*	—	D*	—	—	D*	—	—	—
—	—	—	—	—	D*	—	—	—	—	—	—	—	—
D	—	A	—	—	—	—	—	—	—	—	—	—	—
—	D*	A	D*	D	D*	D*	D*	D*	—	—	—	D	D*
—	—	—	—	—	D*	—	—	—	—	—	—	—	D*
—	—	—	D*	—	—	—	—	—	—	—	—	—	—
—	—	—	—	—	—	—	—	—	—	—	—	—	—
—	—	—	—	—	—	—	D*	—	—	—	—	—	—
—	—	—	—	—	D*	—	—	—	—	—	—	D	—
—	D*	—	—	—	D*	—	—	—	—	—	—	—	—

LIST OF PLENARY INDULGENCES.
(*Continued.*)

MONTHS	DAYS	Plenary Indulgences, TO BE Gained on the Following Festivals. By the Members of the	Purgat. Arch-con-fraternity.	† Scapular of the Immac. Concep.	† Scapular of Mt. Carmel.	† Scapular of the Blessed Trinity.	† Scapular of the Seven Dolors.
MAY		Ascension,	D*	D	D*	D*	D*
	16	St. Simon Stylite,	—	—	D*	—	—
		At the Renewal of Vows,	—	—	—	—	—
	20	St. Bernardin of Sienna,	—	—	—	—	—
	24	Mary, Help of Christians,	—	—	—	—	—
		Pentecost,	—	D	D*	—	—
	27	St. Magdalene of Pazzi,	—	—	D*	—	—
		Trinity Sunday,	—	D	—	D*	—
JUNE		Once a month on a day at option	D*	—	—	—	—
	1	Interior of Mary,	—	—	—	—	—
		Corpus Christi,	D*	—	—	—	—
	11	St. Barnabas, Apostle,	—	—	—	—	—
	13	St. Anthony of Padua,	—	—	—	—	—
	14	St. Basil the Great,	—	—	D*	—	—
	17	St. Paschalis Baylon,	—	—	—	—	—
	19	St. Juliana de Falcantara,	—	—	—	—	—
		Sacred Heart of Jesus,	—	—	—	—	—
	21	St. Aloysius Gonzaga,	—	—	—	—	—
	24	Nativity of St. John the Baptist,	—	D	D*	—	—
	29	St. Peter and Paul, Apostles,	D*	D	D*	—	—
JULY		Once a month on a day at option	D*	—	—	—	—
		First Sunday,	—	—	—	—	—
	2	Visitation of the Blessed Virgin,	—	—	D*	—	—
	9 14	St. Nicholas and Companions, and St. Bonaventure,	—	—	—	—	—
	16	Blessed Virgin of Mt. Carmel,	—	—	D*	—	—
	19	St. Vincent of Paul,	—	—	—	—	—
	20	St. Jerome,	—	—	D*	—	—
	22	St. Mary Magdalen,	—	—	—	—	—
	24	St. Apollinaris,	—	—	—	—	—
	25	St. James, Apostle,	—	D	—	—	—
	26	St. Anna, Mother of the B. V.	—	—	D*	—	—
	31	St. Ignatius Loyola,	—	D	—	—	—
		Last Sunday,	—	D	—	—	—
AUGUST		Once a month on a day at option	D*	—	—	—	—
	2	Portiuncula,	—	D	—	—	—
	5	Dedication of St Mary, ad Nives	—	—	—	—	—
	6	Transfiguration of our Lord,	—	—	—	—	—
	7	St. Albert and Cajetan,	—	D	D*	—	—
	11	St. Philomena,	—	—	D*	—	—
	12	St. Clare,	—	—	—	—	—
	15	Assumption of the Blessed V.	D*	D	D*	—	—
		St. Joachim. Sunday within Oct.	—	—	D*	—	—
		Sac. Heart of Mary. 1st Sunday after the Octav.	—	—	—	—	—

LIST OF PLENARY INDULGENCES.

(*Continued.*)

Scapular of the Passion.	† Third Order of St. Francis.	Absolut'n in Third Order.	† Sacred Heart of Jesus.	Sacred Heart of Mary.	† Confraternity of the Rosary.	Living Rosary.	Confraternity of Precious Blood.	Society of the Blessed Trinity.	† Sodality of Mary.	† Confraternity of Bona Mors.	Society of the Propag'n of the Faith.	Society of Holy Childhood.	Arch-confr. of the Holy Family.
—	D*	A	D*	D	—	D*	D*	—	D*	—	—	—	D*
—	D*	—	—	—	—	—	—	—	—	—	—	—	—
—	D*	—	—	—	—	—	—	—	—	—	—	—	—
—	D*	—	—	—	—	D*	—	—	—	—	—	—	—
—	D*	A	—	D	D*	D*	—	—	—	D*	—	—	—
—	—	—	—	—	—	—	—	—	—	—	—	—	—
—	—	—	—	—	—	D*	D*	D*	—	D*	—	—	—
—	D*	—	—	—	—	D*	—	—	—	—	—	—	—
—	D*	A	—	—	D*	D*	D*	—	—	D*	—	—	D*
—	D*	—	—	—	—	—	—	—	—	—	—	—	—
—	D*	—	—	—	—	—	—	—	—	—	—	—	—
—	D*	—	—	—	—	—	—	—	—	—	—	—	—
—	D*	—	D*	—	—	—	D*	—	—	—	—	—	D*
—	—	—	—	—	—	—	—	—	D*	—	—	—	—
—	—	A	—	D	—	—	—	—	—	D*	—	—	—
—	—	A	D*	D	—	D*	—	—	—	D*	—	—	D*
—	—	—	D*	—	—	—	D*	—	—	—	—	—	—
—	D*	A	—	D	D*	D*	D*	—	—	—	—	—	—
—	D*	—	—	—	—	—	—	—	—	—	—	—	—
—	D*	—	—	—	—	D*	—	—	—	—	—	—	—
—	—	—	—	—	—	—	—	—	—	—	—	V	—
—	—	—	—	D	—	—	—	—	—	—	—	—	—
—	D*	—	—	—	—	—	—	—	—	—	—	—	—
—	—	—	D*	—	—	—	—	—	—	D*	—	—	—
—	—	—	—	D*	—	—	—	—	—	—	—	—	—
—	—	—	—	—	—	—	—	—	—	—	—	—	—
—	D*	A	—	—	—	D*	—	—	—	—	—	—	—
—	D*	—	—	—	—	D*	—	—	—	—	—	—	—
—	D*	—	—	D	—	—	—	—	—	—	—	—	—
—	—	—	—	—	—	—	—	—	—	—	—	—	—
—	—	—	—	—	—	—	—	—	—	—	—	—	—
—	D*	A	—	—	—	D*	—	—	—	—	—	—	—
—	D*	A	D*	D	D*	D*	D*	—	D*	D*	D*	—	D*
—	—	—	—	—	—	—	—	—	—	—	—	—	—
—	D*	—	—	D	—	D*	—	—	—	—	—	—	—

LIST OF PLENARY INDULGENCES.
(Continued.)

MONTHS.	DAYS.	Plenary Indulgences, TO BE Gained on the Following Festivals. By the Members of the	Purgat. Arch-con-fraternity.	Scapular of the Immac. Concep.	Scapular of Mt. Carmel.	Scapular of the Blessed Trinity.	Scapular of the Seven Dolors.
AUG.	19	St. Lewis, Bishop,	—	—	—	—	—
	24	St. Bartholomew, Apostle,	—	—	—	—	—
	25	St. Lewis, King,	—	—	—	—	—
	28	St Augustin,	—	D	—	—	—
SEPTEMBER.		Once a month on a day at option	D*	—	—	—	—
	4	St. Rosalia. St. Rosa,	—	—	—	—	—
	8	Nativity of the Blessed Virgin,	D*	D	D*	D*	—
		During the whole Octave,	—	—	—	—	—
		Holy Name of Mary. Sunday after the Octave,	—	—	—	—	—
		3d Sunday. Feast of the 7 dolors,	—	—	—	—	D*
	14	Exaltation of the Holy Cross,	—	D	D*	—	—
	17	Stigmata of St. Francis and St. Lambert.	—	—	—	—	—
	21	St. Matthew, Apostle,	—	—	—	—	—
	29	St. Michael, the Archangel,	D*	D	D*	—	—
OCTOBER.		Once a month on a day at option	D*	—	—	—	—
	2	Holy Guardian Angels,	—	D	—	—	—
	4	St. Francis of Assisium,	—	—	—	—	—
		1st Sunday. Feast of the Rosary,	—	—	—	—	—
	7	St. Mary Victoria,	—	—	—	—	—
		2d Sunday. Maternity of the B.V.	—	—	—	D*	—
	13	St. Edward, King,	—	—	—	—	—
	15	St. Teresa,	—	D	D*	—	—
		3d Sunday. Purity of Mary,	—	—	—	—	—
	19	St. Peter of Alcantara,	—	—	—	—	—
	23	St. Severin,	—	—	—	D*	—
	28	St. Simon and Judas,	—	—	—	—	—
NOVEMBER.		Once a month on a day at option	D*	—	—	—	—
	1	All Saints,	—	D	D*	—	—
	2	Commemoration of All Souls,	D*	—	—	—	—
	10	St. Andrew Avell.	—	D	—	—	—
	11	St. Martin, B. and C.,	—	—	—	—	—
		1st or 2d Sunday. Patronage of the Most Blessed Virgin,	—	—	—	—	—
	13	St. Didacus, Bp, & St. Stanislas,	—	—	—	—	—
	19	St. Elizabeth of Hungary,	—	—	—	—	—
	20	St. Felix Valois,	—	—	—	D*	—
	21	Presentation of the Blessed V.	—	—	D*	—	—
	24	St. John of the Cross,	—	—	D*	—	—
	25	St. Catharine,	—	—	—	D*	—
	29	All Saints of the Third Order of St. Francis.	—	—	—	—	—
	30	St. Andrew, Apostle,	—	—	—	—	—
		First Sunday in Advent,	—	—	—	—	—

LIST OF PLENARY INDULGENCES.
(Continued.)

Scapular of the Passion.	† Third Order of St. Francis.	Absolut'n in Third Order.	† Sacred Heart of Jesus.	Sacred Heart of Mary.	† Confraternity of the Rosary.	Living Rosary.	Confraternity of Precious Blood.	Society of the Blessed Trinity.	† Sodality of Mary.	† Confraternity of Bona Mors.	Society of the Propag'n of the Faith.	Society of Holy Childhood.	Arch-confr. of the Holy Family.
—	D*	—	—	—	—	—	—	—	—	D*	—	—	—
—	—	—	D*	—	—	—	—	—	—	—	—	—	—
—	D*	—	—	—	—	—	—	—	—	—	—	—	—
—	—	—	—	—	—	—	—	—	—	—	—	—	—
—	D*	—	—	—	—	—	—	—	—	—	—	—	—
—	D*	A	D*	D	D*	D*	D*	D*	D*	D*	—	—	D*
—	—	—	—	D	—	—	—	—	—	—	—	—	—
—	D*	—	—	—	D*	D*	—	—	—	—	—	—	—
—	D*	—	—	—	—	D*	—	—	—	—	—	—	D*
—	—	—	—	—	D*	—	—	—	—	—	—	—	D*
—	D*	—	—	—	—	—	—	—	—	—	—	—	—
—	—	—	—	—	—	—	—	—	—	D*	—	—	—
—	—	—	—	D	—	—	—	—	—	—	—	—	D*
—	—	—	—	—	—	—	—	—	—	—	—	V	D*
—	D*	A	—	—	—	—	—	—	—	—	—	—	—
—	D*	—	—	—	D*	D*	—	—	—	—	—	—	—
—	—	—	—	—	—	D*	—	—	—	—	—	—	—
—	D*	—	—	—	—	D*	—	D*	—	—	—	—	—
—	D*	—	—	—	—	—	—	—	—	—	—	—	—
—	D*	—	—	—	—	D*	—	—	—	—	—	—	—
—	D*	—	—	—	—	—	—	—	—	—	—	—	—
—	D*	—	—	—	—	—	—	—	—	—	—	—	—
—	—	—	—	—	—	—	—	—	—	D*	—	—	—
—	—	A	D*	D	D*	D*	—	—	D*	—	—	—	D*
—	—	—	D*	—	—	—	—	—	—	—	—	—	D*
—	—	—	—	—	—	—	—	—	—	—	—	—	—
—	D*	—	—	—	—	D*	—	—	—	—	—	—	—
—	D*	—	—	—	—	—	—	—	—	—	—	—	—
—	D*	—	—	—	—	—	—	—	—	—	—	—	—
—	D*	A	—	D	D*	D*	D*	—	—	—	—	V	—
—	—	A	—	—	—	—	D*	—	—	—	—	—	—
—	D*	—	—	—	—	—	—	—	—	—	—	—	—
—	—	—	—	—	—	—	—	—	—	D*	—	—	—

LIST OF PLENARY INDULGENCES.

(Continued.)

MONTHS.	DAYS.	Plenary Indulgences, TO BE Gained on the Following Festivals. By the Members of the	† Purgat. Arch-confraternity.	† Scapular of the Immac. Concep.	† Scapular of Mt. Carmel.	† Scapular of the Blessed Trinity.	† Scapular of the Seven Dolors.
DECEMBER.		Once a month on a day at option	D*	—	—	—	—
	3	St. Francis Xavier,	—	—	—	—	—
	7	St. Ambrose,	—	—	—	—	—
	8	Immaculate Conception,	D*	D	D*	—	—
	10	Our Lady of Loretto,	—	—	—	—	—
	13	St. Lucy,	—	D	—	—	—
	15	Octave of the Immac. Concep.	—	—	—	—	—
	18	Expectation of the Delivery of Blessed Virgin Mary.	—	—	—	—	—
	21	St. Thomas, Apostle,	—	—	—	—	—
	25	Nativity of our Lord,	D*	D	D*	D*	D*
	27	For the 3d Mass or the Nativity of our Lord.	D*	—	—	—	—
		St. John, Apostle,	—	—	—	—	—
		On the Feast of the Patron of the Church.	—	—	—	—	—

Plenary Indulges to be Gained in each Month.

1. SUNDAY.—PLENARY INDULGENCES.

For the Confraternity of the Rosary.—D*
For the Confraternity of the Blessed Trinity.—D*.
For the Scapular of the Immaculate Conception.—D.
For the 3d Order of St. Francis, on every Sunday of the year.—D*.
For the Heroic Act of Charity, p. 437, and Monthly Communion.—D.
For the Confraternity of the Sacred Heart of Mary.—D*.
For the Confraternity of the Sacred Heart of Jesus.—D.

2 SUNDAY.

For the Bona Mors Association.—D*.
For those invested with the Scapular of the Immaculate Conception all the Indulgences attached to the Visits of the Churches of the Stations of Rome and the Holy Places, etc.—D*.

The prayer: "O Angel of God," p. 117.—D*. ⎫
The prayer: "O Sacrament, most holy," etc. p. 98.—D. ⎪
3 Our Fathers and Hail Marys, for the dying.—D. ⎬ For saying Daily.
5 Our Fathers and 5 Hail Marys, for the faithful departed.—D. ⎪
The "Sweet Heart." p. 100.—D. ⎪
The "Most Holy Immaculate Virgin," p. 100.—D. ⎪
The "O God, Who," p. 114.—D. ⎭

LIST OF PLENARY INDULGENCES.
(Continued.)

Scapular of the Passion.	† Third Order of St. Francis.	Absolut'n in Third Order.	† Sacred Heart of Jesus.	Sacred Heart of Mary.	† Confraternity of the Rosary.	Living Rosary.	Confraternity of Precious Blood.	Society of the Blessed Trinity.	† Sodality of Mary.	† Confraternity of Bona Mors.	Society of the Propag'n of the Faith.	Society of Holy Childhood.	Arch-confr. of the Holy Family.
—	—	—	—	—	—	—	—	—	—	—	D*	V	—
—	D*	A	D*	D	D*	D*	D*	—	D*	D*	—	—	—
—	D*	—	—	—	—	D*	—	—	—	—	—	—	—
—	—	—	—	D	—	—	—	—	—	—	—	—	—
—	D*	—	—	—	D*	—	—	—	—	—	—	—	—
—	—	—	—	—	—	—	—	—	—	D*	—	—	—
—	D*	A	D*	D	D*	D*	D*	—	D*	D*	—	—	D*
—	—	—	D*	D*	—	—	—	—	—	D*	—	—	—
—	D*	—	—	—	D*	—	—	—	—	—	—	—	—

Plenary Indulgences to be Gained in each Month.
(Continued.)

3. SUNDAY.

For the members of the Holy Rosary.—D*.
Of the Propagation of the Faith.—D*.
Of Scapular of Mt. Carmel when reciting the little office of B.V.—D*.
Of the Scapular of the Immaculate Conception. (See 2. Sunday.)
Sacred Heart of Mary.—D*.
For the Prayer: "Look down," etc. p. 32.—D.

4. SUNDAY.

For the Sacred Heart of Jesus.—D.
The "Angel of the Lord," etc. p. 15.—V.
The Acts of Faith, Hope and Charity, p. 19.—D.
1 Our Father and Hail Mary, in atonement for blasphemies.—V.
The Chaplet of our Lord, p. 119.—D.
The Prayer to the Sacred Heart, p. 129.—D.
The Rosary of the Immaculate Conception, p. 141.—D.
The Prayers of St. Alphonsus, p. 143.—D.
The Prayer to St. Peter and Paul, p. 178.—D.

For saying daily.

(See *Raccolta*, by Mgr. Princivalli—*Nature of Indulgences*, by P. A. Maurel—*Dictionary of Indulgences*, by Abbe Migne—*Manual of the Third Order of St. Francis*, by P. Bruneeler—*Arch-Confraternity of the Sacred Heart of Mary*, by Hubert Leban, etc.

Special Plenary Indulgences.

A Plenary Indulgence:

I. For all the Novenas made in honor; 1) of the Purification of Mary; 2) of St. Gabriel; 3) of St. Joseph; 4) of the Annunciation of the Blessed Virgin; 5) of the Seven Dolors; 6) of the Patronage; 7) of the Sacred Heart of Mary; 8) of the Sacred Heart of Jesus; 9) of the Visitation, Assumption, Presentation and Immaculate Conception of the Blessed Virgin; 10) of St. Vincent of Paul; 11) of the Nativity of our Lord; 12) of the Angel Guardians; 13) of St. Raphael and St. Michael; 14) of the Feast of the Rosary; 15) For the Souls in Purgatory.—D.

II. Those who are invested with the Scapular of the Immaculate Conception, as well as the members of the Third Order of St. Francis, may gain the indulgences attached to the Visits to the Churches of the Stations of Rome, each time they say 6 times the Our Father, Hail Mary and Glory be to the Father, etc., neither Confession nor Communion being required.—D.

III. 1) For the Seven Sundays in honor of St. Joseph, by reciting the prescribed prayers, or seven times the Our Father, Hail Mary, and Glory be to the Father.—D*. 2) On each of the six Sundays, in honor of St. Aloysius—D. 3) On each of the six Sundays—or Fridays, preceding the Feast of the Sacred Heart of Jesus.—D*.

IV. The Plenary Indulgence of the Church of Porziuncula, for each Visit to a Church of the Order of St. Francis, on the 2d of August.—D.

V. At the end of the month of May, for all those who assisted in the Church, at the exercises of piety, and endeavored to praise God in His Sanctuary.—D.

VI. For all those who, in the course of the month of May, endeavored to honor the Blessed Virgin Mary, in public or in private, by prayers and other works of piety.—D.

VII. Those who regularly assist at Catechistical Instructions, Sermons, Explanation of the Gospel, as well as those who give these instructions, may gain a Plenary Indulgence: On the Feast of the Nativity and Epiphany of our Lord, on the Feast of Pentecost and of St. Peter and Paul.—V.

VIII. A Plenary Indulgence for the members of the Purgatorial Arch-Confraternity, once a month on a day at option, if they visit a grave-yard four times a month and pray there for the faithful, departed.—D.

IX. A Plenary Indulgence for each member of the Arch-Confraternity of the Holy Family; 1) on day of admission; 2) on Feast of his (her) patron-saint, and on that of the patron-saint of his (her) division; 3) in the hour of death; 4) on Friday after Passion Sunday; on Whit-Monday; 6) on 2d and 3d Sunday in July.—D*.

NOTE.—The letters D and V indicate the days of indulgences; besides,
D means that the indulgence is applicable to the souls in Purgatory.
V " " " " only to the living.
* " " " requires a visit to a Church.
A indicates the days on which the general Absolution is given in Third Order of St Francis.
† indicates Confraternities which can gain the indulgences of the Churches of the Stations of Rome. See p. 423, No 9.
If the celebration of a Festival is transferred, the indulgences is also transferred.

ALPHABETICAL INDEX.

	PAGE
Abridgement of Christian Doctrine	9
Abstinence, days of	340
Acts of Faith, Hope, Charity, etc.	19
—— before Communion	81
—— after Communion	84
—— of Adoration to Jesus Christ in the Blessed Sacrament	90
—— of Consecration to the Blessed Virgin	89
—— of Devotions for the Time of Death ...211,	196
—— Heroic, of Charity	437
Agony, Prayers for the Time of	192
All-Saints, Vespers on the Festivals of	62
Alma Redemptoris Mater	63
Angel Guardian, Prayer to	176
Apostles' Creed, Vespers on the Festivals of the	50
Arch-Confraternity, the Purgatorian	345
———————— Origin of the	419
———————— Indulgences of the ...421-	425
———————— Patroness of the	431
———————— Privileges of the Directors of the	431
———————— Privileges of the Members of the	432
———————— Manner of establishing the	433
———————— Suitable form for a Certificate of Membership of the	434
———————— Duties of the Directors of the	435
———————— Duties of the Members of the	436
Ave Regina	64
Baptism in Danger of Death	12
—— Prayer to the Patron of	182
Benediction of the Blessed Sacrament	68
Benedictus Dominus, Blessed be the Lord	290
Blessed Sacrament, Visits to	90
Chaplet of our Lord	119
Children, Duties of	327
Christmas-Day, Vespers on	60
Commandments, the Ten, explained	321
Communion, Prayers before	81
—————— Prayers after	84
—————— Spiritual	98

ALPHABETICAL INDEX.

	PAGE
Confession, How to get ready for	71
———— Prayers before	71
———— Prayers after	79
Confessors, Vespers on the Festival of	55
Confirmation, Instructions and Prayers for.	134
Contrition, Act of	75, 344
Corpus Christi, Vespers on the Festival of	62
Creed, Apostles'	50
Death, Prayers for a good	193
———— Protestation for	189
———— Acts of Devotion for the Time of	196
De Profundis, Out of the Depths	293
Devotions in the Morning	13
———— for Mass	21
———— for Confession	71
———— for Communion	80
———— before the Blessed Sacrament	90
———— at Night	17
———— for the Most Holy Trinity for the Dead	312
———— for the Holy Ghost	136
———— for the Blessed Virgin	99
———— for the Saints	156
———— for the Sacred Heart of Jesus	129
———— to the Sorrowful Heart of Mary	152
———— for the Sick	196
———— for the Faithful Departed	221
Epiphany, Vespers on the Festival of	61
Examination of Conscience before Confession	18
Exercise, Devout, for the Dead	299
Extreme Unction, Preparation for	188
———————— Prayer after	189
Faith, Hope and Charity, Acts of	19
Faithful Departed, Mass for	221
———————— Vespers for	236
———————— Matins for	246
———————— Lauds for	278
———————— the Psalm De Profundis for	293
———————— Prayers for the whole week for	295
———————— Novena for	299
———————— Prayers of St. Gertrude for	306
———————— Litany of	309
———————— Invocation of the Most Holy Trinity for	312
Fasting Days of Obligation	340
Fathers and Mothers, Duties of	341

Alphabetical Index.

	PAGE
Festivals of Obligation	340
Good Death, Prayer for	172
Grace before and after Meal	15, 16, 317
Guardian Angel, Prayer in honor of	176
Hail Mary	11
Heart of Jesus, Prayer	129
Heart of Mary, Devotion to the Sorrowful	152
——————— Act of Consecration to the Sacred	89
Holy Childhood, Steps of	115
Holydays of Obligation	340
Holy Ghost, Prayer for the Seven Gifts of the	136
Holy Name, Litany of	131
Husbands and Wives, Duties of	342
Immaculate Conception, Chaplet of	141
Indulgences, Instruction on	426
——————— to Prayers, etc., in this Manual...15, 19, 90, 98, 100, 114, 119, 129, 141, 143, 151, 152, 172, 178, 180, 292	
——————— to be gained by the Members of the Purgatorian Arch-Confraternity... 421-425	
——————— List of	452
Infancy, Mysteries of the Sacred	115
Jesus, Litany of the Holy Name of	131
——— Devotions to, in the Blessed Sacrament	90
Lauds for the Dead	278
Litany of Loretto, in Latin and English	138
——— of the Holy Name of Jesus	131
——— of the Saints	156
——— of the Faithful Departed	309
Magnificat	49
Mary, Devotions to	138-155
———Vespers on the Festivals of	60
———Little Rosary of the Immaculate Conception	141
———Prayers to, for every day of the week	143
———the Prayer "Memorare" of St. Bernard	151
———Prayers to the Sorrowful Heart of	152
———Prayer to, in her Desolation	155
———Visit to	99
———Ejaculation to	100
———Prayer of St. Alphonsus to	100
Mass, Prayer before	21
———Prayers at	22
——— for the Dead	221
Masters, Duties of	344
Matins for the Dead	246

ALPHABETICAL INDEX.

	PAGE
Meal Prayers 15, 16,	317
Meditation or Mental Prayer, Method of............	219
———— on the Pains of Purgatory...........	350
Memorare, the, of St. Bernard...................	151
Morning Prayers...............................	13
Name of Jesus, Litany.........................	131
Night Prayers.................................	17
Oblation, a Daily..............................	165
Office for the Dead............................	221
O Salutaris	68
Our Father....................................	11
Parents, Duties of.............................	341
Practices, Good................................	318
Prayer for Morning........................13,	314
——— for Night...........................17,	317
——— on Approach of Temptation................	319
——— for the Prosperity of the Church..........	210
——— for the Church, Ruling Powers, etc........	164
——— for Renewing the Promises of Baptism.....	183
——— to our Holy Patron of Baptism	182
——— for Parents Deceased....................	244
——— for all Degrees of Men in the Church......	210
——— for the Pope............................	210
——— for Bishops and People committed to them	211
——— for a Congregation or a Family...........	211
——— in any Tribulation	211
——— in Times of Calamity....................	212
——— in Times of Famine and Pestilence........	212
——— in Times of Great Mortality..............	212
——— for Heretics and Schismatics..............	213
——— for Jews................................	213
——— for Pagans..............................	213
——— for our Friends.........................	214
——— for a Friend or Friends..................	214
——— for a Friend in Distress..................	215
——— for Another's Conversion.................	215
——— for the Sick	216
——— for the Dead............................	216
——— before Study or Instructions..............	217
——— for Parents, for Themselves, and for their Children...................................	218
——— for the Faithful Departed in general......	245
——— for a Father and Mother, deceased........	244
——— for Sodalists Departed...................	244
——— for Relations and Benefactors.............	245

Alphabetical Index.

	PAGE
Prayer to the Most Holy Trinity for the Dead	312
——— Look down upon me—before a Crucifix	32
——— to the Blessed Virgin for every day in the week	143
——— of St. Bernard—Memorare	151
——— to SS. Peter and Paul	177
——— to St. Michael	174
——— to Holy Angels	173
——— to St. Patrick	179
——— to St. Aloysius	180
——— to our Guardian Angel	176
——— to St. Joseph	169
——— for all things necesssry to salvation......86,	167
——— in Desolation	181
——— in Sickness or Affliction	186
——— for a Sodalist Departed	292
——— for the Dead for every day in the week	295
——— for the Dead for the nine days preceding All-Souls' day	299
Protestation for Death	189

Psalms—

Ad Dominum cum tribularem—When I was in tribulation	238
Ad te, Domine, levavi—To Thee, O Lord, I have lifted	258
Beati omnes—Blessed are all	62
Beatus qui intelligit—Blessed is the man	269
Beatus vir, qui timet—Blessed is the man	43
Cantate Domino—Sing to the Lord	288
Confitebor tibi Domine—I will praise Thee..42,	240
Credidi, propter quod—I have believed	51
Deus, Deus meus—O God, my God	282
Deus misereatur—God have mercy	284
De Profundis—Out of the Depths............61,	239
Dilexi quoniam—I have loved	236
Dixit Dominus Domino meo—The Lord said to my Lord	41
Domine, Deus meus—O Lord, my God	251
Dominus, illuminatio mea—The Lord is my light	261
Domine, ne in furore—Lord, rebuke me	250
Domine, probasti me—Lord, Thou hast proved	52
Dominus regit me—The Lord rules me	257
Ego dixi, in dimidio—I have said in	284
Expectans, expectavi—Expecting, I expected	266

PSALMS—

    In convertendo—When the Lord brought....... 52
    In exitu, Israel—When Israel went out.......... 46
    Lætatus sum in—I rejoiced at the things........ 58
    Lauda, anima mea—Praise the Lord, O my soul 242
    Lauda Jerusalem—Praise the Lord, O Jerusalem.. 59
    Laudate Dominum omnes—O praise the Lord. 50
    Laudate pueri, Dominum—Praise the Lord, ye children.. 45
    Laudate Dominum de cœlis—Praise ye the Lord from the heavens................................... 284
    Laudate Dominum in—Praise ye the Lord in. 289
    Levavi oculos meos—I lifted up my eyes........ 238
    Memento, Domine, David—O Lord, remember David.. 55
    Miserere, mei Deus—Have mercy on me.......... 278
    Nisi Dominus ædificaverit—Unless the Lord... 59
    Quemadmodum desiderat—Even as the heart.. 271
    Te decet hymnus—A hymn, O Lord................ 280
    Venite, exultemus—Come, let us rejoice......... 246
    Verba mea auribus percipe—Give ear, O Lord. 248

Psalter, the Angel.. 175
Purgatory, Belief in... 346
——— Pains of.. 350
——— Manner of Relieving the Souls in............ 367
——— Motives for Assisting the Souls in........ 396-418
Recommendation of a Soul Departing..................... 201
——————— a Devout................................ 164
Regina cœli.. 65
Rosary, Short Method of saying the....................... 140
——— the little, of the Immaculate Conception....... 141
Rule of Life for a Pious Christian........................... 315
Recapitulation... 448
Sacred Heart of Jesus, Devotions to........................ 129
————————— Act of Consecration to............ 130
————————— Oblation to the 129
————————— Prayer of St. Gertrude to the... 130
Souls distinguished for their Charity....................... 442
Salve Regina... 66
Stations of the Way of the Cross.............................. 102
Steps of our Saviour's Childhood............................. 115
——————— Passion... 112
Servants, Duties of.. 328
Sick, Prayer in Sickness or Affliction...................... 186

	PAGE
Souls in Purgatory, Prayers for the	221
St. Aloysius, Prayer to	180
St. Bernard, the Prayer, Memorare	151
St. Bonaventure, Prayer of	97
St. Gertrude, Prayer of	130
St. Ignatius, Invocations, Soul of Christ, etc	36
St. Joseph, Devotion to	169
St. Michael, Prayer to	174
St. Patrick, Prayer to	179
St. Peter and Paul, Prayer to	177
Tantum ergo	69
Temptation, Prayer in time of	319
Truths most necessary to be known	9
Unction, Extreme, Prayers before and after	188, 189
Vespers, of devotion at	40
———— of All-Saints	62
———— of Apostles	50
———— of Ascension day	62
———— of the Blessed Virgin Mary	60
———— of Christmas-Day	60
———— of a Confessor and Bishop	55
———— of a Confessor, and not a Bishop	57
———— of Corpus Christi	62
———— of the Epiphany	61
———— of Martyrs	55
———— of the Sacred Heart	62
———— of St Peter and Paul	61
———— of the Sunday Office	41
———— of Virgins and of Holy Women	57
———— of the Faithful Departed	236
Virtues, Daily	318
Visit to the Blessed Sacrament	90
—— to Mary	99
Way of the Cross	102
Words, the, of a dying man to Jesus Christ crucified	192

Protest of the Translator.

In obedience to the decrees of Urban VIII., of holy memory, I protest that I do not intend to attribute any other than purely human authority to all the miracles, revelations, graces and incidents contained in this book; neither to the titles holy or blessed applied to the servants of God, not yet canonized, except in cases where these have been confirmed by the Holy Roman Catholic Church and by the Holy Apostolic See, of whom I profess myself an obedient son; and, therefore, to their judgment I submit myself and whatever I have written in this book.

www.ingramcontent.com/pod-product-compliance
Lightning Source LLC
Chambersburg PA
CBHW022103300426
44117CB00007B/571